MW01639708

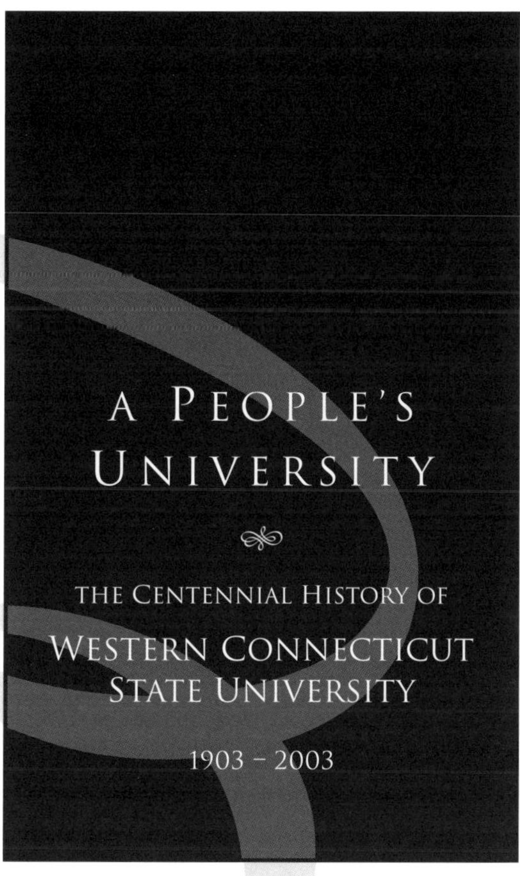

HERBERT F. JANICK, PH.D.

Published in July 2002 by
Western Connecticut State University
181 White Street, Danbury, Connecticut, 06810

International Standard Book Number: 0-9711366-1-0

Library of Congress Cataloging-in-Publication Data is available upon request.

DEDICATION

To my students and colleagues, who made Western Connecticut State University a place worth writing about.

PREFACE

The start of research on this book coincided with my retirement as a full-time faculty member at Western Connecticut State University. Each semester for almost thirty years, I taught an introductory American history course to students who were fulfilling a general education requirement. I saw this assignment not as a chore, but as an opportunity to help them understand how historians "make" history. My focus was not on the accumulation of any set of privileged facts, but on comprehending the way the present shapes the past.

One particular memory from this three-decade educational crusade remains strong. Students were grateful, almost jubilant, whenever they encountered historians who told them where they were coming from and what they were trying to do. In this Preface, I will try to emulate those obliging historians who made my job as a teacher much easier.

From the start, I have tried to answer one basic question: "How did a tiny normal school come into existence and evolve into a comprehensive state university?" Using this query as my focus eliminated the possibility, or the value, of encyclopedic coverage of the activities of all the departments, offices, clubs, and teams that have contributed to the life of the school over the last one hundred years. Instead, I have concentrated on people, organizations and events (on campus and off) that, in my judgment, were most responsible for, or best illustrate, the transformation of the total institution. Much attention has been given in these pages to the chief executives of the school who, due to their position, were most influential in setting a tone and shaping overall policy. Because the school has always been a creature of the State of Connecticut, it has been necessary to explore the attitudes and actions of state educational officials, the governor, and the members of the General Assembly. The relationship between the school and the local community is another essential element of this history.

Although the narrative approach is often maligned today, I framed this history as a story. It is my effort to impose order, admittedly artificial, on hundreds of semesters of events and personalities at a single educational institution. The historian's dangerous assignment is to make choices and to reach conclusions. A review of any chapter will reveal omissions. Many will wonder, for example, how the history of the 1990s could be complete without reference to the link with the Jane Goodall Institute, without mention of the football team's first undefeated regular season in 1999, or without acknowledgment of the chemistry department's certification by the American Chemical Society. My answer is that all history is personal, and that much interesting material about WestConn's past had to be omitted because, in my opinion, it would cloud rather than clarify the story I tried to tell. I will be content if my synthesis—far from being the last word—provides a helpful context for those entering WestConn's second century.

This history is based on solid documentation. The "Note on Sources" section at the end of each chapter lists the principal sources on which that chapter rests. Here I have identified and thanked the many faculty, students, and alumni who generously submitted to recorded interviews. The tapes of these sessions, along with all other data gathered in the course of my research, can be consulted in the Archives of the Ruth Haas Library.

Some contributions are so significant that my appreciation must be repeated here. President James Roach immediately recognized the importance of a university history when we first discussed the subject in 1999. Since then, he has provided constant support for my efforts. I am especially grateful that he afforded me complete freedom to organize and write this history as I saw fit.

In the mid-1970s, when I served as history department chair, Western

Connecticut State College approached its seventy-fifth birthday. With an eye on this anniversary, I persuaded John V. "Jack" Friel, a retired Exxon executive who had returned to school to earn his master's degree in history at WestConn, to research and write this history. Jack spent a year gathering material without compensation (he returned to the school the stipend provided by the WestConn One Hundred Society). Though he was not able to complete the history, he carefully indexed all his data, including tapes of thirty-five interviews with key faculty members, administrators, and community leaders, and deposited it in the Archives of the Haas Library. Without this material, particularly the recorded interviews with individuals now no longer living, I could not have written the early chapters.

Truman Warner made innumerable contributions to WestConn. None were more important than the massive newspaper clipping file that he assembled from the mid-1950s to the mid-1990s. The bulk of this treasure-trove documents the history of Danbury and its surrounding towns. However, five large file boxes deal with the history of the college. Warner's diligence, coupled with his historical training and sensitivity, enabled me to locate pertinent articles from otherwise unindexed local newspapers.

The history of Western Connecticut State University, or for that matter the history of any Danbury institution, could not be written without reliance on local newspapers. Except for one six-year period, Danbury had a single daily newspaper, variously titled over one hundred years. The *Danbury Evening News*, originally a weekly, began daily publication in 1883, under the direction of the legendary "Danbury News Man," James Montgomery Bailey. It remained the sole Danbury newspaper until the rival *Danbury Times* was established by hatting mogul Frank Lee in 1927. Economic woes during the Depression forced the merger of the two publications, in 1933, into the *Danbury News-Times*. In 1953, the Ottaway chain acquired the paper and, in 1962, eliminated "Danbury" from its name. In this book, I have cited the newspaper by the name on its masthead at the time of each reference.

Three former faculty members wrote brief histories of the school, all of which were helpful to me. Longtime librarian May Greene's unpublished essay,

"Danbury Teachers College: A Brief History" (a copy is in the university Archives), sketches key events in the school's life up to 1950. Alumna and Emerita Professor of Education Charlotte Isham's "History of Western Connecticut State College" (1978), written to commemorate the school's seventy-fifth anniversary, is more detailed. Emeritus Mathematics Professor Edwin Rosenberg carefully compiled "A History of Western Connecticut State University (1978-1993)" as part of the 1993 ten-year accreditation process conducted by the New England Association of Schools and Colleges.

Dr. Gertrude Braun came to Danbury in 1946 and retired in 1982. During her career, she served as academic dean, academic vice president, and, on two occasions, acting president. Very little of importance took place at the college during these years that did not involve her. I thank her for sharing her extensive knowledge of WestConn's past with me in three lengthy interviews and in numerous long-distance phone conversations.

The staff of the Ruth Haas Library—especially Joanne Elpern, Russ Gladstone and Vijay Nair—have been extremely helpful during the three years of research and writing. WestConn's pioneer archivist, Mary Rieke, went well beyond the call of professional duty to assist me. A former student and friend, Mary frequently located material that I would have missed and was unfailingly unruffled as I made a mess of her careful filing system. Meg Moughan, the current archivist, continued to provide generous and skilled assistance, particularly in locating photographs.

Librarians at many other institutions eased my task. Of this able group I want to give special thanks to state archivist Mark Jones who facilitated my use of the riches of the Connecticut State Library.

The photographs in this book came from many sources. In addition to those in the Haas Library Archives, two other offices on campus, Alumni Relations and University Publications and Design, collected and preserved a significant number of historical photographs that have now been deposited in the central Archives. Helen Masterson, former director of Alumni Affairs, and her assistant, Janine Brennan, provided critical guidance in locating photographs. They also supplied me with names of alumni to interview. Peggy Stewart, the university photographer, did more than let me rummage through the collection of photographs in the files of Publications; she advised me which photographs to include in the book and then did all of the technical manipulation necessary to prepare them for publication.

A smaller number of photographs came from various other places. Former Danbury Mayor James Dyer served as the official yearbook photographer during his student days and for a few years after his graduation. He made available his carefully indexed collection of proof sheets and negatives capturing campus activities throughout the 1970s. Elizabeth Laws, class of 1942, contributed her snapshots of campus activities in the late 1930s and early 1940s. The photos of Danbury scenes come from the Danbury Scott-Fanton Museum and Historical Society, and from the Greater Danbury Chamber of Commerce. Scott Ames, the sports information director in the WestConn athletics department, promptly answered my request for photographs of the highly successful 1989-90 men's and women's basketball teams. Paul Evans of the *News-Times* was equally efficient in providing a copy of an early photo that appeared in *Images of the Past*, published by the newspaper in 2001.

After finishing a draft of each chapter, I asked five people to read it and make comments on substance and style. Each had a different relationship to WestConn; each helped me in different ways. Former Dean of Arts and Sciences Jim Pegolotti, an author himself, spotted organizational flaws and omissions. English Professor Ed Hagan helped rid the manuscript of clichés and reliance on the pesky verb "to be." Alumnus and historian Steve Flanagan raised important interpretive issues that I had ignored. Two of my sons, Herbert Janick III and Stephen Janick, asked questions that would occur only to "outsiders " to the school. They also proved that their costly educations were worthwhile by correcting their father's faulty grammar. I strained the bonds of friendship and family by asking this group for such sustained criticism, and am deeply grateful for their willing assistance.

At this point my able editor, Connie Conway, went to work. She imposed consistency on the text and made many beneficial stylistic suggestions. The book is a far better literary product because of her expert care.

A team of extremely competent people responded with skill and enthusiasm to the challenge of publishing the university's first book-length manuscript. Jason Davis and Irene Sherlock, the director and associate director of University Publications and Design, guided the entire process from editing to final layout. Dr. Koryoe Anim-Wright, the director of public relations, kept a watchful eye on progress and gave the complete text an attentive reading in search of errors. Peggy Stewart took care of the historical photographs and added some of her own striking contemporary shots. Quietly, master graphic designer Frederica Paine turned typed pages into an eye-catching book. I benefited in many ways from her tact and patience. Yvonne Johnson did heroic duty under a tight deadline as the final editorial reader. The index was swiftly and accurately compiled by Michael Rossa of Plano, Texas. Bob Stone provided expert advice on publication procedures. When I began working with this group, I expected them to be efficient professionals (they were); I was pleased to discover that they were also cooperative and excited about this project.

And finally, my debt to my wife, Mary Jane, is huge. She rescued me from numerous computer messes, patiently endured countless tales of WestConn lore, and resisted the temptation to ask why I devoted so much time and energy to this history. For her support, respect, and constant love, I am deeply grateful.

Herbert Janick
Ridgefield, Connecticut
June 2002

TABLE OF CONTENTS

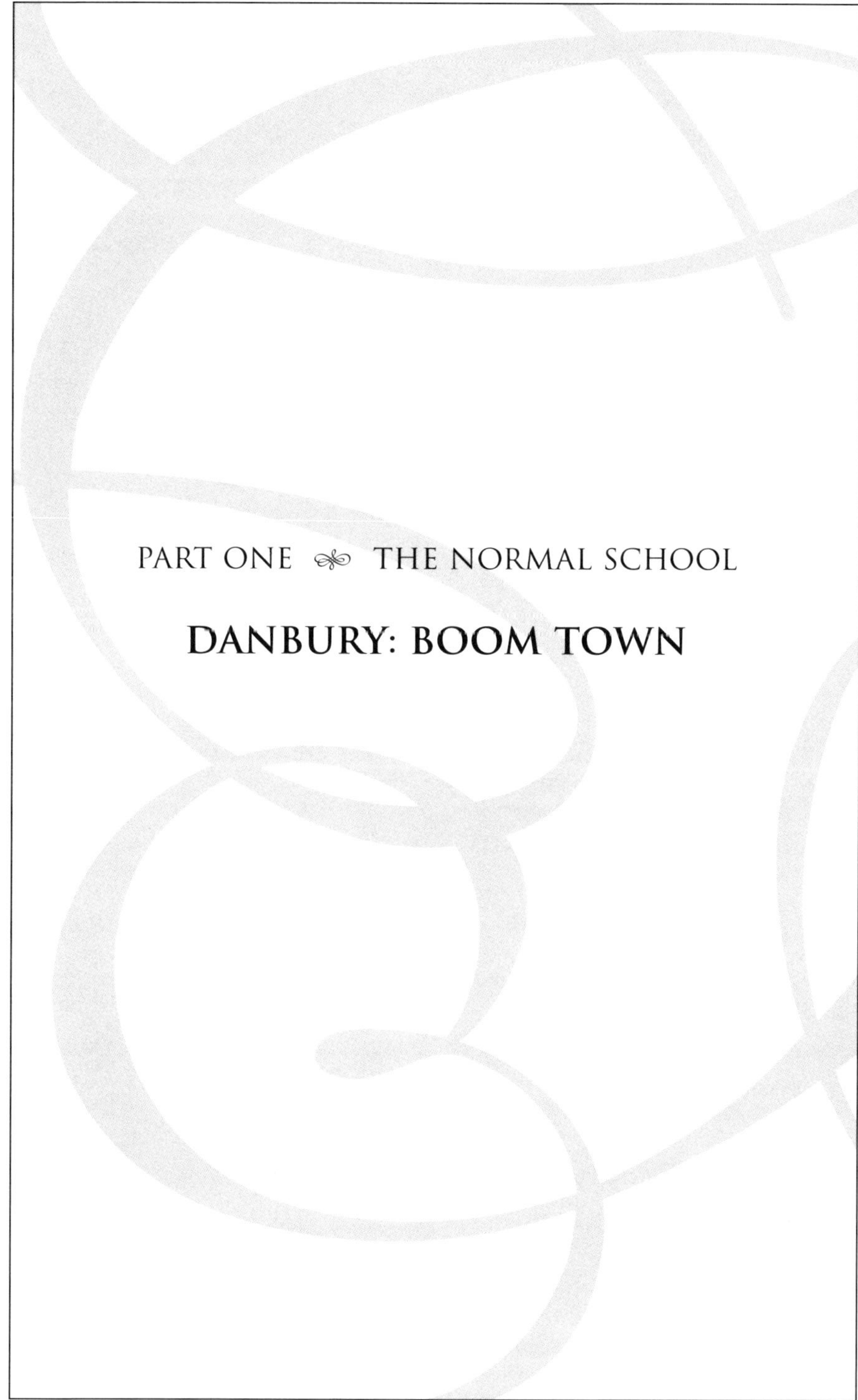

PART ONE ❧ THE NORMAL SCHOOL

DANBURY: BOOM TOWN

Opposite: Danbury's bustling Main Street, looking south from White Street, circa 1920. (Scott-Fanton Museum and Historical Society)

DANBURY: BOOM TOWN

Danbury was grief-stricken by the death of President William McKinley in the late summer of 1901. The parade held that September 19th in memory of the assassinated president was the largest Danbury had ever witnessed. Factories, stores, offices and schools closed down, and bunting in black as well as red, white, and blue draped buildings in all parts of the city. Solid lines of mourners flanked the Main Street parade route from Crosby to Wooster Streets. A long file of military organizations, headed by the Moore-White Post of the Grand Army of the Republic, marched in subdued cadence, followed by fire companies with horse-drawn fire engines covered in black cloth. Knights Templars, Knights of Pythias, and Elks—all the fraternal organizations to which McKinley had belonged—strode together in silence. When the procession reached St. Peter's Church, the voices of five hundred parochial school children lifted into the air, singing "Nearer My God to Thee." Turning at Elmwood Park, the throng of marchers with black arm bands passed the Congregational Church, where no less than a thousand public school pupils repeated the slain president's favorite hymn.

This somber tribute, heartfelt though it was, did not reflect Danbury's real mood during the first decade of the twentieth century. The hatting industry, the key to the city's economy, had recovered from the depression of 1893. All signals pointed to an era of full employment, with a substantial boom in construction of public buildings and private homes. The city's population was on the increase. Optimism characterized the decade. The success of local citizens, in 1903, in persuading the Connecticut General Assembly to locate the state's fourth teacher training institution in Danbury, rather than in rival Waterbury, was evidence of the community's new vigor and a symbol of its confidence in the future.

The home of the state's youngest normal school would be a factory town of approximately twenty thousand residents. The 1906 report of the Connecticut state factory inspector indicated that sixty-two factories operated in Danbury, more than in any city of its size in the state. Of these, thirty-seven were related to the hatting industry. Twenty-two firms made complete hats, both the stiff and soft varieties. Others removed fur from animal skins, produced rough hat bodies, or specialized in finishing hats. The remainder manufactured hat machinery, hat boxes, or silk hat bands and linings. A chamber of commerce survey in 1916 indicated that 76 percent of all local workers were employed in some phase of hatting.

The industry left its mark on Danbury in ways not reflected in statistics. The presence of many medium-size companies, rather than a few giant firms, meant divided power. Most hat factory owners had once been workers themselves and had personal friendships with their employees and intimate knowledge of shop floor culture. Because hat making was less mechanized than many other industries, the workers were not machine tenders but skilled artisans. A strong union protected these skills, guaranteeing a substantial voice for labor in the production process. Comparatively high wages for piece work enabled a significant number of hatters to own their own homes. These factors shaped Danbury into a middle-class community that avoided the extremes of great wealth and abject poverty that characterized other mill towns.

The city was proud that it had emerged from the economic doldrums of the late nineteenth century. The *Danbury Evening News* boasted in August 1901 that eleven hundred makers and about the same number of finishers were on the job earning an average of $3.50 a day, a high wage for factory workers. Local banks opened a record number of savings accounts. Many Danbury hatters who had left the city during hard times returned, while journeymen from manufacturing centers such as Yonkers, New York, and East Orange, New Jersey, and even Philadelphia, settled in Danbury. The publisher of the *Crofut City Directory* confessed in 1902 that he "was astonished to see how many new families have moved into the city in the past year," adding that tenements vacant a year or two before were now filled. He estimated that approximately eight hundred people had settled in the city during the previous year. By 1907, the shortage of skilled workers was so great that hatters remained on the job year round without the normal seasonal layoffs. The federal census of 1910 confirmed this robust picture when it reported that Danbury's population had increased to almost twenty-four thousand, a gain of more than 20 percent in the decade.

Boom times meant expanding factories. So many companies put up additions and installed new machinery that the Danbury and Bethel Gas and Electric Company had to invest in a 750-horsepower electric generator to meet the demand for additional power. Industrialist Arthur E. Tweedy's reaction was typical: he doubled the capacity of his silk mill, where material for hat linings was produced, by purchasing thirty-five more weaving looms. But it was Frank Lee who emerged as the dominant entrepreneur during these expansion years. In 1909, in partnership with Harry McLachlan, Lee built the largest factory in the city on land between South Street and the New Haven Railroad's tracks. Designed by local architect Philip Sunderland, the 900,000-square-foot steel and brick structure would ultimately accommodate more than two thousand workers.

Visitors quickly noticed the upturn in Danbury's fortunes. New buildings appeared everywhere in the downtown. In 1903, those who traveled by railroad, as most still did, entered the city through a modern depot on White Street. Not far from there, on West Street, rose the impressive new headquarters of the Southern New England Telephone Company, which housed the area's first phone exchange. But change was most evident on Main Street. Prominent hat manufacturer John W. Green built the elegant Hotel Green in 1907. In the 1920s and 1930s, it would become a favorite destination for automobile tourists motoring into New England. When the First Congregational Church was destroyed in 1907, it was replaced by a classical temple-style structure for the Savings Bank of Danbury, which was anxious to take its place on the "bank row" stretch of the city's most prestigious street. The Empress Theater, the first theater to be built in the city since the Taylor Opera House in the 1870s, opened its doors to vaudeville and movie audiences in 1912. For Danbury's swelling Catholic population, a second church was built on the northern end of Main Street in 1905. Romanesque in style, St. Joseph's served many of the city's recent Italian, Hungarian, Syrian and Polish immigrants.

The vibrant economy put pressure on local housing stock. In response, developers built dozens of new dwellings each year, especially in areas served by the Danbury and Bethel Street Railway, the primary means of transportation within the city. Even the recession of 1908 failed to slow the building boom. The *Evening News* boasted that during the summer you couldn't walk in any direction in the city without seeing a new home going up. Still, the paper lamented that at least one hundred families were seeking decent living quarters.

The city that welcomed the fledgling Normal School was not without problems. Prosperity muted but did not erase divisions in the community. Labor disputes were frequent as employers, though flush with profits, sought to break the grip of the union, the United Hatters of North America. Old stock Yankees and established immigrant groups (such as the Irish and Germans) often subtly discriminated against more recent arrivals. The temperance crusade, preached from both Protestant and Catholic pulpits, had class and ethnic dimensions.

Yet, the predominant tone of life in the Hat City during the first decades of the twentieth century was upbeat. Energy and optimism were the twin engines of progress. John R. Perkins, the first principal of the Normal School, understood and shared this booster spirit. He commended city officials in 1920 for buying land along White Street for future needs of the public school system. "Old Danbury ideas are dying out," he proclaimed in an interview with the local newspaper. "New Danbury is profiting from the mistakes of the past." Then, looking back over the time he had spent in the changing city, he concluded with satisfaction, "Danbury is now thoroughly awake." ■

Above: Normal School students entered Old Main for the first time on September 5, 1905. (WCSU Archives)

Opposite: This was the auditorium that was located above the gymnasium in Old Main. Students were greeted by Principal John Perkins in this room. (WCSU Archives)

CHAPTER ONE

NORMAL SCHOOL FOR DANBURY

The electric lights in the dining room of the Hotel Groveland burned late on the night of June 4, 1903. Gathered around tables in the popular restaurant on Main Street, members of the Normal School Committee and their supporters celebrated the Connecticut Senate's vote earlier that day to make Danbury the site of the fourth such school in the state. A few hours before, the crowd had greeted Danbury's two General Assembly representatives, Republican Charles Hoffman and Democrat Martin Gorman, on their return from the state capitol, and had escorted them the short distance from the railroad depot to the hotel. After dinner, Committee Chairman Michael T. Cuff, an alderman from the Fourth Ward, lauded the bipartisan cooperation of Hoffman and Gorman and praised the generosity of Bridgeport architect Ernest Southey, the designer of a new Danbury high school then under construction. At a critical point in the House debate, Southey, a member of the city's delegation to Hartford, presented a handsomely framed sketch of the proposed Normal School building; the sketch neutralized the delaying tactics of hostile legislators. The committee, set up six months before by a special town meeting in response to a petition drive, exulted over its success. Astute political observers agreed: the effectiveness of the Danbury lobby was the surprise of the session. It surrounded "the Legislative Jericho" and the walls tumbled down, conceded a chagrined *Waterbury American* newspaper reporter.

Danbury won membership in an educational system that was once considered unorthodox. Conservative Connecticut had been hesitant to embrace the normal school* approach to training elementary schoolteachers. Henry Barnard, the first secretary of the Connecticut Board of School Commissioners, had urged the state to set up "at least one seminary for teachers" in 1839, the year Massachusetts opened the country's first publicly supported normal school. Ten years later, long after Barnard had left the state to become superintendent of schools in Rhode Island, the cautious Connecticut General Assembly concluded that "such schools are no longer to be regarded as a doubtful experiment." When the New Britain Normal School opened in 1850, with Barnard as principal, it was the fifth such institution in the country. For the next forty years, New Britain Normal School, whose student body never exceeded four hundred and often was half that number, was the sole source of Connecticut schoolteachers trained at public expense.

The powerful forces of industrialization, immigration and urbanization, which had slowly transformed Connecticut in the early nineteenth century, accelerated between 1880 and 1900. During these two decades, the population of the state nearly doubled, rising from 527,000 to 908,000. In that same period, the number of factories in Connecticut increased 105 percent to more than 9,000. Products from machine tools to textiles made the state second in the nation in the value of industrial output per capita. Attracted by the promise of manufacturing jobs, thousands of European immigrants flocked into the state. By 1900, 240,000 residents of Connecticut were foreign-born. Only 41 percent of the state's population had parents who had been born in the United States. In cities, the percentage was even smaller. Rural towns shrank in size as their inhabitants moved into urban centers. Sixty-five towns in the state lost population during these twenty years. Urban population soared: New Haven became the first city in Connecticut to contain more than 100,000 people; Bridgeport, Hartford, and Waterbury topped 50,000; seventeen other cities had populations greater than 10,000.

*Though it strikes contemporary ears as strange, the designation "normal school" comes from the French *ecole normal*, meaning "model" or "rules" school. The United States followed the French and German mode of having separate colleges for the training of teachers.

These economic and demographic changes put intense pressure on the public schools, where enrollment had jumped approximately 60 percent from the end of the Civil War to the turn of the century. A compulsory school attendance law, passed in 1872, and a child labor law approved by the General Assembly in 1886, both vigorously enforced by the State Board of Education, boosted regular attendance. The numbers of children of diverse nationalities overwhelmed urban schools. The 1900 census listed forty-three different countries as the birthplaces of Connecticut immigrants. In contrast, rural schools were starved for numbers and resources.

By the late 1880s, the State Board of Education, charged since 1865 with the responsibility of supervising the public schools, realized that the supply and quality of teachers in Connecticut was inadequate. Only a small fraction of the approximately three thousand public school teachers had graduated from a normal school. Turnover was high. The annual report of the state board in 1888 revealed that four hundred new teachers were hired every year in Connecticut. But in that same year, New Britain Normal School graduated only eighty young women. Consequently, standards for hiring dropped, and the quality of education suffered. "A large part of the teachers do not know how or what to teach," was the board's bleak assessment of the situation in New London County. The superintendent of schools in Stamford was equally blunt and more colorful when he described the neglected rural schools in his area. "If you possessed a blooded horse or a valuable dog," he warned parents, "you would put it in the hands of trainers more skilled in their line of work than the teachers of some of these schools . . . are in theirs."

Charles Hine, secretary of the state board from 1883 to 1920, championed the obvious solution of establishing additional normal schools in the fastest growing parts of Connecticut. In 1889, the General Assembly responded to this need by appropriating funds for a second institution in Willimantic to serve the region east of the Connecticut River. Nevertheless, the largest cities in the state were forced to rely on haphazard local arrangements to prepare their teachers. To remedy this situation, the legislature in 1893 authorized the establishment of state normal schools in New Haven and Bridgeport. Only New Haven fulfilled the state mandate to provide a building for the new school, and thus became the home of the third normal school in Connecticut. Bridgeport, hard hit by an economic depression, was unwilling to assume the costs of maintaining a state school building and ultimately decided to continue reliance on a city-run training school, which remained in existence until 1942.

At the start of the twentieth century, only the western part of the state, which included populous and wealthy Fairfield County, had no state teacher-training facility. Waterbury, however, as an industrial center of more than fifty thousand people in New Haven County, confidently expected it would be the home of the next normal school chartered by the legislature. When a bill to set up a school in Waterbury failed, by a narrow margin, to win the approval of the General Assembly's education committee in 1899, the city took steps to ensure that its next request would be looked on more favorably. Republican Senator Cornelius Tracy, a prominent builder and lumber dealer in Waterbury, sought and won the post of chairman of the education committee, which put him in a position to advance the city's interests. A confident Mayor Edward Kilduff of Waterbury appointed a committee in December 1902 to draw up a bill to secure the school.

Waterbury was in for a surprise. As the 1903 legislative session approached, Danbury, for the first time, quietly prepared to present its claim as the logical location for a state teacher-training institution that would serve the 250,000 residents of Fairfield and Litchfield Counties. A special town meeting was called to develop strategy, and a committee of prominent citizens, dominated by lawyers and businessmen, was appointed to spearhead the drive. Without dissent, the same public meeting approved spending $10,000 to purchase land for a school building.

The person most responsible for Danbury's sudden interest in becoming the home of the next normal school was a newcomer to the city. John R. Perkins was thirty-one years old when he became principal of Danbury High School in 1899. This energetic graduate of Dartmouth College had just completed four years of teaching at New Britain High School, where he had come to know and appreciate the normal school system. When Perkins arrived in Danbury, the young teacher immediately saw the need for a similar institution in western Connecticut. The first to suggest approaching the General Assembly for money to build a school in Danbury, he persuaded leading citizens to support the idea. He helped organize the sizable delegations from the region, which testified at legislative hearings, and he even spoke to legislators himself. It was entirely appropriate that Perkins should become the first principal of the Danbury Normal School. With justification, the *Evening News* would describe John Perkins at the time of his death in 1923 as "virtually the father of the movement to establish a state normal school in the city."

The two rival cities took different approaches in their efforts to get a normal school. Waterbury relied on the power of Senator Tracy to gain the endorsement of the education committee. Danbury, conscious of the Brass City's advantage, could not ignore the education committee but concentrated on winning the support of the appropriations committee, which was responsible for considering the cost of construction of all campus buildings. The bill sponsored by Representative Hoffman, authorizing $100,000 to build a normal school in Danbury, was first introduced to the appropriations committee before it was referred to the education committee.

Danbury mobilized for the first set of hearings, held in March 1903 by the legislature's education committee. Characterized by a Danbury reporter on the scene as "one of the most enthusiastic workers in the interest of the normal school," John Perkins spent several days in the capitol coordinating lobbying tactics. Thirty citizens of Danbury traveled to Hartford to testify. Those who could not attend were kept abreast of developments by bulletins posted outside the newspaper's Main Street office in Danbury. Reverend Andrew Hubbard, pastor of the Second Baptist Church and a member of the Danbury school board for thirty years, told lawmakers that at no time had more than 5 percent of the teachers in local schools been graduates of a normal school. He attributed this sorry situation to the fact that most young women in the city who wanted to be teachers came from families of limited means and could not afford to travel or board in New Haven or New Britain. By design, most of the testimony came from legislators and citizens of other towns in Fairfield and Litchfield counties. The superintendent of schools in Stamford, who also represented the Fairfield

County Round Table made up of superintendents and principals, spoke about the need for teachers in his district. He claimed that 80 percent of the Stamford teachers were trained outside of Connecticut normal schools. A normal school in Danbury—convenient by train to southern Fairfield County—would, he asserted, quickly improve this ratio.

On occasion, rational arguments degenerated into partisan bickering. In a heavy-handed manner, Chairman Tracy took time allotted to Danbury speakers for pro-Waterbury testimonials. This so angered the Danbury delegation that two members, Judge James E. Walsh and industrialist N. Burton Rogers, appeared at the Waterbury portion of the hearings the following day to challenge Tracy, who fumed that they were trying to usurp the power of the chairman. The fervor of the rivalry between the two cities is evident in the indignant comment by the *Waterbury American* that Judge Walsh behaved as if he were "berating a witness in a justice court."

It was a foregone conclusion that the education committee would wholeheartedly endorse a fourth normal school. What was shocking was their six-to-three vote in favor of building the school in Danbury. Evidently Senator Tracy's extreme prejudice had alienated some committee members. The number and enthusiasm of Danbury boosters who attended the hearing also proved persuasive and Senator E. Stanley Welles of Newington, one committee member who rebuffed Waterbury, admitted this spirit had convinced him a normal school in Danbury "would be appreciated and supported." In retaliation, an angry Tracy filed a minority report stating in effect that unless a school was built in Waterbury, no other normal school should be authorized. The next battle would be fought in the appropriations committee.

When the appropriations committee held hearings on both the majority and minority reports on May 12, 1903, Danbury was prepared. So many supporters jammed the two morning trains to Hartford that a bemused *Waterbury American* reporter referred to them as a "Coxey-army-like"* group that overflowed the hear-

*Jacob Coxey led an "army" of four hundred unemployed men from Ohio to Washington, D.C., in 1894 to demand that the federal government inaugurate a massive public works program to aid victims of the depression of 1893.

ing room at the capitol and forced the session to be moved to the nearby state supreme court quarters. It was easy to identify the members of the delegation because they all sported blue badges bearing the slogan "Normal School for Danbury."

Judge Howard Scott of Danbury City Court was the principal spokesman at the formal appropriations committee hearings. He stressed the inequality of the present situation, explaining that 92 percent of the teachers in Hartford County were trained in normal schools, compared with only 31 percent in Fairfield County and 23 percent in Litchfield County. This imbalance occurred, Scott charged, because the convenient New Britain Normal School served central Connecticut well, while the southern and western parts of the state were ignored. Strong Comstock, the principal of the Balmforth Avenue School and the authorized representative of both the Teachers Association of Fairfield County and the School Masters Round Table, agreed, pointing out that some towns in Fairfield County were one hundred miles away from any normal school. "One part of the state should be as well looked after as another," Comstock asserted. Charles Merritt, a prominent hat manufacturer, added a blunt nativist argument: western Connecticut, he warned, was filling up with foreigners who did not understand "American standards." A normal school in this part of the state would provide teachers who could inculcate this potentially dangerous group with "the principles of good manners, good morals, and good citizenship."

This time Danbury was disappointed. Despite the persistent rumor that Governor Abraham Chamberlin favored the Danbury bill, the appropriations committee recommended that no money should be spent to establish a school in that city. The real motives of the committee are hard to fathom, but the majority of the members claimed they were troubled by the unwillingness of the Connecticut State Department of Education to go on record supporting the position that another state normal school was needed. This reluctance is also mystifying. Published reports of the department demonstrated that both the New Britain and the New Haven schools, the only ones remotely accessible to western Connecticut residents, were crowded. In addition, Secretary Hine gave private assurances to legislators that another school was justified. Probably nothing more complicated than bureaucratic caution led the Connecticut State Department of Education to leave the decision up to the General Assembly. As one member of the education committee put it, the agency simply "wanted to keep their hands off the thing." Danbury's hopes were still alive, however, because three members of the committee had sent a minority report endorsing the Danbury bill to the General Assembly.

In the final week of the legislative session, first the full House and then the Senate considered Danbury's request. Once again, many Danburians traveled to Hartford to witness the final debate. On June 2, 1903, the now familiar arguments were rehashed with one additional obstacle brought up by Representative Everett Lake, a future Connecticut governor, who contended that no money could be allocated for a school building without an examination of detailed architectural plans. Anticipating this tactic, Danbury's representatives had architect Southey ready to exhibit renderings of the front view of the proposed building, satisfying critics. This shrewd countermove paid off. The final votes were one-sided. The House rejected Waterbury's request and approved money for a Danbury school, both by a comfortable three-to-one margin.

Two days later, just before adjournment, the Connecticut State Senate debate began. Senator Tracy, smarting from his wounds, delivered an emotional speech charging that the Danbury lobby had piloted the bill through the General Assembly by adept logrolling. He claimed that more votes were traded on this bill than on any other in the session. The extent of his animus toward Danbury is indicated by his statement that he was now ready to accept a new normal school in Norwalk. The rest of the discussion was heated, but more civil. Early in the afternoon, two votes were taken. The first, on the majority report of the appropriations committee to reject Danbury's request, ended in an eleven-to-eleven tie, broken in Danbury's favor by Lieutenant Governor Henry J. Roberts.* The second vote, to support the minority recommendation to build a school in Danbury, was anticlimactic. Representatives Hoffman and Gorman rushed back to Danbury to deliver the good news.

*In 1906, Danbury named the street just west of the first Normal School building Roberts Avenue in honor of then-governor, Henry J. Roberts.

During the tense legislative maneuvering over the fate of the $100,000 appropriation, Danbury officials had deliberately postponed consideration of possible sites for a normal school on the grounds that it might cause disagreement among local backers. Now Danbury had the money and needed to find an appropriate location for the new school. Requirements were stringent. Because the land had to be near trolley lines and the railroad station, a downtown location was essential. Yet the two or three acres recommended by the state were hard to find in that crowded central part of the city.

Alexander Moss White, Danbury's most generous philanthropist, provided an ideal solution. A member of a family of ministers and merchants whose roots reached back into pre-Revolutionary Danbury, the elderly White had often been a benefactor of the city. Even though he had not lived in Danbury for sixty years (residing instead in an elegant brownstone in Brooklyn Heights), he operated a fur factory on Beaver Street with his brother William. White's best-known act of civic munificence came in the late 1870s, when he donated funds to build a public library on the site of the family home at the corner of Main Street and Library Place.

Now in his late eighties, White stepped forward to give the city three acres of his three-hundred-acre farm on White Street as a home for the new Normal School. It was a superb location: spacious, with room for expansion, and, since July 1903 when the railroad station relocated to a new building on White Street, even closer to public transportation.

These developments pleased Secretary Charles Hine of the Connecticut State Board of Education. He had always believed that more normal schools were needed in the state and had urged legislators privately to support Danbury's proposal in the last session of the General Assembly. He was so accommodating in working out the details of the cooperative arrangement between the city and the state that the *Evening News* expressed surprise "that the town expected to grant more than the state had asked." Danbury readily agreed to provide the necessary practice schools. Hine, a champion of better rural education, was especially pleased that the city would make several one-room schools available for student teachers.

Hine successfully pressured the Boston architectural firm of Hartwell,

Richardson, and Driver to finish the construction drawings for the school building by the end of the year. On December 30, 1903, the *Evening News* gave citizens their first look at what is today known as "Old Main," reprinting the architect's rendering of the front elevation of the structure. In the accompanying article, the newspaper quoted Hine's description of the building as "handsome and dignified," and added some of its own more pragmatic adjectives: "compact, simple, and thoroughly practical."

In December 1902, a normal school in Danbury had been merely an idea in the mind of the new high school principal, John R. Perkins. One year later, it was almost a reality. In just twelve months, a bitter legislative battle was won, land was obtained, and plans for a building were drawn. Construction would begin in the spring of 1904. ■

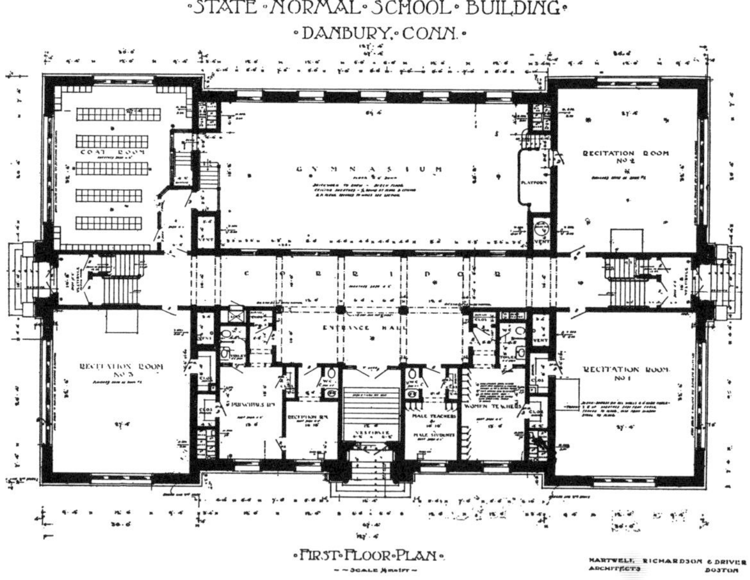

Above: Original first floor plan of Old Main showing location of gymnasium, classrooms, and the principal's office. (WCSU Archives)

Note On Sources

The primary documentation for Danbury's successful campaign to win the Normal School comes from the pages of the daily newspaper, the *Danbury Evening News*, whose masthead justifiably boasted that it was a record of a New England town. Because of the intense local interest in this topic, the newspaper gave full coverage to the lobbying efforts. Stories appeared almost daily, especially in the final weeks of the General Assembly session. The paper printed lengthy articles with verbatim statements made by those who spoke at legislative hearings. "Stenographer's Notes of Public Hearings Before the Joint Standing Committee on Appropriations, Hearing Regarding An Appropriation For a Normal School At Danbury" (May 12, 1903), housed in the Connecticut State Library in Hartford, amplifies this testimony.

Unfortunately, careless microfilming preserved only the special Wednesday issues of the daily Danbury paper of 1903. No original print editions for this period exist. While the Wednesday paper was the largest of the week and contained many summary articles, it was frustrating not to be able to consult every issue published during the legislative debate. A lengthy and thorough research paper about the establishment of the school is located in the Ruth Haas Library Archives, and partially offsets this handicap. Written around 1970 by an unidentified student of Dr. Truman Warner, the paper quotes extensively from the now-destroyed 1903 issues of the *News*, as well as from other Connecticut newspapers.

Donald Averill's Ph.D. dissertation, "The Responsibility of the Connecticut Board of Education for the Education of Teachers in the State from 1865 to 1965" (University of Connecticut, 1966), is the best treatment of the role of the Connecticut State Board of Education in the management of the normal schools. An unpublished article written by Hine's colleague, D. C. Allen, titled "Charles D. Hine and His Public Service," evaluates Hine's thirty-seven-year tenure as secretary of the state board.

Two other University of Connecticut Ph.D. dissertations explore the history of the state normal schools: Richard Pratte's "A History of Teacher Education in Connecticut from 1639 to 1939" (1967), and Michael Pernal's "A Study of State Legislation in the Development of Public Higher Education in Connecticut from 1849 to 1970" (1975). Each of the three other normal schools in Connecticut have published histories of varying age and quality. The oldest and weakest is Herbert E. Fowler's *A Century of Teacher Education in Connecticut: The Story of New Britain Normal School and Teachers College of Connecticut* (New Britain: 1949). Arthur Charles Forst's Ph.D. dissertation, "From Normal School to State College: The Growth and Development of Eastern Connecticut State College from 1889 to 1959" (University of Connecticut, 1980), is well done, but stops at the point when the school becomes a general purpose state college. Southern Connecticut boasts the most comprehensive and scholarly treatment. Thomas Farnham's *Southern Connecticut State University: A Centennial History, 1893-1993* (New Haven, 1993) is a model university history: accurate, relevant, and readable.

Above: John Perkins spearheaded the drive for a teacher-training school in the city. He served as the first principal of Danbury Normal School from 1903 until his death in 1923. (WCSU Archives)

Opposite: Miry Brook School (1912). Danbury Normal School required all students to complete a practice-teaching assignment in a rural school. (WCSU Archives)

CHAPTER TWO

THE FOUNDING FATHER

Bridgeport was an important ally during Danbury's campaign to win a normal school. The largest city in Fairfield County, Bridgeport had been selected by the legislature in 1893 as the site for a state teacher-training institution, but economic and political obstacles stymied the plan. In 1903, one longtime member of the Bridgeport Board of Education, involved in the earlier negotiations with the state, appeared before the appropriations committee of the Connecticut General Assembly to recommend that the school now be built in Danbury. "Bridgeport doesn't want the school and the logical place is Danbury. We would be willing and glad to see a normal school in Danbury," he told the lawmakers.

Twenty years later, in May 1923, the *Bridgeport Telegram* would urge a reconsideration of this position. This was the time, the newspaper observed, to move the school from Danbury to Bridgeport. John R. Perkins, the founding father and first principal of the Danbury Normal School, had recently died, and the newspaper argued that Danbury could not operate the school properly without his leadership and experience.* Partisanship undoubtedly motivated this advice, but the

*Bridgeport grasped any plausible justification for a takeover of the Danbury facility. In February 1923, Bridgeport Superintendent of Schools E. Everett Cortright suggested that Danbury could ease the crowding of its high school by taking over the Normal School building and letting Bridgeport become the home of a state normal school in Fairfield County.

Telegram did capture accurately the extent to which Perkins shaped the Danbury Normal School during its first two decades.

John Perkins was the first of a trio of male Yankee educators who directed the Normal School until after World War II. His route to Danbury, although confined to New England, had many stops. Born in 1868 in Wells, Maine, to parents with lengthy down-east pedigrees but modest means, Perkins was an ambitious and able student. He graduated at the top of his class from Berwick Academy in South Berwick, Maine, where the family had moved when he was twelve years old. Perkins earned a bachelor's degree in 1889 and a master's degree in 1892, both at Dartmouth College. To help pay his tuition, he took time out from college to teach in two small high schools in his native state. A popular undergraduate, his peers admired his unassuming manner and his sturdy independence. "I am the same free trade crank and kicker," Perkins assured his classmates shortly after graduation. He prided himself on his willingness to support members of both political parties. "I recognize the good and the evil in each [party]," he told the Alumni Office in 1893, "and vote as I choose." When Dartmouth published a twenty fifth anniversary report on the activities of the members of the class of 1889, the editor emphasized that "John Perk" was still "not easily bossed."

Perkins entered teaching almost by default. Admitting that he could not make up his mind about a suitable career after finishing college, he accepted a job as principal of a forty-student high school in Mechanic Falls, Maine, a rustic hamlet near the Canadian border. Bored and underpaid, he moved after one term to a position as principal of the high school in his hometown of Berwick. Though relieved to be "once more in civilization," he was restless and resigned after one year to study at Tufts College. He was "following the German model, taking only chemistry," he explained. A year later, in 1893, he was off again, this time to the small community of Washington, Connecticut, to teach science and coach baseball at the Gunnery School.

At this point Perkins re-evaluated his life. His responsibilities had changed. The year he began teaching at the Gunnery, he met and married Mary Whittlesey Brown, the daughter of a prominent local physician. His career goals also were shifting. Since leaving college, where he insisted that his religious creed was simply the Golden Rule, he had undergone a personal religious experience and had become a member of the Congregational Church. Swept along by his developing religious sensibilities, he decided to abandon teaching and enter the ministry. For the next two years, Perkins immersed himself in Biblical studies in Greek and Hebrew at the Hartford Theological Seminary.

Before entering the third and final year of his ministerial studies, Perkins veered back to teaching. The historical record sheds no light on the motivation behind his decision to accept a teaching position at New Britain High School in 1896. It may have been a pragmatic response to the financial pressure of a growing family; his two children were born during the four years he taught in New Britain. Then again, the shift may not suggest anything other than his dedication to teaching. It is clear that Perkins saw his work with students as a legitimate path of Christian service.

The young educator came to Danbury at an opportune time. By the turn of the century, the local economy had improved sufficiently to permit the city to address the woeful inadequacy of its high school facility, a deficiency made worse by the recent addition of a fourth year to the secondary school curriculum. During the five years that Perkins served as principal of Danbury High School (1899 to 1904), he participated in every phase of the planning and construction of a modern school building. This earned him the friendship and respect of the key members of the community's power structure and put him in a position to gain support for his dream of bringing a teacher-training institution to Danbury. He worked closely with members of the high school building committee, which included Alderman Michael Cuff, who became the chairman of the Normal School Committee. Perkins also collaborated with the architect of the high school building, Ernest Southey, one of the heroes of the legislative campaign to win the Normal School. When the new high school, similar in architecture to the first Normal School building, opened at the corner of Main and Boughton Streets in September 1903, Perkins could look back with satisfaction on his role in mobilizing support for a state normal school in the city. It would come as no surprise to him or to the public when the State Board of Education named John R. Perkins as principal of the recently established Danbury Normal School in July 1904.

Construction of the Normal School building on a slight knoll (to minimize excavation costs) on the former White family farm had begun several months before Perkins' appointment as principal. Despite an unstable layer of wet clay soil that even a century later would continue to plague foundations in downtown Danbury (in prehistoric times the area was a lake bed), construction proceeded rapidly. During the summer of 1904, passers-by admired the emerging three-story, red brick and buff limestone building which a newspaper reporter, with forgivable exaggeration, characterized as being in the "Renaissance style." Citizens marveled at the exterior elevator, powered by a massive steam engine, as it effortlessly hauled building materials to the upper floors of the structure. By the time winter began, the masonry walls and roof were completed, allowing interior work to continue during inclement weather.

But Perkins was impatient and unwilling to wait for the building to be completed. Realizing that the new high school had available space, he proposed using a large, unfinished portion of its third floor, described by his daughter many years later as "very box-like storage rooms," as quarters for the first Normal School class. The State Board of Education, anticipating some local resistance, agreed to let Perkins act as principal of both Danbury High School and the Normal School during the transition year, when they would share the same facility.

With that potential obstacle out of the way, Perkins rushed to hire faculty and register students. He decided that he would teach science. Jane Burbank, a Wellesley College graduate, taught literature, and Sarah Armstrong, a veteran Massachusetts public school teacher, taught mathematics. The three were the only full-time employees. Part-time instructors covered other subjects, such as art and music, and one New Haven public school teacher traveled to Danbury one day a week to teach penmanship.

Perkins could devote little time to recruiting students, therefore the thirty-seven pioneers who trudged up the three flights of stairs to the high school attic in September 1904 were, with the exception of two from Norwalk, residents of Danbury or Bethel. Before the school year was over, they were joined by seven more, bringing the size of that historic first class to forty-four. Young (the oldest was twenty-two), and mostly of working class backgrounds, a dozen of them had listed their father's occupation as "hatter" on their application forms. Irish surnames predominated. Seven had previous teaching experience, either in rural public schools or St. Peter's Parochial School in Danbury. All were women, which made Perkins uncomfortable enough to publicize that the school would "welcome and make special provision for young men who want to enter." Although the Normal School was always officially co-educational, very few men entered elementary school teaching until the 1930s.*

At 9 a.m. on Tuesday, September 5, 1905, the tall, bespectacled, slightly rumpled Perkins mounted the small stage in the second-floor auditorium of the completed Normal School building to address a full student body for the first time. An entering class of forty-one juniors, representing fifteen towns, joined forty-three returning seniors in a two-year program that culminated in their state certification as elementary school teachers. There was one important addition to the faculty: Lothrop Higgins, the new science instructor, who presided over the state-of-the-art science lecture room with its tiered seats, skylight, sinks, and demonstration tables. He became Perkins' closest confidant, his informal assistant, and ultimately his successor as principal of the school.

For almost twenty years, however, it was John Perkins who bore the main responsibility of keeping the school afloat in the face of myriad difficulties. Enrollment fluctuated drastically. The school operated for more than a decade before the number of students reached one hundred. For a few years at the beginning of World War I, more than two hundred full-time students registered. But in 1920, enrollment plummeted to sixty-eight. Every dip, such as occurred in 1908, when the total student body numbered thirty-eight, and the following year when only eleven women graduated, provided ammunition for critics in other cities who coveted the school.

Perkins was creative in trying to boost attendance. From 1907 to 1914, Danbury operated a summer school that attracted large numbers of teachers who

*One of the rare male graduates in the early years was Ralph Carrington of the class of 1912. Gertrude Murphy, a classmate who later became a practice school teacher, recalled that he "never seemed embarrassed" by his singular status and concluded that "he evidently wanted to teach and that is what he did."

did not have a normal school degree. In 1912, as many as 325 teachers came to the campus from all parts of the state during the four-week summer session. Perkins himself was a regular summer faculty member, teaching a course called "Duties of Citizenship." Correspondence courses, offered between 1907 and 1914, were also popular. Peak enrollment came in 1911, when 180 students took advantage of these off-campus programs. Perkins mounted a recruiting drive when the number of full-time students dropped during and immediately after World War I. Faculty made visits to local high schools and an annual Field Day brought prospective students to the Danbury campus. When a survey revealed that most young people decided to become teachers during the eighth grade, the Normal School mailed a promotional letter to parents of that target group.

In general, Perkins blamed the pattern of lagging enrollment on the robust Connecticut economy that provided other, more attractive employment opportunities for young women. His annual reports to the State Board of Education are filled with jeremiads about the failure of towns to reward teachers properly. "The amount of money spent in support of schools is pitifully small when compared with the amount spent for amusements, tobacco, liquor," he criticized in 1918. He had no doubt that there was "definitely money in the state to run the school properly if people so desire." Perkins was particularly incensed that school systems were unwilling to pay normal school graduates more than they did teachers who did not have such training. Every public school teacher should be a graduate of a normal school, he insisted.

Entrance requirements were certainly not a barrier to increased enrollment. For most of the twenty years that John Perkins ran the school, he granted admission to any person who had reached sixteen years of age, had graduated from a three-year high school, could obtain two character references, and was willing to declare in writing that she or he intended to teach in a Connecticut public school. After World War I, the criteria were tightened slightly, requiring that applicants also maintain a grade average of 75 in high school classes and complete at least ten hours of academic courses. These stiffer rules could be ignored if the candidate passed a special examination drawn up by the normal school principals. And Perkins, with the approval of Secretary Hine, was willing to bend even these mild requirements. An occasional fifteen-year-old was admitted with the stipulation that she/he could not get a diploma until the age of nineteen. Sometimes a student would successfully plead for entrance to a normal school after only two years of high school. Perkins considered special circumstances liberally. "Exceptions are necessary," was his rule.

A normal school curriculum was not difficult. Students learned to teach the basic elementary school subjects of mathematics, reading, geography, history, literature and elementary science. Perkins understood that a normal school differed from a liberal arts college. In his first published mission statement, delivered in 1905, he was both terse and clear: "The school aims to train students to teach the useful and practical subjects in the best way."* Until the early 1920s, Perkins retained much independence in determining which courses would advance this goal. For many years, Hine would meet monthly with the four normal school principals for dinner and discussion of mutual problems, usually at the Graduates Club in New Haven. But the secretary of the state board did not attempt to centralize control over curriculum.

Even though normal school tuition was free and the state provided text books, the cost of boarding in Danbury handicapped out-of-town students, particularly those from rural areas. Perkins spent much of his time dealing with this problem. As with most other issues, he was flexible, permitting students on occasion to work as paid substitute teachers, tutors, house cleaners, or office clerks while school was in session. He convinced Danbury service clubs to create a fund from which needy students could borrow fifty dollars, with repayment not due until two years after graduation. When one parent of an applicant from Salisbury registered concern about college expenses, Perkins responded with characteristic confident determination: "My advice is that your daughter enter the school expecting that something will come to assist her." He intended that no student be kept away because of lack of money.

*In December 1905, Perkins, along with the other normal school principals, approved of the wording of a letter drafted by Hine and sent to the head of the Yale School of Education. The letter made this same point: "The normal schools are professional schools in the strictest sense as in law and medical schools. The whole time is given to preparation for practice—practice in the school room."

His experience supervising several country school districts as an agent of the state board had made Perkins aware that young women in rural towns, unable to commute to Danbury and without the funds to rent quarters near the Normal School, required special help. He persuaded the General Assembly in 1910 to set up a scholarship system that made it possible for every town with a grand list of less than $1.5 million to have one student enrolled in a normal school at all times, with the state covering the student's living expenses up to a maximum of $150 per year. In return for this subsidy, the student had to teach in her (or his) hometown for a minimum of three years. Many of these "town students" were attracted to Danbury because the school gave special attention to the unique problems of rural education. Danbury's was the only normal school in Connecticut requiring all students to spend time practice teaching in one of Danbury's one-room or two-room schools: Miry Brook, King Street, or Beaver Brook. Demonstration classes, designed to show what could be accomplished in rural schools, were the most popular feature of the annual summer school. A representative of the state board, reporting on the 1912 summer session, praised these model classes where all eight grades were present in one room. They "were crowded by teachers seeking information," commented the impressed official.

The two most vexing problems Perkins faced during his tenure as principal involved not pedagogy, but transportation for commuting students and accommodations for boarding students. The railroad was still the primary form of long-distance travel in early twentieth century Connecticut, and many day students depended on the train to get to Danbury. Because the curriculum in the students' first year concentrated on course work with limited observation in elementary classrooms, the Normal School class schedule could be and was geared to the train schedule. Classes normally did not start before 10 or 10:30 a.m. and ended by 3:30 p.m. to permit students to make train connections. When the need arose, Perkins was willing to make special arrangements. In 1911, he tailored the class-day for juniors commuting from Waterbury to the railroad schedule. Classes for this group began at 9:40 a.m. and were over in time for the return trip to the Brass City on the 2:32 p.m. train. This adaptability, on occasion, prompted gentle warnings from Hine not to let the railroads determine school attendance. "We may labor with the makers of timetables," the secretary admonished, "but schools must look out for their best interests." Perkins tried without success to get the New Haven Railroad to adjust its service to meet the school's needs.

Even relaxed schedules imposed burdens on commuting students. The principal of Newtown High School wrote to Perkins in 1907, asking if he could be lenient with one of his graduates from Sandy Hook who wanted to attend the Normal School. He explained that she had to walk three miles to get a train at the Newtown station—a train that didn't arrive in Danbury until 10 a.m.—and he hoped Perkins would take into account that, in harsh winter weather, she might be late for class. He ended his letter with a familiar lament, "She can't afford to board in Danbury."

During the second year, when a total of twenty weeks of class time was spent in a training school, students were forced to live in Danbury. Student teachers had to be in the classroom at Locust Avenue or Balmforth Avenue, the two primary practice schools, early in the morning (by 8:10, one teacher recalled) to dust and ventilate the room and fill the inkwells. They rarely left before 4:30 in the afternoon. Perkins worked diligently to find boarding facilities for students, many of whom had little money yet voiced definite preferences. His records are filled with requests for living accommodations both "wholesome and refined," often coupled with a reminder that "it is necessary for me to be very economical." "I want a clean, comfortable place, and plain wholesome food. I would prefer a Catholic family," wrote one student in 1910. Perkins responded to all inquiries with lists of acceptable boarding families along with an estimate that the cost would be about five dollars per week. For some years, Mary Howarth, whose daughter was in the first Normal School graduating class, turned her home on White Street opposite the campus into a boarding house for approximately twenty young women.

The Normal School absorbed most of Perkins' energies for two decades. His duties ranged from negotiating with Danbury authorities for more practice classrooms to acting in loco parentis for his "girls." He did not consider it to be inappropriate when a member of the school committee of Cornwall, solicitous of the welfare of the town's student, asked him to "see to it in a fatherly way that she does not overwork, and has good associates." His office and his home were open, even on weekends, to parents who wanted to discuss school issues.

Yet Perkins also believed it necessary to get away from school business. "Charging his dynamo," as his daughter phrased it. He relaxed in ways that told much about the man. The outdoors and the automobile were central to Perkins' non-professional life. He was an ardent hunter who at one time was president of a local gun club. With his pointer dogs "Teddy" and "Dan'l" (named for Theodore Roosevelt and Daniel Webster), he spent leisure hours tromping through the western Connecticut woods. Perkins owned one of the first automobiles in Danbury, a 1905 two-cylinder Ford, and he upgraded models frequently over the years. He was happiest behind the wheel on Sunday excursions or on longer summer motor jaunts through New England. For years he entertained an ambition to drive from Danbury to Maine in a single day. That goal went unfulfilled, but in 1919, after the death of his wife, he and his two children covered nine thousand miles in an adventurous drive to the Pacific Coast. On his return to Danbury, Perkins, ever the careful administrator, sent a letter to the Dodge Motor Company with all the pertinent details of his car's performance on this trek.

Only one aspect of Perkins' career at Danbury frustrated him. Almost from the start of his tenure, he had concluded that a dormitory offered the only effective solution to the school's enrollment problem. He advocated the building of a residence hall for students from distant towns for the first time in his 1907 report to the state board, and hammered that point home in almost every subsequent annual report in succinct and sometimes fractured prose. "A dormitory ought to be part of the Normal School" (1908). "This school needs more than any other one thing a dormitory" (1910). "A dormitory is an essential part of a school plant" (1912). "The need of a dormitory is more pressing than ever" (1913). Construction of a dormitory ultimately became the top priority of a ten-year building program Perkins recommended to the state board in 1920.

To Perkins, a dormitory was more than a way to provide affordable housing for young women residing at a distance from Danbury. He saw it as a mechanism that would change the entire nature of the educational experience. It disturbed him that there was little social life at the school, and that commuting students tended to associate mainly with those from their own towns. Despite his precautions, students sometimes found themselves in off-campus quarters that, in Perkins' judgement, were not refined or morally wholesome. Even though he understood that the primary function of a normal school was job training, he believed that Danbury students should have the same cultural opportunities as his daughter who attended Radcliffe College.* A dormitory would provide an environment where women from working class backgrounds could gain "such habits of manner and attitudes of thought as shall bring a subtle but constant uplifting influence to bear on those children who rarely otherwise come under such influence." His vision was decidedly elitist: the dormitory would be the cultured home he felt so many of the Normal School students lacked.

The Connecticut State Board of Education agreed with Perkins. In 1908, the four normal school principals and Secretary Hine settled on a strategy that gave construction of boarding facilities at Willimantic and Danbury the highest importance. The General Assembly in 1909 rejected a bill to accomplish this goal; it had been sponsored by Representative N. Burton Rogers of Danbury, who had been a force in bringing the Normal School to the city. The legislature killed similar bills in every subsequent session until 1917. In that year, despite the conservative fiscal policies of elderly Governor Marcus Holcomb (a Republican), the General Assembly agreed to appropriate the funds required to build a residence hall in Willimantic and to purchase more land for a future dormitory in Danbury.

Here the modest momentum stalled. World War I and the economic dislocation that accompanied postwar reconstruction altered priorities. It wasn't until 1923 that the legislature was ready to give serious attention to the phantom Danbury dormitory. Another bitter struggle between the education committee and the appropriations committee ensued, reminiscent of the legislative battle that had taken place twenty years earlier when the school was established.

A bill introduced to the education committee by Representative George Andrews of Danbury provided $300,000 to finance construction of a dormitory

*Perkins' daughter, Mrs. Mortimer Camp, in a 1976 memoir, commented that "Until after I had graduated from college, I never realized why my father had pumped me so unmercifully on every single little thing I did at college." She came to believe that he was trying to learn what was missing from college life in Danbury.

on White Street. On February 15th, twenty prominent Danburians testified at a hearing on the bill. Politicians, including Mayor William Gilbert and First Selectman Elijah Sturdevant, as well as businessmen, Normal School faculty and alumni, and members of the Danbury Parent Teachers Association, all joined John Perkins in Hartford to voice their support. A month later, this group brought the education committee to Danbury for a campus tour and lunch at the Hotel Green, where Theodore Bowen of the Booster Club, the most influential civic body in Danbury, presented the city's case. These tactics were effective enough to get the education committee to endorse the Andrews bill on March 30th, although the appropriation was reduced to $225,000. Committee members evidently were convinced that a dormitory was justified because of the Danbury school's demonstrated commitment to the improvement of public schools in rural areas of the state.

Above: Class of 1912 on steps of entrance to Old Main. Among the faculty in the doorway at top are Principal John Perkins (left) and science teacher Lothrop Higgins (middle). The first male graduate, Ralph Carrington, is in the front row. (WCSU Archives)

The Republican Party, whose guiding axiom was economy in government, dominated Connecticut politics during the 1920s. Therefore, it came as no shock when the appropriations committee, the legislature's fiscal watch dog, rejected the dormitory proposal. The reasoning was vintage conservative: business conditions were unsettled and the state could not afford the money. Surprisingly, in this era of firm party discipline, both houses of the General Assembly (for the only time during the legislative session) spurned the advice of the appropriations committee and, on May 18th, approved a scaled-down appropriation of $100,000 for the shrinking dormitory.

One formidable obstacle blocked the realization of Perkins' dream. Governor George Templeton, an acolyte of Republican boss J. Henry Roraback, had already announced that he would veto the dormitory bill. He pulled no punches in his June 5th veto message, declaring that "the erection of a dormitory at the Danbury Normal School is not necessary either for the immediate requirements of the school or for its future needs. All necessary appliances for education should be furnished but the least important need is the dormitory." In the final hours of the session, the legislature flexed its muscles again and attempted to defy the executive. By a vote of twenty to twelve, the Senate re-passed the bill over the governor's veto. Late in the afternoon of June 5th, just before adjournment, the effort of the House of Representatives to do the same thing ended in a 99-99 tie.* In the most dramatic moment of the session, Speaker of the House Leonard Nickerson of Cornwall, soon to be named a judge of the superior court, cast the deciding vote to sustain the governor's veto.

John Perkins was spared the disappointment of this result. On May 14, 1923, while the General Assembly considered the dormitory appropriation, the fifty-five-year-old Perkins died at his home on Terrace Place after a short illness. It would not be long, however, before the vision of the founding father would become a reality. ■

*If Representative Charles Johnson of Sherman, a supporter of the dormitory appropriation, had arrived at the capitol in time to cast his vote, a tie would not have occurred. Instead, his car ran out of gas on the way to New Milford, causing him to miss the train to Hartford. He walked into the legislative chambers five minutes after the roll call vote had been tabulated.

Notes On Sources

"Perkins has not been, in my experience, a voluminous correspondent," noted Dr. David Blakely, the secretary of the Dartmouth College class of 1889. Blakely had been responsible for gathering information about members of the class for the college alumni office, and he reached this conclusion after compiling data for its twenty-fifth anniversary publication. Later historians would agree. Perkins' public comments were few, his letters brief, and his official reports concise.

Fortunately, Dr. Blakely persisted and the Dartmouth alumni records do contain valuable communications from and about the principal. The Western Connecticut State University Haas Library Archives has preserved the completed application forms for members of the Normal School classes of 1904, '05, and '06. Perkins' correspondence with students, parents, and high school principals from 1905 to 1912 is also available, as is the twentieth anniversary material for the class of 1911. The *Danbury Evening News* did its usual complete job of reporting the fate of the dormitory appropriation in 1923. And to give him his due, Perkins' annual reports to the State Board of Education, while not lengthy, do contain essential information about his goals and the school's problems.

John V. Friel generated two vital primary sources for this period in 1976 as part of a history department effort to locate material about the college's early years. John Perkins' daughter, Mrs. Mortimer Camp, then a lawyer living in New Britain, at Friel's urging, wrote a lengthy reminiscence about her father. Friel also conducted a rich interview with Gertrude Murphy, a member of the class of 1912 from New Milford, who for many years was a member of the Locust Avenue training school faculty. In preparation for this interview, Murphy wrote in longhand an eight-page memoir of her years as a student at Danbury. Friel deposited the taped interview and the written memoir, along with the Camp reminiscence, in the Haas Library Archives.

Above: Lothrop Higgins taught science at Danbury from 1905 until he succeeded Perkins as principal in 1923. Here he is lecturing in the then-state-of-the-art science facility in Old Main. (WCSU Archives)

Above: A normal school physical education class in the gymnasium at Old Main in the 1920s. (WCSU Archives)

Above: The early American decor of the "social" room in Fairfield Hall, the school's first dormitory, echoed the Colonial Revival style of the building's exterior. (WCSU Archives)

Opposite: Frank Baisley, Danbury's premier commercial photographer, took this shot of Fairfield Hall shortly after it opened in 1927. (WCSU Archives)

CHAPTER THREE

AN ALTERED RELATIONSHIP

The Danbury Normal School was not autonomous; it was under the direct control of the Connecticut State Board of Education. During most of the two decades of John Perkins' regime, the state board exercised authority with a light hand, confining its attention to fiscal issues, admission policy, and the hiring of faculty nominated by each principal. Individual schools determined all other academic matters, including curriculum, with a minimum of oversight.

In the 1920s, that power-sharing arrangement changed. By the time Perkins died, the business model of bureaucratic organization had won favor in Hartford. Perkins' successor, Lothrop Higgins, would have to adjust to a new relationship in which the state board exercised greater control over all aspects of normal school operation. A good teacher, but equipped with limited leadership skills, Higgins was hard-pressed to cope with a sudden increase in the size of the student body and the still-unmet need for a dormitory. It is no wonder that all photographs of Higgins taken while he was principal show him unsmiling.

Laissez-faire management went out of fashion in 1920 when Albert Meredith replaced Charles Hine as commissioner of education and secretary of the State Board of Education. The two men could not have been more different. Hine, born in Lebanon, Connecticut, and educated at Yale College, was a former high school principal and superintendent who had spent thirty-seven years as a state employee. He operated with a small staff, handled his own correspondence, delivered few public speeches and composed terse, no-nonsense reports. Upon his retirement, the state board paid tribute to his career in the crisp prose that he preferred: "A splendid example of New England service at its best." Meredith, though an 1895 Wesleyan graduate, was really an outsider to the state. He had gained most of his educational experience in New Jersey, where he served as superintendent of schools in Essex County (which included Newark, the state's largest city) and as assistant state commissioner of education. The holder of an unusual advanced degree (Pd.D.—Doctor of Pedagogy) from Muhlenberg College, Meredith's intense ambition drove him to "modernize" Connecticut public education as a stepping stone to a more prestigious job. His approach relied heavily on complicated organizational charts and obtuse written directives.

Once in office, Meredith quickly carried out a series of initiatives intended to heighten the prestige and selectivity of the normal schools. In 1921, he persuaded the General Assembly to give the State Board of Education exclusive control of teacher certification. The board used this power in 1927 to decree that only normal school graduates could teach in elementary schools. Displeased with the number of students who failed to complete the full normal school course, Meredith tightened admission requirements. After 1923, applicants had to have graduated from a four-year high school, earned two-thirds of their fifteen high school credits in academic courses, and received a passing mark of 70 percent in the twelfth grade to be accepted at any Connecticut teacher-training institution. The board also put a ceiling on the size of the entering class at each school. Danbury's quota was 140.

Meredith decided that Connecticut would become one of the first states in the country to require that all applicants pass a "careful physical examination by a woman physician selected by the Board" to gain admission to a normal school. This examination went beyond checking health factors like blood pressure and vision; it was supposed to evaluate such subjective qualities as posture and "good physical appearance." The class that entered Danbury in 1924 was the first group to undergo this ordeal. Of the eighty-one young women tested, fifty-nine were approved and three were rejected. The remaining nineteen were admitted conditionally and had to be re-tested in six months. Doris Salmon, a member of the class of 1932 and later a teacher at Roberts Avenue practice school, still shudders at the memory of being granted conditional admission because she was too thin. Knowing that she had to put on weight in order to stay at the school, she and several classmates in the same predicament visited a candy store on Moss Avenue every noon hour during their first year, to fill up on snacks. It was even more embarrassing for students who lived in the dormitory, where those who were overweight or underweight had to sit at special tables with diets tailored to their situation. "Did they take a riding," Salmon recalls.

Starting in 1925, all Connecticut public schools were required to administer intelligence tests, and then to segregate their entering classes into ability clusters based on the test results. However, this Meredith innovation did not fully affect Danbury. State bureaucrats reluctantly agreed that, because the junior class in Danbury was already broken down into groups with similar commuting schedules, the school was exempt from using IQ tests in this way.

Meredith devoted special attention to the normal school curriculum. The Division of Normal Schools was the only one of the many bureaus and divisions on his intricate department of education organizational chart that Meredith himself headed.* In particular, the lack of uniformity in the curriculum of the normal schools bothered the commissioner. Each school determined the subjects it would teach and how much time would be allotted to each. Meredith was horrified that the practice teaching experience varied "all the way from carefully guided apprenticeships to [a] loose and unorganized chaperonage relation between students and critic teacher." It was clear to him that "for a state as small as Connecticut this was not a condition that should be continued."

In his campaign to reorganize the normal schools, Commissioner Meredith found an eager ally in Lawrence Meader, a distant relative of John Perkins. Meader came to Danbury in 1919, after graduation from Bates College, and taught English for one year at Danbury Normal School. Energetic and eager to

*Meredith headed this division until 1927. During this time, he changed the name to Division of Teacher Training and then to the Division of Teacher Preparation in an exquisite example of bureaucratic tinkering.

please, he attracted the attention of Charles Hine, who appointed him as the state board agent responsible for supervising the schools in four small Litchfield County towns: Kent, Sherman, Washington, and Roxbury.

Shortly after Meredith took over the Connecticut Department of Education in 1920, he put the enterprising Meader in charge of the newly created Division of Investigation and Studies, and directed him to analyze the condition of the state normal schools.

Meader threw himself into the assignment. After two years of gathering data in his Hartford office, he convinced the department to award him an academic leave so he could attend Columbia University Teachers College where, with rich academic resources at his disposal and free of office distractions, he could develop a plan to improve the normal schools. He did not squander his time at Columbia and when he returned from New York in 1923, he brought with him an elaborate scheme for a self-study of the normal schools. Meredith applauded his handiwork and the state board officially endorsed his plan. It gratified Meader to be appointed "Special Agent for Normal Schools" in charge of conducting the self-examination.

A tortuous period for the administration and faculty of the normal schools followed. For six months, from October 1923 to April 1924, in addition to their regular duties, they dissected every aspect of teacher education in Connecticut. Meader kept the process moving by dashing around the state to attend the monthly (in some cases semi-monthly) meetings of the fifteen campus and system-wide committees he had set up. The state board showed the high priority it gave to this marathon by permitting the faculty to spend one week at full pay during the 1924 spring semester on finishing their assignments.

The final report, which was approved by the state board in June 1924, documented the obvious: that the four normal schools had very different approaches to teacher education. The Danbury curriculum, for example, was unique in many ways. It was the only one that included Rural Education or Sewing. No other school had courses such as Principles of Education and History of Education. Danbury students received significantly more instruction in science than those who attended the other schools. They also spent more time in the classroom practicing penmanship than they did learning history and geography combined. Measured by the number of class periods devoted to each subject, New Haven taught nine times more history, and New Britain ten times more geography, than was taught at Danbury. Such diversity, the report concluded, was inefficient for practical as well as philosophical reasons. It complicated budgeting, evaluation, and student transfers. More fundamentally, in the eyes of the true believers, it deprived the state of "the obvious mutual advantage resulting from joint endeavor toward common ends."

The recommendations of the Meader Report, designed to standardize the normal school curriculum, went into effect on September 1, 1924.* Under the new plan, all schools had to implement an identical first-year curriculum. In the second year, students on each campus followed either a primary track (for those who were preparing to teach kindergarten through third grade) or an intermediate track (for those who desired to teach fourth through eighth grade). The two-year program in each school would offer the same number of class hours: 2,000. Previously, no school had come close to this number; the Danbury total was 1,418, second highest to Willimantic's 1,600. Each institution was permitted some freedom to experiment, but it could not deviate from the formula that required 50 percent of the curriculum be devoted to subject matter courses, 25 percent to professional courses, and 25 percent to practice teaching.

The sweeping reorganization did not ignore the faculty. In an effort to upgrade the quality of instruction, the standard teaching load was reduced to sixteen class periods per week. An effort was made to raise faculty salaries, revealed by Meader's statistics to be well below normal school pay in other states. In the next few years, the percentage of the normal school budgets earmarked for faculty pay rose substantially. When Meader began his study, only New Haven and New Britain allotted as much as 60 percent of their budgets to salaries. Danbury used only 48 percent of its funds for this purpose because some elementary school teachers from the training schools acted as part-time Danbury Normal School teachers, a practice discontinued in 1923. By 1927, the salary item in the four

*By 1924, Meader had moved on to replace the retired Arthur Morrill as principal of New Haven Normal School.

normal school budgets soared to 84 percent of the total, prompting a warning from Alfred Simpson, the new director of the Division of Teacher Preparation, that "we have absorbed in salaries about all that present appropriations will permit."

This increase is deceiving; much of the money financed the hiring of additional faculty, rather than boosting individual paychecks. In 1923-24, the average Danbury Normal School teacher's salary was $2,500. Only two members of the faculty, both male, earned $3,000. The lowest salary—paid to a female librarian—was $1,800. The principal earned $4,500. Four years later, the average salary had crept up to $2,600. Higgins' $5,004 salary topped the schedule. The staff of the practice schools benefited most from the financial reforms. In addition to matching the elementary school pay level in Danbury, the state board agreed in 1928 to add an extra $100 to $700 to the remuneration of each teacher at the Balmforth Avenue, Locust Avenue, and Miry Brook model schools.

An experienced normal school principal would have had difficulty keeping pace with the torrent of directives that flowed out of Hartford in the 1920s. The drastic shift in the balance of power engineered by Meredith and Meader presented an even more daunting challenge to a novice like Lothrop Higgins. Higgins was the senior Danbury faculty member who succeeded Perkins in 1923, but his credentials, like the man himself, were solid but unspectacular. Born in 1876 to a family with a seafaring tradition in Charlestown, Massachusetts, Higgins had attended Brown University, where he excelled in his studies and earned Phi Beta Kappa distinction but was otherwise not active in campus life. After graduation in 1899, he spent one year of special study at Massachusetts Institute of Technology before taking a job as a high school science teacher in Clinton, Connecticut. In 1905 he came to Danbury, where he concentrated on improving the caliber of science education through his writing and teaching. Between 1903 and 1923, Higgins authored four elementary and high school science textbooks for a national publishing company, and two other elementary texts that were distributed by the State Board of Education.

One of his teaching devices was particularly innovative. To help Danbury students who were going out to teach in rural schools with no laboratories, he packaged science kits in small wooden boxes that contained the chemicals necessary to conduct basic experiments. Even though he was a resourceful teacher, Higgins had no illusions about his career. When his alma mater asked him to summarize his accomplishments since graduation, he replied modestly, "Have tried to do my work as well as I could and to be reasonably useful. Have written a little and talked a little in following out this general effort."

When Higgins shifted from the classroom to the principal's office, he moved out of his element. For one thing, he did not have a commanding appearance. Tall, thin, and bald, almost delicate-looking, he usually wore a dark suit with a high celluloid collar and tie. He was solemn and formal—"very, very formal," one 1928 graduate stressed. A member of the class of 1926 voiced a universal sentiment. "I don't think that he ever smiled," she remembered. Corrine O'Connell, a Danbury alumna and longtime teacher at Balmforth Avenue School, emphasized how uncomfortable Higgins was with little children. On one of his visits to the practice school, he was embarrassed by a bold first grader who, without waiting for the principal to be introduced, blurted out, "I know! He's an undertaker!" It seems almost poignantly appropriate that he once chose to deliver a school assembly lecture on the career of Calvin Coolidge.

Students and faculty agreed that Higgins was kind, considerate, and totally dedicated to the school. However, his rigidity and need to control situations impeded his ability to respond flexibly to change. He devoted inordinate attention to keeping the classrooms and building neat and orderly. One faculty member was amused, on entering Higgins' office, to see thumbtacks on the floor marking the spots where every piece of furniture should be located.

A puritanical streak that some felt stifled creativity presented a more serious obstacle. He did not permit staff members to smoke, and was upset when a woman teacher with long hair, hired in the spring, showed up at the start of fall classes sporting a fashionable short haircut. In a 1933 speech to the Forum, a college club, he attacked contemporary society for putting too much attention on the "perishables," which he identified as "automobiles, dancing, card playing, [and] cosmetics."

His tendency to control and his overt moralism were evident in Higgins' relationship with the Student Cooperative Government Association, an organization that he himself had founded in 1926 to promote student morale. Higgins made sure that the by-laws of the group permitted the principal to attend all meetings, a privilege he often exercised. He had to approve of every candidate for office, adding or subtracting names as he saw fit. He officiated at the swearing-in of new members, but only after reading them the oath of office and discussing it "clause by clause," as a long-suffering secretary noted in the minutes of a 1926 meeting. Higgins drafted a model constitution that the student association prudently decided to use when chartering clubs. The phrase "this is referred to Mr. Higgins" was a frequent entry in the student government records. Single-minded in purpose, Higgins transferred his preoccupation with proper behavior to the students. At a meeting in October 1928, the principal reprimanded the student representatives for spending too much time on trivial issues such as choosing school rings, pins, and songs, and urged them to "take note of such things as conduct, honesty, highest standards which the faculty might not be so apt to hear of or see." The Student Cooperative Government Association on occasion acted as an honor court in which offenses such as taking books from the library without checking them out were deliberated.*

A sudden enlargement of the student body made Higgins' transition from teacher to administrator even more difficult. From a low point in 1919, enrollment had been slowly creeping upward; but then the unexpected happened. In 1923, Bridgeport decided to close its teacher-training school and transport all its second-year students to Danbury. During Higgins' first year as principal, 253 students packed the school. The 1924 graduating class of 170 students, including forty-nine from Bridgeport, was the largest in the school's history. This abrupt increase in size called for physical and psychological adjustments. Space was precious. Seventy student desks were installed in the physics and chemistry laboratory, and a curtain was hung to divide the manual training room in the basement,

*The March 10, 1927, meeting dealt with the "library situation." During the discussion, it was pointed out that, if a trial were necessary, the name of the person accused would be inscribed in the minutes of the Student Government Association. The recording secretary then asked incredulously, "Would any teacher wish such a stigma attached to her name?"

allowing space for a lunch room. Not willing to abandon his commitment to rural schools, Higgins sent student teachers in groups of four to the Sherman Center School to relieve the overtaxed Miry Brook School.

Assimilating a large group of seniors who had spent their first year at another school was a delicate operation. Higgins acknowledged that the Bridgeport transfers "have not wholly caught our attitude of service to the state." Nevertheless, there are ample indications that the two groups blended smoothly. They cooperated to produce *The Anchor*, the school's first yearbook. The two highest awards presented at the 1924 graduation went to students from Bridgeport.

Enrollment pressure diminished when Bridgeport reopened its training school after one year. Through the rest of the decade, the size of the Danbury student body stabilized at about 150 per year. The tempo of campus life did not differ much from earlier years. Commuter students now traveled by bus as well as by train. Helen Tucker, class of 1929, walked two and one-half miles each school day to catch the New England Transportation Company bus in Brookfield, which arrived in Danbury at about 8 a.m. Ridgefield students took advantage of regular bus service on Route 7 that connected the two towns. Boarding the small jitney at the news store opposite Ridgefield Town Hall at 7 a.m., the young women got off in front of the Pershing Building on Danbury's Main Street a half hour later. They had plenty of time to make the long, often cold, walk to the campus before classes began. Helen McGlynn Cutting, class of 1926, was glad to have this early morning period to study, as well as two post-class hours before the 5:30 p.m. return trip to Ridgefield.

Seniors engaged in practice teaching continued the school tradition of agonizing over visits of Supervisor of Training May Sherwood, a Normal School graduate who had joined the faculty in 1914. "How many hearts have stood still as Miss Sherwood came to the training schools on her tour of inspection!" This caption, printed under the yearbook picture of a benign looking Sherwood, conveyed restrained apprehension. Doris Salmon, class of 1932, was more direct when she confessed that "she scared me to death! I can still feel her writing in my Crit Book [which contained a student teacher's lesson plans] in the back of the room."

Higgins worked hard to make the campus a more vibrant place during the

1920s. One of the main tasks of the Student Cooperative Government Association was to award charters to student clubs. The Dramatics Club, Rural Club, Glee Club, Athletic Club, Nature Club, Camera Club, and the Forum, competed for scarce meeting time during the school day. The process of choosing such identifying school symbols as a seal, stationary, pin, song, and colors promoted school spirit. For the first time, the school published a handbook that contained an obligatory warning about dishonesty. Typically, the always vigilant Principal Higgins, while pleased with the activity, worried that students would join too many clubs to the detriment of their studies.

One long-standing obstacle to progress remained firmly in place. It became increasingly apparent that as long as students returned home or scattered to boarding houses each day after class, the Danbury Normal School could not grow in size or influence. Once again, the college and community united to try to persuade the General Assembly, during the 1925 biennial session, to fund the construction of a dormitory in Danbury on adjacent land purchased by the state for this purpose in 1917 and 1919. This time they faced stiff competition from New Britain Normal School and the agricultural college at Storrs; both of these also wanted state money to build badly needed student residences.

The Booster Club, whose membership roster listed every important business and political figure in Danbury, took charge of applying political pressure.* The members appointed a special committee headed by Judge Samuel Davis, who had taken part in the unsuccessful 1923 dormitory drive to guide a Danbury appropriation bill through the legislature. The composition of the committee, which included Mayor A. Homer Fillow, Charles Peck (owner of a hat machinery factory), and hatting mogul William Mallory, testified to the importance local leaders attached to the well-being of the Normal School.

When the General Assembly's education and appropriations committees held a joint hearing on the Danbury bill on March 25, 1925, the Boosters sprang into action. Banker Martin Griffing, the Boosters' president, canceled the club's

*The Booster Club was organized in 1919 and functioned for a few years as an informal branch of city government. In the early '20s, for example, the members were so irritated with the failure of elected officials to see the potential of aviation that they bought the land for the present Danbury Airport and gave it to the city.

regular meeting that day so members could travel to Hartford to attend the hearing. A convoy of automobiles left the Hotel Green at 10:30 a.m. to transport thirty luminaries, including Judge Martin Cunningham and Frank Lee, owner of the city's largest hat company, to the Senate hearing room in the capitol. There, these determined dignitaries testified on behalf of a bill requesting $300,000 for dormitory construction. Unlike 1923, when the Connecticut Department of Education remained aloof, Commissioner Meredith strongly endorsed Danbury's request.

While community leaders, school officials, and elected representatives all spoke in favor of the bill (indeed, there was no overt opposition), it was left to Lothrop Higgins to present the official rationale for building a dormitory in Danbury. His statement reveals much about his traditional mind-set. He briefly reviewed the familiar arguments about the high cost of boarding in the city, the increasingly unreliable railroad service that made commuting difficult, and the opportunity dormitory living would provide for greater socialization of students. But his major contention must have raised some eyebrows, as it so clearly rested on a deep suspicion of industrial cities like Danbury. He told the committees that a dormitory would enable the school to attract more students from rural towns—the type of students, he said, who on the whole made better teachers than those from urban centers. No doubt this remark mystified the city fathers, who had brought their powerful presence to the battle. Mayor Fillow must have been particularly startled. He had just delivered his own speech, in which he proudly boasted that by educating students from the city of Danbury, the State of Connecticut would be getting "genuine American girls as teachers."

Evidently the subtle fissure within the Danbury delegation went unnoticed, for the General Assembly, in May 1925, exactly twenty years after John Perkins first expressed the need for such a facility, authorized $200,000—still one-third less than the amount requested in the original bill—to construct a dormitory on the corner of White Street and 7th Avenue. The reduced appropriation led to further delay. In 1926, another state agency, the Board of Control, set up by Roraback Republicans to curb any unexpected legislative urge to spend, refused to award the construction contract to the chosen Bridgeport company, whose bid was slightly more than $200,000. Pressure from the Booster Club and Commissioner Meredith on high state officials, including Governor John Trumbull, failed to get the Board of Control to add the needed $10,000 to the appropriation. After months of wrangling, plans for the building had to be scaled back to stay within the approved limit.

On September 7, 1927, the second dormitory to be built on a Connecticut normal school campus (Willimantic's dormitory was constructed in 1921) opened its doors. Named Fairfield Hall by the first class to reside there, the new facility provided accommodations for eighty-six young women, along with a suite of rooms for a dean of women. In addition to fulfilling a long-postponed need, the design of the building made powerful aesthetic and cultural statements. The Colonial Revival style chosen by architect C. Z. Zeoli of Westport, with its simplicity, symmetrical balance, columns, and cupola, expressed the cultural nationalism in vogue at the time of the nation's 150th anniversary. A style based on a domestic, rather than a foreign, model seemed to be appropriate for a public institution charged with the training of teachers who would have the responsibility of Americanizing large numbers of children of recent immigrants.

With the opening of the dormitory, Danbury Normal School entered a new era. From now on, the school would attract a larger and more diverse student body and offer greater advantages. In the exuberant mood of the Jazz Decade, few suspected that awesome challenges lay ahead. The national economic depression that hit Connecticut particularly hard in the 1930s would threaten the very existence of the school. ■

Note On Sources

Because of the central role played by Lawrence Meader, principal of New Haven Normal School from 1924 to 1928, the reorganization of the Connecticut State Department of Education during the 1920s is presented in detail in Thomas Farnham's *Southern Connecticut State University: A Centennial History, 1893-1993*. Columbia University Teachers College published Meader's research findings and recommendations concerning the Connecticut normal schools in 1928, under the title *Normal School Education in Connecticut* (Columbia University Contributions to Education, #307). The biannual reports of the Connecticut State Board of Education to the governor, particularly the report for 1924-26, document the changed relationship between the state board and the normal schools.

University archival records for the 1920s, while scanty, are important. The detailed minutes of the Student Government Cooperative Association meetings between 1926 and 1930, written in legible teacher-ready penmanship, tell much about student life and about Principal Higgins. Fortunately, one copy of the first yearbook, the 1924 *Anchor*, is also in the archives. Connecticut State Archivist Mark Jones discovered, in the State Library in Hartford, a box of material pertaining to the Danbury Normal School and had it officially transferred to the Ruth Haas Library in 1999. One of the important items in this file box is a folder that contains annual salary records for normal school and practice-school teachers during the 1920s.

Many people connected with the Danbury Normal School as students or teachers during this period were willing to be interviewed. Without the cooperation and the good memories of the following individuals this chapter could not have been written: Margaret Perkins Camp, Mary Creagh, Helen Cuming, Ann Girlometti, Helen Budd Mason, Elizabeth McNamara, Gertrude Murphy, Corrine O'Connell, Doris Salmon, Jennie Stone, Helen Tucker, and Minnie Benham Warner.

Upper left: A typical spartan dormitory room in the 1930s. Fairfield Hall, the only campus dorm for almost thirty years, originally housed eighty-six young women. (WCSU Archives)

Upper right: The nearby Balmforth Avenue school served as a primary practice facility for Normal School and Teachers College students. In this 1930 photo, Principal Higgins makes an inspection visit. (WCSU Archives)

Left: After graduating from Danbury Normal School, May Sherwood joined the faculty in 1914. She supervised student teaching, operated a one-person job placement office, and was the liaison with school alumni until her retirement in the early 1950s. This snapshot was taken by a student in 1926. (WCSU Archives)

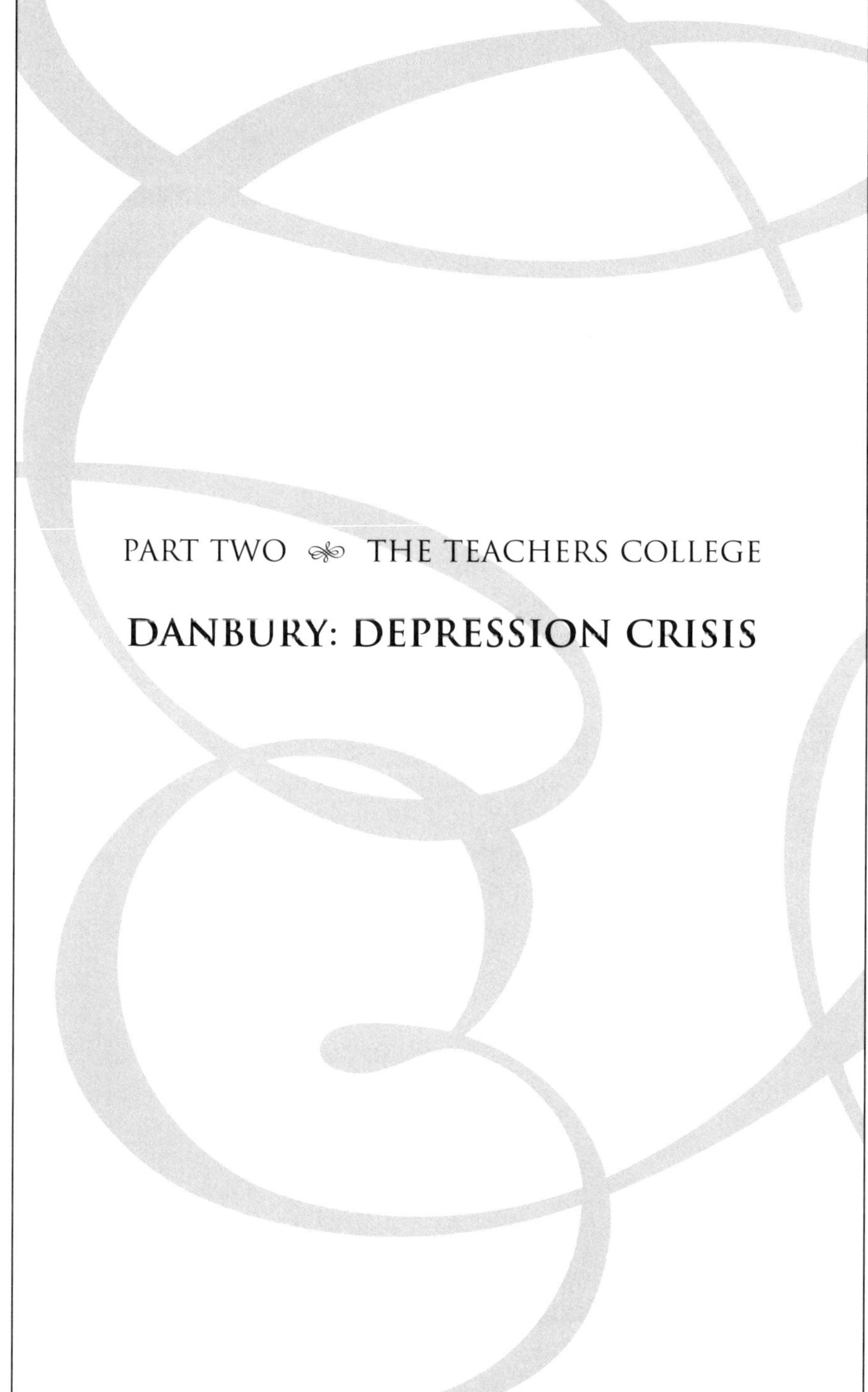

PART TWO ❧ THE TEACHERS COLLEGE

DANBURY: DEPRESSION CRISIS

Opposite: Shift change at the Frank H.Lee Company hat factory, Danbury's largest, in 1931. (Scott-Fanton Museum and Historical Society)

DANBURY: DEPRESSION CRISIS

On a spring day in 1935, eighteen-year-old Elsie Lauricella, soon to be graduated from Greenwich High School, traveled to Danbury to undergo the required examination and interview for admission to the Danbury Normal School. Her mother had wanted her to attend a private women's college in another state but Elsie was determined to be a teacher in Connecticut, and she believed that a normal school diploma would help her achieve her goal. Her first impression of Danbury, however, was far from positive. As her father drove the family Buick down West Street to Main and then up White Street to the school, the number of men standing idle on street corners shocked the young woman. Years later, when interviewed shortly before her sixtieth class reunion (the school had become Danbury Teachers College during her time as an undergraduate), Elsie still expressed astonishment at the visibility of the Depression in the Hat City.

What Elsie and her father saw on their first trip to Danbury was not misleading. The economic collapse of the 1930s left its mark on the community, just as it was responsible for the challenges and uncertainty faced by the Normal School itself at this time. High unemployment had created relief needs that neither private charity nor municipal government could meet. Business failures and unpaid taxes slashed municipal revenues, making it difficult to provide such essential services as education, fire-fighting, and police protection. Overcrowded elementary schools, an antiquated waste disposal system, downtown traffic congestion, and the lack of recreational facilities—all ignored during the prosperous 1920s—could be remedied only with massive federal assistance during the Depression decade.

Hatting, a fashion industry subject to unpredictable shifts in taste, temporarily shielded the local economy from the onslaught of the Depression. In the summer of 1931, hat factories worked frantically to fill orders placed by milliners for the stylish new Empress Eugenie women's felt hat. National media portrayed the city as a haven for those seeking work, and soon officials were forced to warn desperate job seekers from other parts of the country not to come to Danbury.

The boom was short-lived. During the winter of 1931-32, the number of unemployed workers skyrocketed. Frank Lee, the owner of the largest hat factory in town, could not live up to a pledge made the year before to hire all unemployed hatters in Danbury by stretching out available jobs. Dwindling orders stymied the "Share the Work Plan" so confidently advocated by hatting company executives. Jeremiah Scully, president of the Danbury Hat Makers Association, set up a soup kitchen, dubbed the Danbury Unemployment Restaurant, on Crosby Street in January 1933. Supported by donations of money and labor, the restaurant served breakfast and supper to an average of 250 people a day during the winter months. The Danbury Unemployment Commission, a citizens' group funded by private contributions, bore the brunt of the relief effort until the federal government, under the New Deal, began operation in the city in December 1933. The severity of the Depression in Danbury can be measured by the fact that fifteen hundred out-of-work people registered to participate in the inaugural federal works projects in the city.

The New Deal provided jobs and, equally important, badly needed infrastructure improvements in Danbury. It did not, however, end the Depression. A census taken in November 1937, at the time of yet another unexpected economic downturn, revealed that a staggering total of 3,074 people in Danbury (close to 12 percent of the total population of twenty-seven thousand) were either unemployed, under-employed, or already on government relief rolls. By January 1938, town government was providing relief services for 550 families, a record high. An office in the City Hall basement dispensed free food to the unemployed. Less than five months into the 1938 fiscal year, the entire annual budget for relief had been spent and the city was forced to borrow from a local bank. When the first selectman proposed a special tax to take care of this emergency, a stormy town meeting —so crowded that the audience spilled out of City Hall onto the sidewalk— rejected it. One resident called it the "ugliest" session he had witnessed in the thirty-five years he had attended town meetings.

The specter of labor violence revealed another ugly side of the state of the economy in Danbury. In July 1933, state police had to be called when a mob of angry workers slashed tires and hurled stones at the cars of those who refused to quit George McLachlan's hat shop to protest the discharge of five hundred union employees. A year later, the Reverend Nicholas Wehby of St. George's Antiochian Orthodox Church on Elm Street organized the United Fur Workers of Danbury. The one thousand mostly-Lebanese members went on strike for fourteen weeks in an unsuccessful effort to gain recognition for their independent union. On June 5, 1934, strikers wrecked three taxis carrying "scabs" to a fur factory on River Street; then they clashed with police, injuring the chief of police seriously enough to send him to the hospital. Eleven strikers, including several women, were arrested.

The Depression plunged city government into a fiscal crisis. The tax base had shrunk by almost $250,000 dollars, due primarily to a decline in consumer purchasing of automobiles that were subject to a personal property tax. At the start of 1932, the city was owed an estimated $500,000 in back taxes. Desperate for revenue, officials tendered taxpayers a 6 percent discount for taxes paid early, but the offer failed to attract many takers. More drastic measures were tried. In late 1932, the wages of teachers as well as firemen and policemen were cut by 10 percent. All city employees went from July to November of that year without any pay—the longest of several pay interruptions they endured during the decade. Teachers received no salary increases for four years.

Pressing emergency needs coupled with the disarray of city finances made local solutions to long-range problems impossible. The State Water Commission had designated the Still River, for years a convenient receptacle for hat factory waste, the most polluted body of water in Connecticut. An outmoded sewer system combined storm water with industrial and residential discharge. The city filtration plant, built in the 1890s to serve twelve thousand people, had been designed to accommodate an annual flow more than 750,000 gallons. By the 1930s, it groaned under a load of more than two million gallons per year. No elementary schools had been built in the city since the nineteenth century. The Balmforth Avenue and Locust Avenue schools, used as practice schools by Normal School students, were outmoded. After an inspection visit in 1930, the State Board of Education termed the Balmforth facility "nothing but a fire trap." Despite periodic grumbling from citizens, Danbury had refused to invest in public parks. The Lions Club funded and operated the only playground in the city at the corner of Osborne Street and Locust Avenue. Candlewood Lake lapped Danbury on the north, but as yet there was no public recreational access to its waters. No action had been taken on an offer by Cephas Rogers to exchange twenty-two acres of swamp land that he owned at the intersection of Main and South Street, usable for a park, in return for forgiveness of $6,000 in back taxes. City officials had failed to ease the congestion caused by the automobile. Nothing had been done, for example, to relieve or even study the volume of traffic that was choking Main Street between West and White Streets, the nexus of two major federal and four state highways.

All of these problems were ultimately addressed, but only through federal subsidies. Money from Washington would largely pay for modernization of the sewage treatment plant, completion of a state-of-the-art sewer system, preliminary work on Lake Candlewood and Rogers Parks, a survey of traffic flow on Main Street, and construction of the Beaver Brook School and an addition to the South Street School. New Deal spending brought about a change in attitude toward federal involvement in local affairs. Welcome replaced suspicion. In 1940, when Danbury was chosen as the site for the first federal prison to be built in New England, the *Danbury News-Times* expressed this new relationship with a banner headline that rejoiced: FEDERAL FUNDS ARE POURING IN. ■

Above: In 1936, England's Lord Marley spoke to the Forum annual banquet in the Peacock Room of the Hotel Green. Katherine A. Sutton, Forum adviser, is at the speaker's immediate right. Principal Ralph Jenkins is seated in front of the flag staff to the speaker's left. (WCSU Archives)

Opposite: Ruth deVillafranca, the bulwark of the music department from 1934 until her retirement in 1957, rehearses the school chorus. (WCSU Archives)

CHAPTER FOUR

THE FACULTY BELONGS TO US

January 4, 1939, was cold and blustery. The people lining the inaugural parade route from the Hartford Club to the state capitol noticed that elderly outgoing Democratic Governor Wilbur Cross, riding in an open car, buttoned his coat up to his chin to ward off the raw wind and snow flurries. Raymond Baldwin, the forty-five-year-old Stratford lawyer who was about to become the first Republican governor of Connecticut in eight years, sat beside him, waving his high silk hat to supporters. After arriving at the capitol, Baldwin took the oath of office from Chief Justice William Maltbie and then delivered his inaugural address to the General Assembly. He made brief but pointed comments about education. Because the state had too many teachers, he urged the legislature to close some teacher-training facilities. The new governor stressed that these schools "must be considered as state institutions rather than as local institutions," and emphasized that "local pride should yield to the welfare of all the people." Two weeks later, in his budget message, he was more specific: the legislature should shut down the New Haven and Willimantic schools and, within two years, consolidate all teacher education at New Britain and Danbury.

Irate constituents deluged Baldwin with letters, postcards, telegrams, and petitions of protest. Most were sent by residents living near the two schools the governor wanted to close. But one poignant handwritten defense of the teachers colleges came from a self-described "very ordinary mother" from Danbury, who was struggling to raise four children on her husband's weekly paycheck of $32. Even though she had completed only the eighth grade, she told the chief executive, she wanted her children "to live under better circumstances and gain an increased knowledge of the world and its ways." The only possibility of higher education available to them was Danbury Teachers College, where her oldest son and daughter were enrolled. After reminding him that she was a Republican who "did vote for you," she chided Baldwin for wanting to block an avenue of upward mobility for ordinary citizens by centralizing teacher education.

Baldwin's public pronouncement and the Danbury housewife's personal appeal illustrate the two outlooks toward the teacher-training schools—outlooks that clashed frequently during the 1930s. Regardless of party affiliation, the governor and the executive appointees in the Department of Education gave the highest priority to economy and efficiency on a statewide level. They believed the purpose of the teachers colleges was to produce the best teachers in the right quantity at the lowest cost. Residents of the areas where these schools were located saw the school's primarily as precious regional resources that provided educational opportunity for individuals of average means, as well as economic benefit and cultural enrichment for the local community. The state's precarious financial situation during the Depression intensified this conflict. Ultimately, the General Assembly had to choose between, or reconcile, these clashing positions and, in the process, determine the future of the Danbury Normal School.

The Depression had hit Connecticut hard. Dependent on manufacturing, the state felt the economic slump immediately. Companies that fabricated durable goods, such as metal products and machinery, began to cut production in 1930. Although the impact on consumer industries like hatting was delayed, eventually the sag in demand forced factory lay-offs, reduced wages, and shortened hours. In 1932, a Metropolitan Life Insurance Company study revealed that the number of people engaged in manufacturing in the state had dropped by 45 percent in three years. The grim situation persisted without significant improvement until 1939, when war contracts rekindled factory production. This climate restricted the funding of taxpayer-financed educational services.

There had been signs during the prosperous 1920s that Connecticut was training too many teachers, and the normal schools were targets for down-sizing. The state's birth rate had been falling steadily since 1917. Almost ten thousand fewer children were born in Connecticut in 1928 than were born in the state ten years earlier. This decline translated into a drop in public school enrollment that started in 1928. At the same time, the number of elementary school teachers employed in the state began to shrink. The redoubtable May Sherwood, who both supervised practice teaching at Danbury Normal School and placed graduates in teaching jobs, noted that in 1927, for the first time, she was not able to find employment for all her charges.

This downward trend worsened during the Depression. The birth rate, and consequent public elementary school enrollment, continued to plummet. High unemployment and a diminishing tax base forced communities to cut costs. Beleaguered school boards, unable to meet payrolls, laid off teachers and combined classes. Art, music, and industrial arts programs were discontinued. As a result, 746 fewer teachers were employed in the state in 1931 than in 1928. When Charlotte Isham graduated from Danbury Normal School in 1932, she decided to continue her education because, as she recounted with passion in a 1976 interview, "There were no jobs. I didn't have any money!" Isham was not alone. Statistics gathered by the State Board of Education indicate that fifty-seven of the seventy-one Danbury graduates in that year could not find teaching positions. The employment situation remained bleak throughout the 1930s. At the end of the 1934-35 school year, Danbury officials reported that only twenty-two of the seventy-five graduates had been hired to teach.*

Commissioner Meredith, shortly before leaving Connecticut in 1930 to head the School of Education at New York University, urged the state board of education to extend the normal school curriculum to three years—as Massachusetts, New York, New Jersey, and Rhode Island had already done. Prodded by school superintendents and the head of the Teacher Preparation Division, Alonzo Myers,

*Because hard-pressed public schools delayed hiring until well into the summer months, more 1935 graduates ultimately obtained teaching jobs. Nevertheless, only 74 percent of Danbury Normal School graduates seeking school positions in that year were successful.

Meredith argued that, besides curbing the oversupply of teachers, this longer period of training would make Connecticut's beginning teachers more competent and thus more competitive with those educated in the surrounding states. The state board agreed with this reasoning and voted to add one more year, effective September 1930, to the course at the New Haven Normal School, where the oversupply of teachers was most extreme. The board approved an additional year for the other three normal schools but did not specify any timetable for implementation.

The three-year plan was an emergency measure. Since the board provided no additional funds to support the extra year, it was assumed that the current faculty and plant at each school could accommodate the altered situation. Little thought was given to what should be taught in the increased class time. As a result, the two-year curriculum was merely spread out over the longer period.

The first class to follow a three-year elementary education program at Danbury entered in 1932.* The previous year, twenty-four young women had come to the campus to embark on a three-year course in commercial education, which represented a radical departure for the Connecticut normal school system. For the first time, some students—those preparing to teach business subjects—were being trained to work in secondary rather than elementary schools. This innovation brought benefits and problems to the Danbury Normal School.
It provided a welcome new pool of applicants at a time when there was concern about unused space in the dormitory which the state expected to be full, but it also demanded changed procedures and additional costs. Applications had to be screened for the required high school courses in shorthand, typing, and bookkeeping. Tests of proficiency in dictation had to be administered to candidates. Two new faculty members with special commercial skills were hired, and business machines were purchased. Practice-teaching opportunities were established in high schools, not only in Danbury, but in more distant places like Hartford, Milford, New Haven, Shelton, and Stratford. Placement was particularly difficult; only seven of the nineteen graduates in the first graduating class in 1934 received

*In 1933, a group of students who had finished the two-year program was admitted for a third year. For the first time, the school enrolled three classes.

teaching jobs. Danbury's involvement in business education proved to be a brief interlude, as in 1935 the state board moved the entire program—students, faculty, and equipment—to New Britain.

Ernest Butterfield, who replaced Albert Meredith as commissioner of education in 1930, thought that extending the normal school curriculum to three years was only a partial remedy. He was horrified to find that "in normal school development, Connecticut has lagged behind the other states." He was not timid in stating his view that Connecticut should join other progressive states in stretching out the normal school course to four years. Butterfield also felt strongly that Connecticut's normal schools were too small to be run efficiently. A first-class institution, he insisted, required at least five hundred students, about three times the current size of the Danbury student body. Centralization was the obvious solution.

Inspired by Butterfield's rhetoric, the Connecticut State Board of Finance and Control, searching for ways to rein in spending at the nadir of the Depression, recommended to the General Assembly in 1933 that the New Haven, Willimantic, and Danbury Normal Schools be consolidated into a first-class, four-year teachers college at New Britain. The commissioner and the State Board of Education applauded this initiative. Butterfield believed that any other course of action was unrealistic. "The state obviously will not and cannot be expected to develop four strong teacher training institutions. Both the cost and the need for teachers forbid such a program," he asserted. The outspoken commissioner did not hesitate to go on record with his conclusion that "It is clearly to the advantage of the state, financially as well as educationally, to merge the four normal schools into one teachers college."

During four consecutive biennial legislative sessions in the 1930s, the General Assembly debated restructuring the state's teacher-training institutions. In 1933, legislators took several contradictory actions. They enacted part of the Department of Education's plan to centralize facilities by making the New Britain school a four-year, degree-granting institution with the imposing title of 'The State Teachers College of Connecticut." They refused, however, to abolish the other three normal schools. Rather, they ordered the state board to report to the 1935 session on the feasibility of making all the normal schools four-year teachers colleges. The General Assembly also decided it was time to end the policy of free teacher education and accepted the need for a small tuition charge.

It was up to the Department of Education to make sense of this compromise. Far from discouraged, the energetic Butterfield grasped the opportunity to bring coherence to teacher preparation in the state by making New Haven, Willimantic, and Danbury three-year units of the central campus at New Britain. Rather than four separate normal schools, Connecticut now had a single teachers college with semi-autonomous branches. All four schools would have the same admissions policy and similarly qualified faculty. Although it retained administrative independence in local matters, the Danbury Normal School became officially "The Danbury Unit of The State Teachers College of Connecticut." Like its two step-sisters in Willimantic and New Haven, the school's mission would be to prepare candidates for elementary education certification. Students would have to transfer to New Britain for their fourth year if they desired a college degree. Specialized programs designed to train junior high and high school teachers, such as the newly implemented commercial education program at Danbury, would be moved to New Britain. In 1933, a ten-dollar-per-semester tuition charge went into effect, an amount that would not be increased until 1956.

When the General Assembly convened in 1935, the question of teacher education was again on the agenda. Supporters of the three normal schools resented their inferior status. State Senator Nathan Spiro of Danbury promptly introduced a bill that would turn all the schools into four-year teachers colleges. The state board bitterly opposed this action and argued that "to transform each of the normal schools into an independent teachers college would give the state four small teachers colleges and would mean poverty of equipment and high cost of maintenance." Commissioner Butterfield was more dismissive in his weekly newsletter. Under the headline "A Prolonged Normal School Is Not A Teachers College," he scoffed at the notion that the present integrated plan should be replaced "by a group of small, weak, and expensive teachers colleges."

An overflow crowd of five hundred people attended the education committee hearing on the Spiro bill, forcing proceedings to be moved into the

Senate chamber. Butterfield was the only one to speak in opposition. Listening to the voices of the voters rather than the professional advice of the commissioner of education, the General Assembly, with scant disagreement, declared the normal schools to be four-year teachers colleges. At this point, Governor Cross intervened. The former college professor vetoed the bill, troubled by what he saw as both legislative intrusion into academic curriculum decisions and the lawmakers' irresponsible failure to provide additional funds for the schools' expanded mission.

The outcome was different in 1937. Pressure from organized interest groups in New Haven, Willimantic, and Danbury continued. A bill making the three normal schools into four-year institutions with powers equal to New Britain's sailed through the General Assembly. Mindful of the governor's previous objection, the legislature added a minuscule $37,500 to the budget of each of the three schools to ease the transition. At the same time, it deducted $22,000 from the annual budget of New Britain. This ruse satisfied Governor Cross, who signed the bill that transformed Danbury Normal School into Danbury State Teachers College.* It also infuriated Commissioner Butterfield, who resigned a few months later.

The future of the infant teachers colleges was far from secure. Republican Governor Baldwin's surprise recommendation, in his 1939 inaugural speech, to consolidate teacher education at New Britain and Danbury, the two campuses he judged had the most modern physical facilities, revived the controversy. Public opinion, and a majority of members of both parties in the legislature, strongly opposed the governor's suggestion. Even the new commissioner of education, Alonzo Grace, hesitated to back such a drastic step without more research. An astute politician, Baldwin backed off. He set up a special commission on education, which included such noted experts as the president of the Carnegie Foundation and the dean of the Graduate School of Education at Harvard University, and gave them a meager six weeks to come up with yet another report about teacher preparation in Connecticut. When this prestigious body concluded that the state should consolidate "as soon as practicable" the preparation of

*Cross's hypocrisy in this matter is revealed by his subsequent order to the Department of Education to reduce its spending by $90,000 to offset the increase in the teachers colleges' budgets.

teachers at New Britain, and "gradually . . . over a period of time" discontinue teacher training at Danbury, Willimantic and New Haven, the prudent governor buried the report.

The local community mobilized to resist every threat to Danbury Normal School by the forces of centralization during these years of unsettled economic conditions. The Federation of Civic Clubs, an umbrella organization formed in 1931, remained in existence through the decade to coordinate and sustain efforts to defend the Normal School. Led by Thomas Bowen, an executive of Mallory Hat Company, its membership roster was a veritable *Who's Who* of Danbury industry and society. Every major special interest group, from the Daughters of the American Revolution to the Businessmen's Association, participated. The group lobbied the legislature. So many Danburians wanted to be present at the hearings on the Spiro bill in 1935 that the Federation had to charter a bus to transport them to the capitol where they affirmed the comments of their spokesman, Lynn Wilson, the editorial writer of the *Danbury News-Times*. A few weeks later, the group brought the General Assembly's education committee to the city to impress on them the value of the school to Danbury.

Why was the Danbury community so aroused at the possibility that the state institution would be eliminated? One obvious answer was that the school provided the only way that many local students could get a college education. The parents of Danbury students were not affluent. The families of most of the students, according to figures submitted by school officials to the state board in 1935, had an annual income of between $1,000 and $2,000. Danbury High School was justly proud that eighty-two members of the graduating class of 1937 were going on to college. More than one-third of that number, thirty graduates, would attend Danbury Teachers College. In 1939, almost half the student body at the school came from Danbury or the immediately contiguous towns. Only eleven of the 212 students came from outside Fairfield or Litchfield Counties.

The economic impact of the institution on the community had macro- and micro-dimensions. The Connecticut State Department of Education stated that the college buildings and land were worth $370,000. The Civic Federation placed the value of the campus real estate much higher, over a half million dollars.

According to school officials, in the school year 1935-36, the average Danbury student spent $155 in the community in addition to boarding costs.

The most powerful and often-used argument in defense of the teacher training school in Danbury, however, was cultural, not economic. Mrs. John Downs, the wife of the president of the Union Savings Bank of Danbury, represented the Federated Women's Clubs at the 1933 state education committee hearings on the proposal to close all the normal schools but New Britain. She pleaded with the legislators, saying, "If the Danbury Normal School is taken away, the cultural life [of the city] will be taken." When the education committee members came to Danbury in 1935, they received a more complete picture of the way the scholarship of the college faculty and students benefited the community. The Federation of Civic Clubs presented them with an eloquent document that began, "We of Danbury feel that the presence of the Normal School in our city is one of our very greatest cultural assets. Any economic value that institution has to our business life is negligible . . . in comparison with the great cultural enrichment the school contributes to our social and civic life." The statement then enumerated the myriad ways in which the college faculty and students provided "free and willing and able help" for every local organization. The petition asserted in emotional language that there was no wall between town and gown in Danbury: "The faculty of the school is a real part of us. We feel the members 'belong' to us."

The late Rabbi Jerome Malino felt the same way. Moving to Danbury in 1935 to minister to the city's small Jewish population, he found a mill town with a difference: the presence of the teachers college set it apart from other industrial cities. Sixty-five years later, the esteemed religious leader looked back at those early years and agreed with the sentiments expressed in the 1935 petition. The college had provided spiritual sustenance to the community and intellectual companionship for him. "The college was my oasis, my refuge, and my nourishment," he acknowledged.

In particular, two Danbury faculty members personified the ideal of the scholar-citizen that Rabbi Malino and the Civic Federation so admired. Katherine Augusta Sutton, who taught history and International Relations, and Ruth deVillafranca, the director of the music program, were not only the most popular and accomplished teachers at the school, they also reached across campus boundaries to the wider community. Their careers illuminate the strong bond between Danbury Teachers College and its home city in the 1930s.

The two women were similar in many ways. They were about the same age. Sutton was born in 1888, deVillafranca in 1892. They looked alike, both tall and slender. They were flamboyant in dress and manner. Alumni remember Sutton appearing in class wearing a broad-brimmed hat and a silk scarf that she flourished dramatically, and they recall as clearly deVillafranca's vividly colored clothing. The strong personalities of the two women dominated faculty and students. In a genteel manner, they competed to bring talented students into their orbits. Sutton was thirty-three years old when she came to Danbury Normal School as a student in 1921. When deVillafranca became the music instructor at the school in 1934, she was forty-two.

Sutton's career paralleled the evolution of Danbury from normal school to teachers college. Born on a farm in New Canaan to a family with deep New England roots, Katherine Augusta Keeler married a local boy when she was nineteen years old. Her husband, Raymond Sutton, died suddenly in 1912, leaving her with two small sons. Teaching became her refuge from grief. For the next seven years, she was in charge of the one-room Smith Ridge School, which was heated by a pot-bellied coal stove and was without running water, but was conveniently located adjacent to the family homestead. In 1919, tragedy struck again. Her youngest son, who had been one of her pupils, died of pneumonia, a complication of the flu epidemic.

At this low point, Sutton, seeking to rebuild her life, began her association with the Danbury Normal School. In 1921, after a single year of study, she obtained her state certification and was hired to teach in the Balmforth Avenue practice school. One year later, Principal John Perkins was so impressed by her energy and creativity that he promoted her to the Normal School faculty. She quickly became the most feared and admired teacher in the school. "K-A," as she was called by the students (though certainly not to her face), was intense and demanding. Hundreds of alumni learned to read *The New York Times* because Sutton required it. The memory of Elizabeth McNamara, class of 1928, is typical.

"I read the *New York Times* in the morning so I could say a few words in class. She always asked us." On the second floor of Old Main, in a classroom decorated with the flags of the world's nations, Sutton shattered the provincialism and apathy of her students. As the 1924 yearbook put it, she challenged them "to get a vision—and get to work."

Sutton was not content to be a competent normal school teacher without a four-year college degree. She drove herself to acquire academic credentials even though she was restricted to part-time and summer study. In 1928, she earned a BS degree from Columbia University, and two years later, an MA in political science from the same institution. Her ambition was not satisfied, however, until she received a doctorate in education from New York University in 1940, the first Danbury teaching faculty member to reach that academic level. Dr. Sutton—she was justly proud of the title—supplemented her formal education with world travel. In 1931, she spent time at the League of Nations headquarters in Geneva, Switzerland, and on another trip, in 1934, focused on Russia and Central Europe. On academic leave in 1937, she traced the globe-circling route followed by Wendell Wilkie and described in his book, *One World*. She was in Japan when the Sino-Japanese war broke out, and in China during the bombing of Shanghai.

Sutton considered the entire Danbury region to be her classroom. The Forum, a college club she organized in 1928, became the area's locus for discussion of public affairs in the 1930s. Each year, until Sutton's illness and subsequent retirement in 1946, the Forum brought together students, faculty, and citizens in a variety of formats, on campus and off, to discuss national and international issues. The featured event came each December, when the Forum banquet invited foreign policy experts, such as Professor James Shotwell of the Carnegie Endowment for International Peace, to Danbury. By 1936, the annual dinner had become so popular that it had to be held in the elegant Peacock Ballroom of the Hotel Green. That year, four hundred guests clad in evening gowns and formal attire dined by candlelight before listening to Lord Marley of the English House of Lords discuss "Our Future in the Pacific: Does it Lie With Japan?" The *Danbury News-Times* described the affair as "one of the largest and most brilliant dinner gatherings ever held in this city."

Although that banquet and a less formal tea held in Fairfield Hall each spring were the highlights of the year, the Forum maintained a busy schedule of meetings, lectures, and round tables. Sutton herself spoke dozens of times every year to community groups. In the fall and winter of 1935-36, for example, she delivered twelve lectures to the League of Women Voters. Students were trained and encouraged to speak to non-college audiences. In 1939, student members of the Forum addressed twenty-one different community groups. Club president Ralph Braibanti, later to become a distinguished professor at Duke University, spoke on that year's study topic of Latin America to civic organizations, such as the Rotary Club, on no less than ten occasions.

Just as K. Augusta Sutton was the primary intellectual ambassador to the Danbury community in the 1930s, Ruth deVillafranca was the main cultural emissary. In 1934, she brought her rich background in music education to Danbury. A graduate of Oswego (New York) Normal School with a bachelor of science degree from New York University, she had taught in the public schools of Winsted and Meriden and in St. Petersburg (Florida) Junior College. Over the next three decades, she would build the music program at Danbury into the school's strongest academic asset. By the time deVillafranca retired in 1957, Danbury State Teachers College trained all the elementary and secondary music teaching students in the state system.

In the early years, deVillafranca's task was daunting. As the sole music instructor, she had to prepare even the most tone-deaf student to be an elementary school teacher able to read simple music and identify a tune on a piano. She did it with drama, confidence, and enthusiasm. Her style, though appreciated, could be painful to those without aptitude. It is easy to envision the author of the 1935 yearbook tribute to deVillafranca shuddering as she wrote: "None of us can forget her frank and energetic manner of dealing with our uncertain musical ability." On the other hand, deVillafranca's impact transformed students with more talent. Richard Wanzer, class of 1943, a retired Air Force pilot, wrote from Georgia in 1995: "Wonderful Divvy— she instilled a love of group music in me that still burns. At 76, I'm the narrator in our church choir as well as one of its baritones."

Students proficient in music got special attention. Some, like Mort Johnson, class of 1942, came to the college in Danbury so they could sing in the a cappella choir that deVillafranca trained. This elite group sang in churches and school auditoriums all over Fairfield and Litchfield Counties. The expert performance of the choir impressed guests at the 1940 banquet of the Eastern States Association of Professional Schools for Teachers, held in New York City in the Grand Ballroom of the Hotel Pennsylvania. Local audiences praised deVillafranca's production of Gilbert and Sullivan's "Iolanthe," staged in the outdoor amphitheater behind Fairfield Hall in May 1940.

When deVillafranca arrived in Danbury, she discovered a community that was not "backward musically" so much as "merely starved for lack of fine music." In 1934, with other music devotees, she allied with Donald Tweedy, a composer-pianist with a music degree from Harvard and the scion of a wealthy hatting family, to end this artistic isolation. Together they formed the Danbury Music Centre. For the next twenty-five years, deVillafranca would be a key figure in organizing the Centre's annual concert series, bringing world class musicians to the small industrial city and maintaining the Danbury Symphony Orchestra, which from 1936 on provided an outlet for skilled local musicians. Even after her retirement from the college, she remained active, serving as executive director of the Music Centre from 1957 to 1960.

In 1939, less than a year after Governor Baldwin threatened to consolidate the state teachers colleges, the advocates of centralization backed down. On November 27th, Connecticut Commissioner of Education Alonzo Grace came to Danbury to address the recently formed Regional Council of the Connecticut Council on Education, one of five citizen's groups that Grace hoped would improve communication between the public and the Department of Education. Glancing at the audience gathered in the Fairfield Hall lounge, he recognized Thomas Bowen, the chairman of the new regional organization, as well as Lynn Wilson, Judge Martin Cunningham and other stalwarts of the Federation of Civic Clubs who had fought for almost ten years against efforts by the state educational apparatus to centralize teacher education in Connecticut. In a politic move, Dr. Grace began his remarks by proclaiming the end of the war against Danbury

Teachers College. Danbury had won. From now on, Grace vowed, the Connecticut State Board of Education would help the college grow and respond to the specific needs of western Connecticut.

In reality, Dr. Grace and the state board had already begun their retreat. Shortly after Grace became commissioner in 1938, Franklin Pierce, the director of the Department of Education's Teacher Preparation Division, died. Grace decided to turn over his responsibilities to a committee consisting of the four teachers college presidents and chaired by the capable Finis Engleman of New Haven. In the future, this collective body would supply much of the impetus for increasing local autonomy. A few months later, Grace convinced the state board to take an even more significant step, setting the precedent for the state colleges to do more than train teachers. In June 1939, the board voted to broaden the curriculum of the four colleges "to serve the wider needs of youth" by devoting the first two years of study to general education courses. At the end of this period, students would receive the equivalent of a junior college certificate. On the basis of their classroom performance, the best students would be selected for the professional education sequence confined to junior and senior year. The decade that had begun so ominously for the Danbury Normal School ended with the promise of dramatic growth for Danbury Teachers College. ■

Left: Katherine Augusta Sutton, who taught history from 1922 to 1946, accompanies her students on a trip to Washington, D.C., in 1925. She is fourth from the right. (WCSU Archives)

Note On Sources

The official papers of Connecticut's governors at the State Library are an important source of information about educational policy in the state in the 1930s. The papers of Wilbur Cross (1930-38) and Raymond Baldwin (1938-40) contain valuable, if random, material. Baldwin's papers from his first term include a bulky folder filled with pro and con responses to his 1939 effort to close two normal schools. "A Program of Teacher Preparation for Connecticut" (1939) is the report of the special commission charged by Governor Baldwin to make recommendations for improving teacher education in the state.

The *Danbury News-Times* provides much detail about the close relationship between the local community and the Danbury Normal School (later, the Teachers College). The May 4, 1935, issue contains the complete text of the petition presented by the Danbury Federation of Civic Clubs to the legislative committee on education during its visit to Danbury. This document explains the many ways in which the college faculty contributed to the cultural life of the community. Stenographic transcripts of hearings held by the education committee of the General Assembly during every session in the 1930s are available at the State Library. They record what the local citizens who traveled to Hartford told the legislators about the value of the college to Danbury.

Materials at the New Canaan Historical Society make it possible to recreate the early life of Katherine Augusta Sutton. A large scrapbook of newspaper clippings, located in the Haas Library Archives, details the activities of the Forum from its founding in 1928 until Sutton's retirement in 1946. Professor Ralph Braibanti, an extremely active member of the Forum while he was a student at Danbury, remained a close personal friend of Dr. Sutton's, and generously shared his memories and his materials. The late Rabbi Jerome Malino, one of the founders of the Danbury Music Centre, was the best source of information about Ruth deVillafranca. Interviews with former students, particularly Mort Johnson and Truman Warner, provided information about her teaching style and extraordinary influence on her students.

Left: The class of 1936 with faculty in back row. Principal Ralph Jenkins is in the center. Jesse Brill, Dean Ruth Haas, and Ruth deVillafranca are to his left. Phebe Harrison and Grant Finch are to his extreme right. (WCSU Archives)

Above: In June 1944, college and practice-school faculty and students produced an elaborate pageant dedicated to "Our Latin American Neighbors," in the outdoor amphitheatre. (WCSU Archives)

Opposite: The outdoor amphitheatre was constructed behind Fairfield Hall by the Works Progress Administration (WPA) in 1936. (WCSU Archives)

CHAPTER FIVE

WITH HENRY BARNARD AS GUIDE

Charlotte Isham was startled when Principal Lothrop Higgins, clad in his trademark dark suit, high white collar and tie, turned his old Ford automobile into the driveway of her family farm in Woodbury one summer morning in 1933. The young woman had recently graduated from the Danbury Normal School and, as she recalled years later, the visit was a "real shocker" because she had never seen the principal away from the campus. Higgins trudged down to the barn, shook hands with Isham's father, and asked him to consider sending his daughter back to Danbury for a third year of study that the school now offered. When the farmer pleaded that he didn't have enough money to pay for another year of training, Higgins promised to cobble together an available town scholarship with part-time employment to defray Charlotte's boarding expenses. Thanks to Higgins' persistence and ingenuity, Charlotte Isham became a member of a special third-year class at Danbury.

Higgins needed all the resourcefulness he could muster to cope with what he termed the "extraordinary difficulties" faced by the Normal School in the early years of the Depression. Dealing with declining enrollment, empty dormitory rooms and sub-standard practice schools, along with constant worry about the ethical standards and conduct of the students, drained his energy. A casual remark made to a practice-school faculty member betrayed the stress that he was under during this period. After asking about the teacher's health, Higgins commented, "I don't know what it is to wake up and feel well."

While Higgins' anxiety may have been too extreme, the problems faced by the school were serious. At a time of economic hardship, the rapid extension of the teacher-preparation period from two to three and then to four years, though welcomed by Higgins, discouraged many young people from entering the field of elementary education. Secondary school teaching, which also required a four-year degree but offered much higher pay, attracted the best candidates. The need for students to relocate to New Britain for their fourth year in elementary education also made enrollment at Danbury less appealing. Higgins fretted about losing the popular commercial education program to New Britain. In 1933-34, one-third of the 185 students at Danbury were training to be business teachers.

In 1933, for the first time since it had opened five years earlier, Fairfield Hall was not full. Higgins sensed several interlocking factors had altered the composition of Danbury's student body. The Depression deterred many students from undertaking a four-year program unless they could pare costs by commuting. The automobile and a good highway system in Connecticut now made it possible for students from distant parts of Fairfield and Litchfield Counties, who would earlier have boarded at Danbury, to commute by car. Some chose to drive to New Haven or New Britain for classes, rather than to Danbury. As a result, the Danbury Normal School became predominately a day school. In 1927, 75 percent of the Normal School students came from beyond the local area and had to board in Danbury; ten years later, the same percentage lived in Danbury or in contiguous towns. Higgins, who believed this trend deprived students of the valuable boarding experience, did everything he could to stimulate attendance beyond the commuting radius. He suggested that the state give Danbury a monopoly on students from Fairfield and Litchfield Counties, require that all rural scholarship holders live on campus, and "possibly" insist on a period of dorm residence for "all whose daily commutation prevents their full participation in the extra-curricular activities of student life." In 1935, he went on a personal campaign, with some success, to persuade commuters to take up residence at Fairfield Hall. Charlotte Isham's third-year program was part of this effort to fill dorm rooms.

Higgins battled on other fronts, as well. He complained that the outmoded practice schools provided by the city of Danbury made it impossible for the Normal School to attract the best students. Locust Avenue and Balmforth Avenue Schools, both built in the late nineteenth century, he deemed obsolete. Containing only classrooms, they lacked teachers' offices, preparation areas, assembly space, or a gymnasium. As early as 1930, Higgins began urging the state to build a modern practice school on the Normal School grounds.

Higgins did not permit attention to these fundamental problems to deflect him from preoccupation with student behavior. In 1933, the student council, at his urging, drafted and posted in prominent spots on campus a terse list of "Accepted Standards For Conduct," which detailed proper decorum in study rooms, the library, the assembly room, and corridors. The emphasis in all places was on quiet and order. In school halls, for example, "all conversations should be in low tones only." Higgins added a final admonition that pertained to actions "On the Street, In Cars, or In Any Public Place." He specified that "smoking and other practices that reflect unfavorably upon our student body are out of place." He completed the guidelines with the dogmatic admonition: "A woman of refinement always avoids attracting attention by her appearance, voice, or actions." Higgins abhorred dishonesty and took elaborate steps to stamp out any vestiges of it at the school. In Wilsonian fashion, he presented the student council with "14 Points" that he wanted the group to consider. The first two, "Keep at work on the thief question" and "Keep at work on the matter of cheating," made clear his righteous agenda.

Lothrop Higgins' health was never robust. By early 1935, intimates noticed that the strain of guiding the school through uncertain times had taken its toll. While not ill, he suffered from chronic fatigue. In an effort to regain his energy, Higgins and his wife traveled to Atlantic City on February 22nd, where he planned to combine attendance at the mid-winter National Education Association meeting with a seaside vacation. After participating in a few sessions of the convention, the Danbury principal contracted pneumonia and was confined to his room in the Hotel Traymore. On March 6, 1935, he died at the age of fifty-nine.

Ralph Jenkins, who became the third and last principal of Danbury Normal

School in 1935, and the first president of Danbury Teachers College in 1937, resembled his predecessor only in their common Yankee background. In appearance, personality, administrative style, and educational experience, the two men were worlds—more accurately, centuries—apart.

Jenkins, forty-three years old when he was hired, had New England roots, seemingly a prerequisite for Danbury principals. Born in 1891 in Springfield, Vermont, to working class parents (his father was a pattern maker in a machine shop), the young Jenkins showed unusual interest in science. As a teenager he had an article published in *Popular Mechanics* magazine. After graduation from local schools, he entered Dartmouth College in 1910, where, of necessity, he combined study with part-time employment. While earning a BA degree with a major in English and a minor in biology, the ambitious Jenkins worked variously as a jeweler's assistant, a reporter for the Springfield newspaper, and a railroad telegrapher (which required proficiency in Morse code).

After receiving his undergraduate degree from Dartmouth in 1914, Jenkins began a lifelong commitment to teaching that brought him deep satisfaction. Years later, in 1943, he would close a speech to a Danbury Teachers College assembly with this sincere declaration: "I can honestly say as your President that I have never regretted for a day that I chose the profession of education and have stuck to it constantly for nearly 30 years."

His single-minded dedication to education paid off. During the two decades between leaving Hanover and arriving in Danbury, Jenkins held a series of increasingly more responsible administrative positions in the field. He progressed from assistant principal at Burr and Burton Seminary in Manchester, Vermont, in 1915; to principal at Black River Academy in Ludlow, Vermont, in 1916; to superintendent of schools in Plymouth, Connecticut, in 1917; to superintendent of schools in Putnam, Connecticut, in 1922. There was only one brief detour, between 1920 and 1922, when he became a salesman of educational publications for the American Book Company.

In 1928, the highly focused Jenkins returned to Vermont for his first job in higher education. As principal of Johnson Normal School, a tiny two-year school located in a heavily French outpost forty miles below the Canadian border, he established a reputation for cautious innovation and skill in marketing. He added a third year to the program of study and increased the number of faculty. In 1931, he replaced the conventional curriculum with the grandiose sounding "Johnson Plan of Training for Vitalized Teaching," which became the distinguishing feature of the college. This approach aimed at the development of each student-teacher by integrating the three parts of the college experience: formal classes, practice teaching, and social life. The Johnson Plan impressed Connecticut Education Commissioner Butterfield; in 1935 he brought Jenkins to Danbury.

The new Danbury principal looked and acted like a modern college chief executive. Tall, slightly overweight ("burly" was a word his son used to describe him), Jenkins was a handsome man who wore expensive suits set off with a Homburg hat. His personal life, while highly moral, was not puritanical. He smoked five or six cigars a day, drank socially, and enjoyed playing bridge. Change did not paralyze Jenkins. On the contrary, he was comfortable in unfamiliar situations and welcomed challenges. He was active in many educational and civic organizations, an amateur actor whose love of public speaking made him popular. A faithful Rotarian, Jenkins addressed the local club in terms the members understood. In his first appearance as a guest speaker in early 1936, he described the Normal School as a business, sprinkling his talk with terms like "plant," "raw materials," "finished goods," and "the ultimate consumer." He referred to rising enrollment at the college by declaring that "sales are decidedly picking up." His unpretentious manner was so effective that the *News-Times* the next day praised his speech in an editorial entitled "Our Splendid Normal School." Because of his many contributions, Rotary International selected him as a district governor in 1941, the first Danburian to receive that honor.

The facade of an affable administrator disguised a complex nature. Jenkins loved music. His rich baritone voice graced numerous church choirs. For many years he headed the music committee of the First Congregational Church in Danbury. He traveled widely to hear the nation's best symphony orchestras and regularly listened to classical music on the radio. One of the ways he hoped to attract more able students to Danbury was by specializing in music education as a "distinctive type of service."

To a degree that would make many uncomfortable today, Jenkins did not separate his religious commitment from his directorship of a secular institution. "Teaching As a Vocation," a speech he delivered to the Bradford Club of the First Congregational Church shortly after he arrived in Danbury, made clear that, in his judgment, a good teacher had to have a deeply religious nature. He did not have a problem including prayers and hymns in student assemblies, or in lecturing students on "The Value of Church Attendance." Although he was an active lay leader in the Congregational Church, Jenkins tolerated all creeds. His unembarrassed and uncomplicated message was that church membership would sustain students just as it nourished him.

It would be an overstatement to term Jenkins a scholar, but it is accurate to say that he was a dedicated student. His son recalled that he continually attended school. He earned a master's degree at Middlebury College in 1919 while teaching in secondary school. When he headed Johnson State, he moved his family to Boston in the summer of 1933, in order to complete his master's in Educational Administration at the Harvard Graduate School of Education. In 1937, after more summers of trekking into New York City, he received his doctorate from New York University.

It was as a graduate student at NYU, in a course taught by former Director of Teacher Preparation Alonzo Myers, that the Danbury school president discovered the state's first commissioner of education, Henry Barnard. From that point on, Barnard became a fixation and an inspiration for Ralph Jenkins. Jenkins wrote his doctoral dissertation about Barnard. He then recirculated his research in a short book published by the state teachers association, as well as in numerous scholarly and popular articles and in lectures to groups such as the Connecticut Historical Society. Jenkins testified at length before the General Assembly on behalf of a bill to commemorate the one hundredth anniversary of the establishment of the Connecticut State Board of Education. He told legislators that Barnard was as great "if not a greater educator than Horace Mann." Unwilling to let the board's centennial pass without a proper celebration, Jenkins mobilized the Danbury community to honor Barnard. On June 16, 1938, a cast of hundreds, including college students and faculty, practice-school teachers and their students, and members of numerous civic organizations, dramatized the life of Barnard in an outdoor pageant.* Jenkins himself played the role of Barnard in his adult years and led the cast and audience in the singing of "America the Beautiful" as a grand finale.

On September 30, 1937, state and local dignitaries assembled in nearby Danbury High School's auditorium for the first Danbury State Teachers College academic convocation and the formal installation of Jenkins as president. On this auspicious occasion, the culmination of Jenkins' career, he delivered an address entitled "With Henry Barnard As Guide." He told the audience he had expected his intense study of Barnard's life would help him develop a coherent philosophy of education. Instead, after reading more than two thousand letters written by the famous Connecticut educator, he had concluded that action, rather than theory, interested Barnard. Jenkins applied this insight to his own presidency, saying, "If I can do the work first, the necessary work, perhaps after a period of prolonged study I can announce with some finality what my philosophy is and even some of the objectives of our college." He promised only that his administration would be marked by action.

The action had already begun. When Jenkins had assumed command of the Normal School in 1935, he immediately redefined the role of the principal. He first streamlined administrative procedures. Recent reorganization of Connecticut government had required all state agencies to file quarterly budgets, to abide by the merit system in hiring, and to seek competitive bids on all purchases. These rules imposed a heavy burden on the small staff in the principal's office. Once office routines had been systematized, Jenkins concentrated on a list of priorities. He wanted to make the school more selective. In order to reach his goal of admitting only 50 percent of those who applied, he spent time promoting the college. The General Assembly had to be convinced to spend more money on higher education, especially with the pressing need for an adequate practice school on campus. Jenkins saw the value of extension classes on Saturday and on late weekday

*During the summer of 1936, the WPA had transformed the low area behind Fairfield Hall into an outdoor amphitheater, complete with stage and dressing rooms. A hedge screened the area from the athletic fields behind.

afternoons to serve alumni who did not have college degrees. When Danbury became a four-year school, Jenkins threw his energy into fulfilling the requirements for accreditation issued by the American Association of Teachers Colleges. In order to accomplish this formidable task, the library holdings had to be expanded, the faculty upgraded, and physical education facilities improved.*

While Jenkins had little time left to deal with students, he could delegate authority. Fortunately, an administrator already at Danbury had the capacity to take on more responsibility. In 1931, Lothrop Higgins, in one of his shrewdest personnel decisions, had hired Ruth A. Haas as dean of women to supervise the boarding students. The young, attractive, vivacious Haas, a recent graduate of Syracuse University, moved into an apartment in Fairfield Hall and quickly became the most popular person on campus. Students appreciated her honesty and open friendliness. Jenkins recognized that, although Haas was not much older than many of the Danbury students, she was the ideal choice to become, in effect, the academic dean. In 1936, her duties were expanded—though her title was not changed—to include all student-related matters, such as discipline, attendance, and scholastic progress, as well as control of the curriculum. For ten years, Ruth Haas, under Jenkins' tutelage, managed all the internal affairs of Danbury Teachers College, an arrangement congenial enough to persuade her to decline the offer of at least one higher-paying job offer from another college.

Haas' promotion changed the atmosphere on campus. She projected reasonableness and moderation. Enforceable rules that permitted students to smoke in the lunch room until 4:30 p.m. and in the dorm basement "Frolic Room" after dinner until 10 p.m., and all day on Saturday and Sunday, replaced Higgins' ban on smoking. Underachieving students who had to meet with her about their grades remembered that she balanced firmness with understanding in these dreaded conferences. Haas was no pushover, however—as a January 21, 1938, entry in the student council minutes illustrates. The secretary of the organization recorded that "She [Haas] spoke tersely and unflatteringly about the Council's ineffectiveness and laxity in doing its duty."

*The American Association of Teachers Colleges accredited the school in 1941.

Jenkins elevated the goal of making Danbury a truly co-educational institution above all his other aims. As he told the Rotary Club in 1936, "I want more boys to enjoy the splendid advantages Danbury Normal School has to offer. Five boys in 30 years are not enough."* His immediate objective was to have fifteen to twenty males enter the school each year. To bring this about, he revamped the college catalog to make it more appealing to men. Starting in 1936, a special section in bold type explained how men could easily find jobs in teaching. The 1940-41 catalog, under the banner headline "OPPORTUNITY FOR MEN IN TEACHING," tried to counteract the stigma of men teaching in female-dominated elementary schools with the guarantee that "Qualified men may look forward to moving on from the classroom to service in an administrative capacity." Men were highly visible, well out of proportion to their numbers, in photographs printed in the catalogs. During the winter of 1936-37, the school played its first men's intercollegiate basketball schedule. High school students flipping through the 1938-39 catalog couldn't miss spotting a picture of the "Boy's Basketball Squad" below an even larger formal group photo of "The Men of the College." Alfred Geddes, a recent graduate of Arnold College and Boston University, who would have a lengthy career at Danbury as dean of men, was hired in 1938 to teach physical education and coach men's sports. Jenkins also took to the stump to convince high school boys of the wisdom of enrolling at Danbury. He told Danbury High School students, during a visit in the spring of 1937, that they could live at home and earn a college degree for the low cost of eighty dollars.

External circumstances beyond Jenkins' control enhanced the appeal of this message. The Depression made it impossible for many young men to pay tuition at a private college or to afford the expense of attending a distant university. Truman Warner felt that he was like most of his male classmates because he came to Danbury Teachers College in 1937 (after graduation from Danbury High School), "in some ways by default." After 1937, Danbury became even more attractive to men because it was no longer a normal school preparing students to

*As soon as he took over the reins in Danbury, Jenkins asked May Sherwood who, among her many duties, was head of the Alumni Association, to make an accurate count of the number of male students who had attended the school. She came up with a list of five male graduates.

teach exclusively in elementary schools. Many men (and some women) who came to Danbury after the four-year program had begun, never intended to teach at this level or, indeed, to teach at all. They saw the teachers college as a cost-effective step toward another career.

Beginning in September 1936, when twenty young men enrolled, Danbury had a significant male presence. In 1940-41, the first year that had men in all four classes, there were fifty-five in a total student body of 198. Many had extraordinary ability and went on to distinguished careers. Arthur Coladarci, class of 1940, became dean of the School of Education at Stanford University after getting his doctoral degree from Yale. Theodore Shannon, also class of 1940, after earning his doctorate at the University of Wisconsin, remained at the Madison school as professor and dean. Ralph J. D. Braibanti, class of 1941, received his Ph.D. from Syracuse University and became a professor of political science at Duke University with an international reputation as an expert on the Middle East. His classmate in 1941, Truman Warner, earned a doctorate from Columbia University and taught anthropology at his alma mater for more than thirty years.

Men altered the dynamics of campus life. For one thing, they challenged the overwhelmingly female faculty. Some teachers, such as K. Augusta Sutton, relished having able and aggressive male students. Others encountered discipline problems with the more boisterous males who were bored with some aspects of the curriculum. Most men students, but only a few women, had taken math and science in high school; they found the courses in these areas repetitious. The gender issue increased pressure already felt by a veteran Normal School faculty to upgrade their credentials for college teaching.* In 1938, all but one of the fourteen faculty members were taking courses at Yale, Columbia, or New York University. Eight of them had already received master's degrees from Columbia Teachers College. Jenkins held the only doctorate.

Men added a third pattern of daily activity at the small school. They lived at their Danbury area homes or boarded in the city and drove their cars to school.

*At Jenkins' installation as president in 1937, Grant Finch, one of two male faculty members, gave a short talk. He claimed that fourteen members of the faculty, practice-school faculty included, had served under all three Normal School principals.

After 1936, jalopies appeared parked at the curb on White Street. Mort Johnson, class of 1942, was a long-distance exception who drove to Danbury each day from his home in Norwalk in an effort to stay under his budget ceiling of fifty cents a day. Almost all men had to work. Warren Laws, class of 1942, who hailed from Stratford, boarded with a relative in Danbury. He drove a school bus before and after his college classes and also clerked in a grocery store. Many, like Laws' roommate, Donald O'Connor, put in several hours a day in a hat factory. Their straited circumstances concerned Jenkins. Urging the alumni to contribute to a scholarship fund in 1939, he told them that many of the students "are living from day to day with but a few dollars between them and failure to keep on."

It is possible to exaggerate the impact of co-education at Danbury. True, women seemed to defer to men's leadership; all of the classes in the early 1940s elected men as president. But women still made up three-quarters of the student body during these transition years. Under the watchful eye of Dean Haas, eighty-five of them lived in Fairfield Hall, where they ate lunch and dinner together, dressed properly and seated eight to a table. Anyone late for 6:15 p.m. dinner had to explain the reason for her tardiness to the dean. Each student took a one-month turn as a waitress. No one could leave the dining room until the faculty finished eating. Students could have one evening "date" a week but had to return to the dormitory by 10 p.m. Failure to abide by the curfew meant confinement to campus for the next week. This rigid routine prompted complaints, but it also promoted camaraderie that would later dominate the recollections of the alumnae. A smaller group of women, about fifty in number, were day students who sometimes felt the distance between themselves and their boarding sisters. They developed rituals of their own. Marie Tomaino Prebenna, class of 1942, described cooperative lunches cooked by commuting students on a gas stove in the basement of Old Main.

Even though the three components of the Danbury student body (dormitory residents, women commuters, and men) had different living experiences, the small size of the school was a powerful, unifying force. The four class years were divided into "A" and "B" sections with no consideration of gender or on- or off-campus status. Each section took the same classes at the same time with the same teacher. Frequent field trips to geological sites or to Broadway plays promoted friendship, especially when the entire freshman or junior class could be transported in a single bus. A variety of clubs, musical productions, and plays gave everyone a chance to participate, regardless of ability. Truman Warner, the president of the a cappella choir when he was as an undergraduate, appreciated this opportunity. "At Yale I could never have been one of the Whiffenpoofs," he recalled, "but I was a member of the quartet here." The entire student body gathered in the auditorium twice a week for mandatory Monday and Thursday assemblies planned by a joint student-faculty committee. Students spent much more time in what censorious English instructor Phebe Harrison called "The Den of Iniquity," a basement room in Old Main where smoking and playing bridge were permitted. Everyone had to participate in the first two years of the student-teaching process that began in freshman year with two weeks of observation in a practice school. During sophomore year, this was expanded to include four weeks as an elementary school classroom aide. It is no accident that the classes of 1940, 1941, and 1942 have held regular joint reunions since their graduation.

Pearl Harbor changed Danbury State Teachers College as it changed everything else in the nation. The most obvious alteration was the disappearance of male students. This did not happen suddenly because Jenkins, in line with government policy, urged young men not to leave school to volunteer for the armed forces. The December 18, 1941, *Campus Crier* recommended that "the most sensible, the most courageous thing to do at this time is to continue to specialize yourself in that field which you have already chosen." The front-page article emphasized, "So, until you are called, stay in school."

The Army and Navy, in an attempt to establish an orderly induction process, set up reserve programs that permitted students to enlist while remaining on campus until they finished their courses. To help students graduate more quickly, the college adopted, in September 1942, a tri-semester schedule of twelve-week segments that virtually eliminated the summer vacation. During the winter of 1942-43, evening classes accommodated students working the day shift in war plants. Under the compressed schedule, students could complete their four-year course in three years. Two graduations were held, in April and in

December. Jenkins put these emergency actions into perspective in September 1942, when he told a student assembly that the campus had mobilized for war. The new mission of the school, the principal fervently proclaimed, "is to make a total contribution to the total war. All of the student body are merely kept here in trust by our government in order to better prepare yourselves for the time when you will be called in some way to serve your country."

By mid-1943, almost all male undergraduates and some women had entered the armed services. When Jenkins addressed the Alumni Association meeting at the Hotel Green on May 22nd, he reported that only four male students remained on campus. While he was proud that Danbury students were serving their country, he also expressed disappointment. "I have lived to see the Danbury Teachers College grow from a college for girls to a coeducational institution and back again," he said. At the same time, he was quick to remind women students that the government had designated teaching an essential occupation and that they were fulfilling their patriotic duty by preparing to instruct young children. The 1944-45 catalog reiterated this gospel of dual service: "There is just as much need to use the finest of woman power to protect the American way of life at home as there is to draft the best of man power to defend democracy in foreign lands."

Given his penchant for action, Jenkins did not allow much time for regret. He kept a hectic schedule of public speaking at war bond rallies. During one six-month period, he delivered an average of one speech a week. As district governor of Rotary, he traveled all over the state to urge the members of the twenty-eight clubs under his jurisdiction to contribute to the war effort. Jenkins was the chairman of the Community Chest Speakers Bureau and, in 1942, became president of this volunteer organization that coordinated fund raising for local charities. He saw this activity as another form of patriotic service. "The common defense demands that we eliminate every useless movement," he reasoned.

There were times during the war when homefront sacrifice seemed insignificant. One particular event dramatized the steep cost of the war. After the student assembly held on November 22, 1943, a white service flag with a red border flew from the flagpole outside Old Main for the duration of the conflict. In the center of the flag were blue stars for the 111 Danbury Teachers College graduates and faculty (86 men, 21 women, 4 faculty) who were then in military service.* The Alumni Association presented this powerful symbol to the school as part of a memorial service for Anthony Palermo, who was killed in an Air Force training crash in Georgia on October 27, 1943, and Warren Laws, a bomber pilot declared missing in action after being shot down over Europe on September 6, 1943. Ruth deVillafranca, faculty adviser to the class of 1941, eulogized Palermo. K. Augusta Sutton, faculty adviser of the class of 1942, paid tribute to Laws.**

Despite such vivid reminders, the war had less impact on the campus after 1943. The three-year accelerated program became optional, although 95 percent of the students continued to take some advantage of it. Jenkins felt the time had come to look to the future. In December 1944, he appointed a Postwar Planning Committee, headed by Sutton and made up of faculty, students, alumni and community leaders, to study the long-range needs of the college. The challenges were daunting: an expected surge in enrollment, including increased numbers of men; a demand for more varied programs to meet regional requirements, especially in the fields of health care and technology; and the need for additional campus buildings. Jenkins gave the members of the State Board of Education an indication of what lay ahead when he warned them in early 1945 that the citizens of Fairfield and Litchfield Counties wanted more than a teachers college in Danbury. "The people of Western Connecticut want a people's college in this area," he declared. ■

Note On Sources

The material about Ralph Jenkins comes from a variety of sources: the Alumni Records of Dartmouth College; Kenneth Raymond, *The History of Johnson State College* (1985); The *Danbury News-Times*; campus publications (*Dee Tee Cee*, *Campus Crier*, *The Inkling*) that covered Jenkins' activities and printed many of his comments; and interviews with faculty and students. One of the most helpful interviews was with Dr. Ward Jenkins, who supplied many insights about his father. The Ruth Haas Library Archives has a copy of Jenkins' dissertation and most of his numerous publications about Henry Barnard.

*In all, 123 persons connected with the school served in the armed forces during World War II.

**Laws survived. He parachuted from his plane and, although severely burned, escaped to Spain with the assistance of the French Underground. In early 1944, he made his way to England and safety.

The Papers of the State Department of Education (Connecticut State Library, Record Group 10, Box 24) contains lengthy unpublished annual reports of Higgins and Jenkins to the Department of Teacher Preparation for the years 1933 to 1938. They are supplemented by detailed statistics on the training schools.

The picture of campus life is based on material in publications such as the school catalog, school newspapers, and yearbooks. The personal details come from the memory of the following former students and faculty: Gertrude Braun, Ralph Braibanti, Ann Titsworth Carey, Charlotte Isham, Mort Johnson, Elizabeth Minck Laws, Mary Brennan Musnicki, Elsie Lauricella Rader, Elizabeth McNamara, Barbara Warner Obeda, and Truman Warner. Ann Titsworth Carey supplemented her interview with a detailed written reminiscence of the daily routine in Fairfield Hall. Marie Tomaino Prebenna spoke about her life as a Danbury student and as an elementary school teacher, during a symposium on "Women in Education," sponsored by the Western Connecticut State University Department of Education on March 1, 1994. Helping to bring this era to life are four bulging scrapbooks in the Haas Library Archives. Covering the years 1934-1944, these were compiled by the publicity committee of the Cooperative Student Government Association. Truman Warner and Elizabeth Laws generously donated to the college archives fascinating and scarce memorabilia related to their student days.

Above: The 1938 men's basketball team. Alfred Geddes (top row, middle), who will later serve for many years as dean of men, is coach. (WCSU Archives)

Left: During its first academic year (1904-05), Danbury Normal School conducted classes on the third floor of the new Danbury High School on Main Street. (Postcard courtesy of Stephen Flanagan)

Below: The members of the first graduating class pose for a picture in front of Old Main. Principal John Perkins is in the top row center. Lothrop Higgins is to his right. (WCSU Archives)

Left: The first Normal School building (Old Main), under construction in the summer of 1904. The initials of the general contractor, H. Wales Lines Company of Meriden, are displayed on the building front. (WCSU Archives)

Left: Students line up in front of the Locust Avenue "model" school (currently the home of Danbury public school system's Alternative High School) in this 1910 photograph. Old Main is in the background. (WCSU Archives)

Above: Danbury was the only Connecticut normal school to require practice-teaching in a rural school like the one-room Miry Brook school shown in this photograph (circa 1907). Note: The flag has only 46 stars. (WCSU Archives)

Left: Members of the Normal School "Senior A Division" on a geography field trip, in February 1926. (WCSU Archives)

Right and bottom: These snapshots, taken by an anonymous student, give two views of the 1925 Field Day. At right is a synchronized flag routine; at bottom, members of the senior class dance around the Maypole. (WCSU Archives)

Above: White Street was the educational center of Danbury in the 1930s. Left to Right: Danbury High School and Fairfield Hall (both opened in 1927), as well as Old Main. The high school was purchased by the State of Connecticut and became White Hall in the mid 1960s. (WCSU Archives)

Left: A Teachers College student explains an experiment in a Higgins Hall science lab (late 1940s). Visiting education professor Norman Reed is on the right. (WCSU Archives)

Above: The 1940-41 Danbury Teachers College catalog called attention to the recreational opportunities at the school. "Sports Day" was held on the athletic field behind Fairfield Hall. (WCSU Archives)

Left: Teachers College students perch on the rocks above the Housatonic River on a geography field trip in the 1930s. (WCSU Archives)

Right: "The Hut" served multiple functions from 1946 until it was replaced by Memorial Hall in 1959. Music professor Ruth de Villafranca and two students participate in a recording session in 1949. (WCSU Archives)

Above: Students in 1940 prepare for a bicycle outing. (WCSU Archives)

Right: Students in the 1950s wait in line for coffee at the snack bar in the Hut. (WCSU Archives)

Left: Members of the Social Science-History Department meet in the Higgins Hall lounge, adjacent to their offices (mid 1960s). From left: Chairman Carl Petteresch, Truman Warner, Martha Counts, Adam Bilecky, Tom Godward and Arnold Stinchfield. (WCSU Archives)

Above: Classes in the 1960s vied for honors in the float competition, one of the highlights of Spring Weekend. (WCSU Archives)

Left: After its construction in 1954, Berkshire Hall became the principle academic building on campus. Here in the late 1950s, students take a final examination in a first floor classroom. (WCSU Archives)

Right: Academic Dean Gertrude Braun meets with students in the 1960s. (WCSU Archives)

Below: In the early 1980s "Project Acorn" revived the spirit of "Do Day." Biology Professor Howard Russock (standing) and student Chris McDonough plant shrubs around Haas Library. (WCSU Archives)

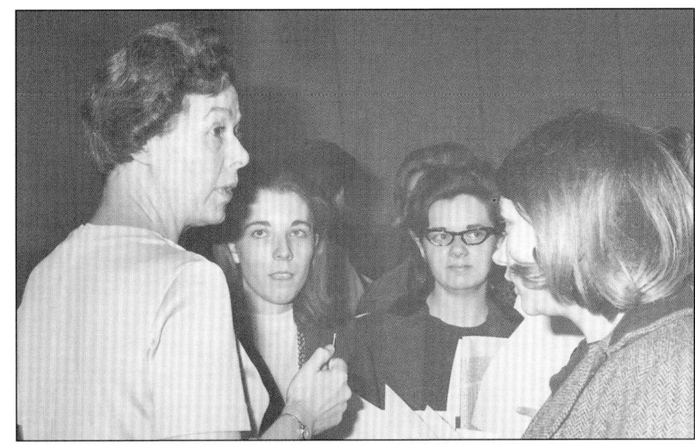

Right: Prior to the 1990s, students registered in person each semester in the Bill Williams gymnasium. Here, during the 1970s, students demonstrate that the time-consuming process did not dampen their good humor. (WCSU Archives)

Following page: Aerial view of the Midtown campus, spring 2002. (Photo by Peggy Stewart)

Left: Local musicians helped popularize the Charles Ives Center with informal concerts in the late 1970s and early 1980s. The University's Westside campus was still under construction. (Photo courtesy of the Ives Center)

Below: Aerial view of the Westside campus, spring 2002. (Photo by Peggy Stewart)

Left: The classroom building on the Westside campus opened in 1982. The pyramidal sculpture, a product of Connecticut's "One-percent for Art" program, was created by Warren Owens and installed in 1983. (Photo by Peggy Stewart)

Right: For the ninth consecutive year, the Middlefort Pipe Band led the parade of graduates who received their degrees at the 2002 commencement on the Westside campus.
(Photo by Peggy Stewart)

Below: When the William O'Neill Center finally opened on the Westside campus in 1994, it filled a long-standing need for a modern athletic facility.
(Photo by Peggy Stewart)

Right: The thirty-three-acre Westside Nature Preserve opened to the public in 1997. Dr. Stephen Wagener led a biology class along the two-mile trail.
(Photo by Peggy Stewart)

Following page: Students gather for a memorial tribute to the victims of the September 11th terrorist attacks. In 1916, Marguerite Wheeler's kindergarten class planted the red oak tree. (Photo by Erin Kiernan, News-Times)

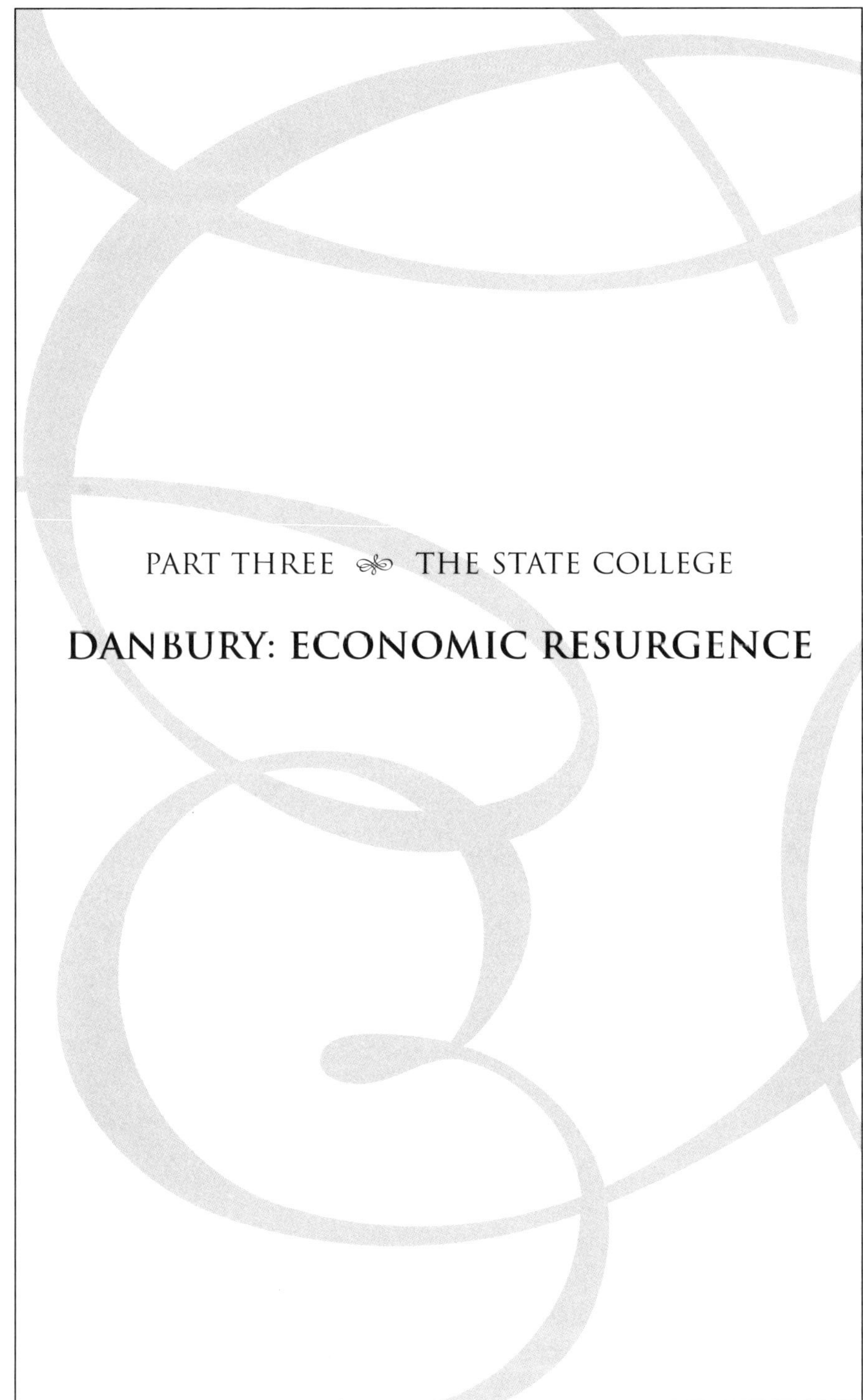

PART THREE ❧ THE STATE COLLEGE

DANBURY: ECONOMIC RESURGENCE

Opposite: White Street near Main during the October 1955 flood. The need to control the Still River sparked an extensive urban renewal program in downtown Danbury.
(Scott-Fanton Museum and Historical Society)

DANBURY: ECONOMIC RESURGENCE

Mill towns all over New England died in the middle of the twentieth century. Everywhere, the pattern was the same. The dominant industry in each community closed or moved away, leaving behind vacant factories, stranded workers, and ruined economies.

Danbury escaped this fate. The collapse of hatting after World War II did not devastate the city that had been so dependent on this industry for a century. Rather, a simultaneous influx of companies manufacturing sophisticated technical products, many in the aerospace and communications fields, sparked an economic resurgence. By 1957, the Danbury economy was so robust that the head of the Connecticut Development Commission could refer to the former Hat City as the "hottest spot in the state for new industries." The experience of one of the first high-tech companies to locate in the city indicates the magnitude of the transformation. In 1943, the Barden Corporation, manufacturers of precision ball bearings for the Norden bombsight, began operation in the former Tweedy Silk Mill on East Franklin Street. Less than twenty years later, the firm employed thirteen hundred people—as many as were still working in all of Danbury's hat factories.

World War II damaged the already tottering hatting industry in several crucial ways. The conflict interrupted the normal supply of fur from Europe and Australia. Because hatting was not considered an industry essential to the war effort, skilled hatters were not granted deferments from military service. Most hat factories were of wood-frame construction, unsuitable for heavy machinery, and therefore could not be converted easily to mass production of war-related items. As a result, Danbury did not benefit significantly from military contracts. Instead, hundreds of workers left the city each day during the war years, traveling by bus and in car-pools to jobs in Bridgeport, Stratford, Waterbury, Norwalk, New Haven, and even as far away as the Pratt and Whitney factory in East Hartford.

Hatting continued its rapid decline after the war. When the Mallory Company, one of the oldest and largest hat manufacturers in the city, sold out to the Stetson Company of Philadelphia in 1947, it marked the first time a Danbury hat factory was not locally owned. Stetson steadily cut back production at the Mallory plant, ultimately closing the facility altogether in 1965. Two years earlier, the Philadelphia firm had shut down the Frank Lee factory, which it had purchased in 1960. Approximately 60 percent of the local work force was engaged in hatting in 1947; ten years later the figure had plummeted to less than 20 percent. During the same interval, the number of hat factories in the city dropped from over forty to only five.

Long before hatting faded, Danbury leaders attempted to diversify the city's economy. As early as 1918, local businessmen organized the Danbury Industrial Corporation, a non-profit private development company that at first had minimal success in attracting varied industry to the city. Between 1940 and 1960, however, more than sixty companies opened or settled in Danbury. Many occupied facilities built by the community-owned Industrial Corporation. Energetic, innovative and flexible entrepreneurs flocked to the city during this period. Individuals like John Douglas, the founder of Republic Foil, were eager to take advantage of the many scientific breakthroughs made during the war.

Danbury offered migrating industry many advantages. A pool of workers, including a large number of women, were accustomed to, and content with, factory jobs. Vacant hat factories provided low-cost start-up quarters. The emerging interstate highway system made Danbury an affordable alternative for companies stymied by the high cost of real estate closer to New York City. Even though the expressway by-pass around Danbury would not be completed until the early 1960s, plans were far enough along a decade earlier to stimulate development on the fringe of the city. In 1955, Seymour Powers opened Commerce Park, the first suburban industrial park in Danbury. A year later, Eagle Pencil left New York City and built a modern factory near the projected route of the Yankee Expressway, the local term for the segments of Routes 6 and 7 that would soon be incorporated into the interstate system.

Danbury's 1950 population of about thirty thousand individuals, a modest 9 percent increase over the 1940 total, surged ahead in the next decade. Lawrence Moore, a consultant with Technical Planning Associates of New Haven, put this growth in perspective in his first report to the city planning commission. Moore pointed out that Danbury had added eight thousand people in the thirty years between 1920 and 1950; while in just the seven years from 1950 to 1957, the city's population expanded by nine thousand people and the rate of increase did not slow in the following decade. By 1970, Danbury's population topped fifty thousand.

A change in leadership and attitude accompanied this economic renaissance and population rise. A younger generation of men and women, many of them executives with the recently arrived high-tech corporations, were determined to make Danbury a more progressive place. During the 1950s and 1960s, the new power elite tackled big problems. They supported a massive school building program, brought about consolidation of city and town government, and advocated the physical rejuvenation of the downtown coupled with flood control of the Still River.

Public schools felt the town's growth pains most acutely. Enrollment burgeoned during the 1950s. The Board of Education tried to keep pace with this growth by authorizing construction of five new elementary schools, all but one of which were replacements for outmoded structures described caustically by one school board member as "probably the most decayed public buildings that I ever went into." Nevertheless, elementary schools remained seriously overcrowded. The high school, built in 1927 to accommodate eleven hundred students, shifted to double sessions in 1957. When a high school building referendum was defeated in 1959, a number of concerned citizens banded together in a grass roots campaign to push through a comprehensive $9.5 million school construction program. Known as the "Committee of 1000," this volunteer group combined a massive, face-to-face lobbying effort with impressive radio and newspaper advertising that earned them national magazine coverage. The 1961 report of a professional consulting firm hired by the school board buttressed their arguments. In three short years, warned the expert, the high school would have to resort to triple sessions to handle a projected twenty-four hundred students. Voters were finally convinced. Despite a mid-winter blizzard on voting day in 1962, they flocked to the polls to approve the ambitious plan by an overwhelming margin. As a result, Danbury built four new elementary schools and one of the largest high schools in New England during the 1960s.

Rapid expansion exposed the weakness of Danbury's archaic form of dual government that retained separate political systems for the city and the town. As settlement grew outside the borders of the city in the 1950s, it became clear that city taxpayers carried an inequitable burden of rising taxes to pay for sewers, water, police and fire protection for the larger town. Joint town-city committees studied the subject with inconclusive results. Local industrialists, however, particularly the new breed of corporate executives, insisted that more efficient government was necessary if the city were to continue to attract desirable companies. The Greater Danbury Association, led by prominent Republican politician T. Clark Hull, responded to this threat by endorsing reform. When businessman J. Thayer Bowman was elected mayor in 1961 on a platform advocating consolidation, it appeared that Danbury might soon join most other Connecticut cities in abolishing dual government. However, it took another massive educational effort by many of the same people who had championed the school building program before voters, by a narrow margin, ended 143 years of divided rule in 1963.

In 1955, Danbury had been in the process of shedding its image as a one-industry mill town when the Still River, a small stream that usually meandered unobtrusively through the city, flooded in August and again in October. These unexpected acts of nature caused an estimated $3 million in damage to the downtown and low-lying industrial areas. Far from being a tragedy, the floods presented an opportunity to address some serious urban problems. Businessmen, especially those who had recently settled in the city, formed the Citizens Committee for Flood Control Action. F. E. Erickson, president of the Barden Corporation, whose factory had been inundated in both floods, minced no words when he told the group, "If we get another flood we're through . . . We can't stay in Danbury." Under the leadership of John McCann, head of the Chamber of Commerce and an executive at Sperry Products, the flood committee pressured city government to seek federal assistance for harnessing the Still River. The U.S. Army Corps of Engineers' recommendation that the estimated $16 million cost for necessary flood-control measures could not be paid by the federal government shocked and disappointed Danbury officials.

However, the flood committee and the city government were resourceful. They devised a more comprehensive approach that combined flood control with a new federal program designed to rehabilitate slum neighborhoods. To tap into available federal largesse, Danbury needed only to pay one-sixth of the cost of an urban-renewal project in the Wooster Square section of downtown that was hardest hit by the floods. Conveniently, the federal government would pay two-thirds of the cost while state government would match Danbury's contribution. Such generosity was irresistible. In April of 1956, voters enthusiastically endorsed a $1.5 million bond issue to finance the local share of this plan.

The redevelopment process unfolded over the next decade. As federal rules required, the city set up a planning commission, which drafted Danbury's first master plan of development. The mayor appointed a redevelopment commission to administer the renewal program. The Still River was straightened, channeled, and speeded through the downtown. At the same time, buildings in the flood plain were bought and leveled to make way for more upscale tenants. Roads were relocated and widened to improve traffic flow. A large indoor shopping mall, the most ambitious new construction in the downtown, replaced the decrepit hat shops and tenements in the Rose and River Street area in 1968 but folded within a decade.

The influential coalition of young professionals and long-time city residents paid less attention to some of the region's social problems. David

Wilder, a Columbia University sociologist, who in 1965 spent August and September investigating the social needs of the city at the request of the teachers college, emphasized in his report the seriousness of racial inequality. He pointed out that, in the fifteen years from 1950 to 1965, the number of African Americans in the city had grown from less than five hundred to an estimated three thousand, an "increase which easily exceeds that of the region as a whole and one that is not approached by any other ethnic group." Few unskilled jobs were available for workers of any race. Although no Black ghetto existed in Danbury, confinement of recent migrants to sub-standard housing scattered throughout the city prompted a highly critical 1966 report of the Connecticut Civil Rights Commission. Serious problems plagued youth. The dropout rate for African Americans in the high school class of 1966, for example, was three times that of other students. Police had to be summoned in 1965 to deal with racial violence involving teenagers.

The same forces that challenged the city of Danbury affected Danbury State Teachers College. The 1950s and 1960s were a time of dramatic growth for the school as well as for the city. Enrollment increased, programs proliferated, more faculty were hired, and the campus expanded. Racial tension appeared for the first time. In these tumultuous decades, the mission of the school broadened beyond the exclusive training of elementary school teachers to embrace the multiple aims of a regional college. ■

Above: Ruth Haas, shown at her desk in Old Main in the early years of her presidency, had a greater impact on the school than any other single person. She served as dean and then president from 1931 to 1975. (WCSU Archives)

Opposite: "The Hut" served as the school's cafeteria, bookstore, and social center from 1947 to 1960. (WCSU Archives)

CHAPTER SIX

RUTH HAAS BREAKS THE MOLD

Thursday, October 3, 1946, was Governor's Day at the Seventy-sixth Danbury Fair, the first fair held since 1941. Honoring a long tradition, Governor Raymond Baldwin, soon to become a United States senator, began his Danbury visit with lunch at the Hotel Green as a guest of the Rotary Club. Radio newsman Lowell Thomas, a resident of nearby Pawling, New York, spoke at the event about his recent trip to witness the atomic bomb tests at Bikini atoll. At two in the afternoon, Baldwin and his party arrived at the fairgrounds. In his brief formal remarks, the astute politician promised the crowd he would order state engineers to redesign the nearby highways in an effort to avoid a repeat of the horrendous traffic jam that accompanied the record-breaking attendance of forty-two thousand on the previous Sunday, the opening day of the fair.

That morning in 1946, Ralph Jenkins hurried back to Danbury from Crawford Notch, New Hampshire, where he had been participating in a week-long meeting of educators, in order to attend the Rotary luncheon for the governor. After finishing the meal, he walked down White Street to the campus, greeted his secretary cheerfully, went into his private office to the left of the center entrance of Old Main, and, uncharacteristically, closed the door. Five minutes later, the secretary tried to inform Jenkins of a phone call and found the president had suffered a fatal heart attack. When Dean Ruth Haas informed the

Connecticut Department of Education by telephone of the death of the fifty-four year-old Jenkins,* Commissioner of Education Alonzo Grace immediately appointed her as acting president. At their next regular meeting on November 13th, which was held coincidentally in Danbury, the state board named Ruth Haas the second president of Danbury State Teachers College. She had never actually applied for the job; the board never considered choosing anyone else.

In one sense the selection of Haas was routine. She had an unmatched knowledge of the workings of the school, the city, and the state. During her fifteen years as dean, she had earned the respect and affection of the college and civic communities. However, because extraneous factors were involved, the decision was pathbreaking—even courageous. Haas was the first woman to head a public college in Connecticut. Unlike her male predecessors who were New England Protestants, Ruth Haas was a practicing Roman Catholic from upstate New York. Governor James McConaughy, himself a former Wesleyan University president, speaking at Haas' installation, commended the state board for ignoring irrelevant considerations and seeking only "the best 'person'" for the job.

In later years, whenever she was asked about becoming president, Haas insisted she had been surprised at her selection and had been "frightened, truly frightened" at the prospect of running the college. Still, it is hard to imagine that she was not eager to assume a leadership post that would fulfill the aspirations planted by her family and nurtured by her alma mater, Syracuse University, an institution that championed women's advancement.

Haas was born in Solvay, New York, a suburb of Syracuse, in 1903, the same year Danbury Normal School was established. Her father, Frederick, exerted decisive influence in her life. Of German extraction, he had migrated as a young man from his native Prince Edward Island in Canada to central New York state, where he married, attended night school to get a background in business law, and became a purchasing manager for Solvay Process Company. Enamored of politics, he served as chairman of the board of education in Solvay. In 1917, this

*Roberta Mower, Jenkin's secretary, worried that her resignation letter—made necessary by family responsibilities and on the president's desk when he returned to the office—might have triggered his heart attack. Actually it was a recurrence of a heart condition that had first been diagnosed shortly after Jenkins' arrival in Danbury.

ambitious, strong-willed man moved his wife and three daughters (Ruth was the eldest) to Amherstburg, Canada, near Windsor, to help establish a factory for Bruner, Mond Limited, a subsidiary of Solvay Process. Although he never relinquished his American citizenship, Frederick Haas plunged into local affairs. When he died in 1942, the Amherstburg newspaper needed half a page to list his civic contributions.

Haas idolized her father and inherited his resolute but reserved personality. Family members recall her summer vacation routine during her early Danbury years. After a grueling twelve-hour drive to Canada in her Buick automobile, she would first present her father with a made-in-Danbury fedora and then spend countless hours with him discussing politics. Given the fascination of both father and daughter with politics, it is surprising that Frederick vetoed his daughter's desire to pursue a career in law. Instead, he insisted Ruth and her sisters go into teaching, a field he felt held more opportunity for women.

When Haas enrolled at Syracuse University in 1920, she entered a supportive environment that for the next decade would foster her leadership skills. She was a competent student, majoring in European history and political science, but it was outside the classroom that she made her mark. A versatile athlete, she excelled in track, baseball, basketball, and tennis. Her prowess as a softball player was so great that one of her classmates referred to her as "the girl with the elastic arm." Beneath the picture of a handsome, pleasant-looking young woman, the 1924 *Onondagan* detailed Haas' involvement in women's activities: membership in the Women's Glee Club, the Women's Class Advisory Board, on both the board and the cabinet of the Women's Student Government Association, and chair of the vocational committee of the YWCA. The quiet, non-abrasive feminism that would characterize Haas' career as a college president had deep roots.

After graduation in 1924, Haas accepted a position as a high school history teacher in Watertown, New York, without severing her ties to Syracuse University. By taking summer courses, she earned a bachelor of science degree in education in 1925 and made progress toward a master of arts degree. When high school teaching proved unsatisfying, she turned to a former college teacher for advice. She confided to Professor Alexander Flick, then the New York State

Historian, that despite being "considered quite successful for a novice" at Watertown (the school had boosted her $1,400 starting salary by $75 in recognition of her good work), she was looking for an opportunity in history and education "outside of the teaching field." Undeterred by Flick's warm but pessimistic response,* Haas decided to return to Syracuse as a full-time graduate student in 1927.

The next four years were critical in shaping Haas' professional career. She hoped that the master's degree in political science she received in 1928 from the Maxwell School of Citizenship and Public Affairs would lead to a college teaching job, a goal encouraged by her mentor, Professor Finla Crawford, the vice-chancellor of the university. Twenty years later, Crawford, still one of her most loyal backers, would be the featured speaker at President Haas' inauguration in Danbury.** Unfortunately, political science in the 1920s, like most academic fields, was a male-dominated discipline with few openings for women. Consequently, Haas remained at Syracuse as an adjunct faculty member for four years. She was a teaching assistant at the Maxwell School and offered an introductory sociology course to freshmen women students in the College of Home Economics. When Crawford learned that Danbury Teachers College sought a dean of women in 1931—Haas recalled that it was "the first opening that anyone on campus had heard of"—he advised his protégé to put aside her academic ambitions "and make a way for herself" in educational administration.

Thanks to her training at Syracuse, this shift in career focus did not require additional preparation. From 1927 to 1931, Haas had participated in a pioneer program, set up by Dean of Women Iva Peters, that was designed to enhance the life of women students. Rather than assigning freshmen women to large, intimidating dormitories, Syracuse placed them in nearby former private homes that

*In a March 1925 letter, Flick wrote that positions in historical research were "at present rather limited," and gently advised that "it would be wiser for you to continue in the field where there is opportunity and in which you have been reasonably successful."

**Shortly after Haas had been named acting president in 1946, Crawford sent a congratulatory letter urging her not to consider it as a temporary appointment. He advised her to "act positively; increase that confidence which the faculty has for you now." He predicted that "the trustees will have great difficulties in finding a person as well suited for the permanent job as yourself."

had been purchased and remodeled by the university. A female graduate student was in charge of each of the fifteen "cottages." For four years, Ruth Haas served as a dorm chaperone for one of these family-style residences. She gained valuable experience helping young women adjust to college life, master social etiquette, and excel in the classroom. In 1931, her last year on the Syracuse campus, Schultze Cottage, where she was head resident, earned the highest academic average of all women's living centers. Haas was so effective with students that she became a member of the dean of women's staff during the time that the innovative Student Dean Program was being developed.*

Her credentials seemed to fit Danbury's needs so perfectly that Lothrop Higgins was willing to take the unusual step of traveling to Albany to interview the young applicant for the position of dean of women. Haas was skeptical about the job. She had no academic experience outside New York state. Even her master's thesis on the fiscal problems of education dealt exclusively with school systems in New York. The fact that she had never taught in an elementary school made her uncomfortable with the prospect of a normal school post. Surely the job would demand a grasp of the needs of children in the early grades. And, although she was a champion of expanded opportunities for women, she had never been associated with what was, in effect, a single-sex college. Her reservations were so strong that she accepted the job with the intention of staying only two years. Never a dynamic public speaker, she also took the opportunity to extort from Higgins a promise that she would not be required to make any speeches.

Haas' first years in Danbury were an extension of her life at Syracuse. She had an apartment in Fairfield Hall, supervised the living arrangements of eighty-five women, and taught an occasional history class. Her energy and athletic ability impressed Danbury students as they had those at Syracuse. Alumni recall fondly her willingness to accompany them on nightly forays through the tunnel that connected the dorm with Old Main to play basketball. Like the cottage residents at Syracuse University, the women who lived in Fairfield Hall appreciated her

*From 1931 to 1969, the Student Dean Program at Syracuse University offered women a graduate degree in student personnel work combined with experience as a dorm resident leader.

openness, candor, and concern for each individual. These same qualities won over the male students, who entered the college in greater numbers after 1937 and who had frequent contact with Haas in her expanded role as academic dean.

Of the many congratulatory letters Haas received from alumni when she became president, two in particular capture the warmth of the student-dean relationship. One, from Charlotte Blight Valois, is especially poignant. The writer first identified herself as "one of the 'lesser lights' in school, back in 1933," and therefore someone the new president would probably not recall. The Chester, Pennsylvania, resident then presented a heartfelt tribute. "However, I've always remembered how very much you added to making life pleasant, especially for a shy and frightened freshman—and I know there are many, many more former students who can look back on those days and remember your kindness." Mary LaCava, summing up her note to the popular dean, wrote that the members of the class of 1943 all agreed: "You can go to Dean Haas with anything and feel better after you've talked to her."

Throughout her twenty-seven-year tenure as president, Ruth Haas maintained this close bond with students. She heeded the warning of Finla Crawford that her promotion brought with it the danger of losing touch with students. "Avoid that at all costs," the veteran Syracuse administrator cautioned in November 1946. "One of the tragedies of the chief executive is isolation." This never became an issue for Haas, as she prided herself on not limiting her contact with students to prescribed hours. Whenever she was in her office in Old Main, which was often because her work day began at 7 a.m., she welcomed all members of the campus community. She never deviated from this "open-door policy," as she termed it. Even during the activist 1960s, when groups of irate undergraduates would crowd into her office to present their "demands," Haas met them face to face—much to the consternation of a campus security force worried about the president's safety.

Armed with an honorary Doctor of Laws degree bestowed by her proud alma mater in 1947, *Dr.* Haas took over at a turbulent time in American higher education. Veterans of military service in World War II were taking advantage of the educational subsidy offered by a grateful government and flooding college campuses. New buildings had to be built and additional faculty hired to accommodate increased enrollments. Courses had to be added to reflect a higher priority being given to science and technology. Although Danbury State Teachers College responded to these developments in much the same way as did all other colleges and universities, in one respect Danbury was a unique and exciting place. During the late 1940s and 1950s, the still-small school, profiting from a close relationship with Columbia University Teachers College, earned a national reputation for curriculum reform that emphasized learning by doing. Dean of Women Claire Trish Geddes, one of the young, idealistic faculty members caught up in these experiments, captured the spirit of innovation that pervaded the campus when, years later, she said with pride to an interviewer, "We weren't afraid to break the mold."

Anyone who might have read the February 1945 report of the Post-War Planning Committee appointed by President Jenkins had a right to be skeptical of its claim that western Connecticut could support a college of seven hundred students. At that time, Danbury had only 172 students, all of them women. Only rarely during the first forty years of its existence did the size of the student body exceed two hundred. In the next fifteen years, however, Danbury State Teachers College twice doubled in size. By 1960, the school had almost reached the visionary seven hundred figure; official full-time enrollment was 698. For the first time, the college, strapped for dormitory space, had to reject qualified applicants.

Three engines pushed enrollment upward: the G.I. Bill, the appeal of a more varied curriculum, and the extreme shortage of qualified elementary school teachers. Passed by Congress in 1944, the Serviceman's Readjustment Act provided educational benefits for all who served in World War II and was partly responsible for the surge of growth. From 1947 to 1950, veterans made up about 20 percent of the Danbury student body. Although fewer ex-G.I.'s enrolled than expected (satellite campuses set up by Danbury in Torrington and Norwalk in 1946 to accommodate those returning from the war closed after a single year because of low registration), veterans significantly increased the number of male students on the Danbury campus. These older men called attention to their distinctive status by organizing a social club called ERUTMA, an anagram of the word "mature." Whether they were veterans or simply young male high school graduates, by 1950 almost half of Danbury's 362 students were men.

Several new programs inaugurated in 1945 attracted additional students. Danbury became the first state school to offer a four-year degree in music education for both elementary and secondary teachers. Limited by the state board to one hundred students, the program became increasingly selective, requiring candidates to audition for admission. Two-year tracks in electronics, pre-engineering and lab technology, as well as a two-year curriculum leading to a bachelor of science degree for registered nurses, responded to the perceived needs of the region. In addition, the school offered extension courses in communities throughout Fairfield and Litchfield Counties.

Demography was probably the most important factor in boosting enrollment at all the teachers colleges. The birth rate in Connecticut soared in the post-war years as returning veterans married and started families. More than forty-four thousand babies were born in the state in 1947, double the total born during 1935, the mid-point of the Depression. As children born in the late 1940s and early 1950s entered school and moved through the educational system, they created a huge demand for teachers. Connecticut tried to fill this void by enticing back into the classroom women with teaching certificates who had left to raise their families, and by granting provisional teaching certificates to liberal arts graduates who could complete education courses during summer. The first class of fourteen members of the Intensive Program for College Graduates easily found teaching jobs after just eight weeks of summer training at Danbury in 1949. Still, the supply of teachers fell far short of the demand. In September 1956, one hundred classrooms in the state could not be staffed. This shortage could be remedied only by increasing the output of the state's teachers colleges.

The size and composition of the college faculty changed significantly during the post-war years. Between 1945 and 1960, the number of faculty grew from seventeen to fifty. Veteran normal school stalwarts like Grant Finch, Jesse Brill, and May Sherwood retired. Younger teachers, all with master's degrees and a significant number with Ph.D.'s, took their place. The self-study conducted for the American Association of Colleges of Teacher Education in 1953 as part of

Danbury's reaccreditation revealed that eight faculty members had doctorates, compared with only one in 1945. It also highlighted the recent arrival of most of the teaching staff: twenty-five of the thirty-four faculty had been hired within the previous four years.

The larger size of the school also forced administrative adjustments. Dr. Haas was serious when she assured the students shortly after she assumed the presidency, "There isn't any change in our standing. In the future our relationship shall be the same as in the past, only better." To underscore her determination to maintain personal contact with the students, she retained responsibility for academic advisement.

However, the task proved too formidable. By 1949, Haas realized that she could not continue to be both dean and president. Consequently, she named F. Burton Cook to a new post as dean of the college. Cook, in some ways, was an awkward choice. Even though he had a doctorate from Yale, he demonstrated little scholarly depth. His pre-war academic career had been primarily in high school administration, and before he came to Danbury he had been an advisor at the Bridgeport Veterans Center. But another part of his résumé impressed Haas. Cook had served in the United States Army from 1941 to 1945, emerging with the rank of lieutenant colonel. In his first years at Danbury as director of extension programs and head of audio-visual services, he exhibited efficiency, common sense and reliability. Cook, who remained as dean until he became president of Post Junior College in Waterbury in 1970, was in effect Ruth Haas' chief of staff.

When Danbury residents drove down White Street during the 1950s, the constant sight of construction equipment reminded them that Danbury State Teachers College had become one of the fastest growing institutions in the city. In the course of a single decade, eight new buildings sprouted on the tiny downtown campus, and additional land was purchased for more expansion. This building spree contrasted vividly with previous inactivity. With the exception of three surplus government Quonset huts put up in 1947 behind Old Main, no construction had taken place since the completion of Fairfield Hall twenty years earlier.

Campus expansion followed no master design. Such long-range comprehensive planning was difficult for two reasons. First, financing of capital improvements depended on a fickle legislature. Despite constant badgering by the State Board of Education, which adopted a ten-year building program for the teachers colleges in 1948, the Connecticut General Assembly was frugal. Each biennial session triggered a new battle for funds with an uncertain outcome. The legislature considered a total of forty-seven bills dealing with physical facilities at the four state colleges between 1949 and 1959, but it approved only twenty-six. Second, Ruth Haas was also responsible for the incremental pattern of campus growth. She did not yearn to build monumental structures. Unlike many college presidents, Haas did not even think of physical facilities on a grand coordinated scale. Rather, her natural inclination to deal with building needs in a fragmented, piecemeal manner made her comfortable with the legislature's tendency to consider construction requests on a situation-by-situation basis.

When Ruth Haas became president, the college desperately needed better facilities. Nearly a half century of use had taken its toll on Old Main, the single all-purpose academic building. State Senator Alice Rowland of Ridgefield told her colleagues on the education committee in 1947, "No institution in the State of Connecticut that I have visited since last January has had such bad conditions as I find at Danbury." Science rooms were particularly dismal. All the science courses shared a single lecture hall and cramped laboratory that accommodated only fifteen students at one time. The remaining facilities in Old Main, including the gymnasium with its low ceiling and an undersized auditorium, had been designed to serve two hundred students. In addition, ever since the 1930s, the inability of the city of Danbury to provide a suitable practice school for student teachers had frustrated college officials.

The legislature responded to these pressing needs grudgingly. In 1947, the General Assembly appropriated $400,000 for a new science building. Higgins Hall, named after the school's first science teacher and second principal, opened in September 1950. Originally a small structure creatively described by the *Danbury News-Times* as "semi-Colonial," it housed all the science classrooms, laboratories, and offices within its two floors and basement. It was quickly outmoded. An addition that doubled the size of Higgins Hall would be opened in 1959.

In 1949, the legislature appropriated one million dollars for construction of a classroom building with an auditorium seating six hundred and a respectable gymnasium. The state comptroller put this action in proper perspective when he ordered Danbury architect Philip Sunderland to come up with a simple design "without frills." Sunderland, who would leave his imprint on several campus buildings, attempted to comply, but a combination of escalating construction costs and a shortage of steel brought on by the Korean War forced him to delete the gymnasium from the plan. When Berkshire Hall opened in 1954, even without the gym, it was the school's largest building, containing more than twice the combined space of the three existing structures. Delay in adding the gymnasium was expensive. The final cost of the athletic wing, completed in 1959, was double the original estimate.

The General Assembly balked at funding a new "lab" school for the college. Senator Rowland's bill, which proposed that the state share costs with the city for an up-to-date elementary school to replace the decrepit Balmforth Avenue School as a training facility for student teachers, was defeated in 1949. The most the legislature would do was authorize the transfer of state-owned land on Roberts Avenue to the city. Undaunted, Danbury voters, prodded by an energized parent-teacher association, approved a bond issue in 1951 covering the entire cost of a new practice school on this site. The Roberts Avenue School, staffed by college faculty, welcomed 450 students for the first time in September 1953. It would continue to be operated by the college until 1968.

After several lean sessions, the General Assembly was more generous with the state colleges in 1955 and 1957. Along with financing the addition to Higgins and the gymnasium, Danbury spent its share of the appropriation on a forty-six room extension to the rear of Fairfield Hall in 1957, and on a modern heating plant and the remodeling of Old Main, both in 1959. Additional land was purchased on White Street for another dormitory, and on Osborne Street for athletic fields.

The final building erected in the decade, the student union, was completed in 1960, and was more than just another functional structure: it summed up a decade of change. Since 1947, a snack bar, book store, and social room had been crammed into a World War II government surplus corrugated metal relic so tiny the same staff operated the bookstore and the food service, which meant the bookstore had to close each day during lunch. Officially named Curley Hall in honor of Thomas Curley, a popular student and Navy veteran who died unexpectedly in 1948, the students and faculty affectionately referred to the meager informal space available to them as "The Hut." Memorial Hall, the bland, impersonal designation given to the building that replaced this Quonset hut, contained ample meeting rooms, lounges, and a dining room that accommodated three hundred at a single sitting. The alteration in scale, ambiance, and even in name of the new student center indicates the distance traveled by Danbury State Teachers College in the 1950s.

Yet the school's commitment to educating teachers remained constant in this decade of change. In 1954-1955—the year the school first exceeded four hundred full-time students—Danbury was still very much a teachers college. Two hundred and fifty of the 420 students were preparing to be elementary teachers, while fifty-six more were majoring in music education. Students had to earn admission to the education program. The faculty evaluated each student's performance after the first two years of liberal arts courses. Even though jittery sophomores worried about being "screened out" of education, in fact more than 90 percent won faculty approval for professional training.

Rejecting the top-down approach of Meader and Meredith, the State Board of Education no longer imposed a standard curriculum on the teachers colleges. On the contrary, Commissioner of Education Alonzo Grace (1938-48) and his successor, former New Haven Teachers College President Finis Engleman (1948-1956), encouraged local experimentation. Both believed, as Grace phrased it, that "Growth from the bottom is infinitely sounder and more durable than domination from the top." Grace first sanctioned this freedom to innovate when he assured college officials in 1945 that "Unity does not mean uniformity. Each faculty may determine its own [curriculum] pattern and a basic pattern is not necessarily desirable."

Ruth Haas seized this opportunity. She sensed that the time was right to find a fresh path that would provide a more substantive education for students, take advantage of the creativity of the young and eager faculty, and—not incidentally—mark her administration as forward-looking and innovative. One of Haas' strengths as an administrator was her willingness to seek expert advice. In 1947, she hired an old friend, Professor Florence Stratemeyer, an elementary education curriculum specialist at Columbia University Teachers College, as a consultant "to stir the pot," as one faculty member characterized it. Brimming with ideas, Stratemeyer had been at the forefront of the crusade for experiential learning at Teachers College. In the 1930s, she was a bulwark of the faculty at New College, Columbia's avant-garde undergraduate education school which required students to complete demanding off-campus internships. In the post-war years, when Teachers College shifted its priority away from operating model campus schools to acting as a resource for public schools, Stratemeyer became an ambassador to receptive teacher-preparation institutions around the country. During the ten years Florence Stratemeyer served as consultant to Danbury State Teachers College, she helped make the school a vibrant educational laboratory, an outpost of Columbia University Teachers College.

Columbia also channeled promising graduates to Danbury. Dean of Women Claire Trisch Geddes and Coordinator of Elementary Education Paul Williams were New College alumni. Martha Counts, the daughter of well-known Columbia professor George Counts, received her master's from Teachers College in 1949. Urged by Columbia faculty to accept a position at Danbury in 1954, she became the head of the social science and history department a few years later.

Morningside Heights was also the favorite destination for Danbury faculty seeking a higher academic degree. Gertrude Braun, who during an illustrious thirty-two year career would serve as academic dean, academic vice president and twice as acting president of the school, came to Danbury in 1945 after finishing her master's at Yale, to replace K. Augusta Sutton, then on the verge of retirement. Chair of the powerful curriculum committee in the late 1950s, Braun earned her Ed.D. in 1956 from Teachers College, where Florence Stratemeyer served as her mentor. Carl Petteresch, the first graduate dean, received his Ph.D. in history from Columbia in 1957. Throughout the decade, approximately one-third of the Danbury faculty possessed an advanced degree from Columbia.

From 1948 to 1951, the faculty, spurred on by Stratemeyer, went through an excruciating process of trying to codify how good teachers behave in five areas: with children, with colleagues, in the community, in their professional lives, and (predictably the most controversial category) in their personal lives. What came out of this soul searching was an eight-page, single-spaced document entitled "Good Elementary Teachers' Do's" that enumerated hundreds of ideal characteristics of successful teachers. The list ran the gamut from the mundane "lives within income" to the sublime "attempts to develop sensitivity to beauty." Before distributing the report, the curriculum committee felt obliged to preface it with the reassuring caveat that "Not all teachers will do all these things."

The next step was more concrete but equally challenging. After the faculty approved these guidelines in June 1951, at what had become an annual week-long post-graduation workshop, it set out to fashion courses and develop out-of-class experiences that would promote such positive qualities. Two structures with almost comic acronyms emerged. All faculty who primarily taught freshmen or sophomores banded together into what were labeled the Freshman Instructional Team (FITS) and the Sophomore Instructional Team (SITS). Each member of these teams assumed responsibility for advising six to eight students. A two-hour block of time was set aside in the weekly class schedule, so each team could meet to share information about advisees, to coordinate course assignments, and to find ways of linking the classroom with the larger world. Despite a heavy five-course teaching load, the faculty eagerly met, talked, planned, and eternally evaluated. They organized ambitious field trips. In April 1953, the entire sophomore class and its teachers traveled to Boston to visit literary, historical, and cultural sites for three days. Two years later, the freshman class and faculty trekked to New York City for two days to fulfill six carefully defined educational purposes including "to gain direct experience with foreign cultures through contact with the people in their groups." It was a "tremendously exciting time," recalled Alice Donnelly, the head of the physical education department.

In 1948, the college returned to a two-semester calendar from the accelerated wartime schedule, thereby creating another opportunity to get students off campus and into the community. For the next ten years, all freshmen and sophomores were required to spend a month between semesters in a non-paying position with a business, government agency, or non-profit association. The rationale was simple. As Dr. Haas told prospective sponsors in 1951, "The community needs teachers whose interests extend beyond the walls of the school." Administered by a faculty committee, the Interim Program, as it was called, placed between two hundred and three hundred undergraduates each year in a wide range of positions. Most were in Connecticut, but many were out of state. Ben DaSilva, class of 1952, learned much about life in his freshman Interim assignment at the Danbury Federal Correctional Institution, where he witnessed a fight between two knife wielding inmates. The experience of Diane Rebenstein, class of 1954, working at the Boston University radio station WBUR, was more tame. Her daily log, neatly recorded in a three-by-five-inch notebook, reveals that she also learned valuable life skills, not the least of which was how to live in Boston for a month on $100.72! Each faculty member monitored eight to ten undergraduates. Many members traveled as far as Washington or Boston without reimbursement of their expenses. Most faculty (like Edwin Rosenberg, who came to Danbury in 1956 after getting his M.A. at Columbia Teachers College) willingly accepted the rigors of the Interim Program even though it required donning boots to trudge through the mud to visit a student working on a farm one day, and dressing up to travel to New York City to supervise several interns at the American Association for the United Nations a few days later.

Although unconnected with the curriculum, "Do-Day," the brainchild of young Science Professor John Murphy, reflected the school's belief in learning by doing. Beginning in 1948, faculty and students spent one day each spring performing maintenance tasks around the campus. An elected male dean of women supervised the work of female students while men were bossed by an elected female dean of men chosen in campaigns that were often zany and always creative. One enterprising candidate, for example, made a speech from the top of a fire truck ladder. Another flaunted a letter of endorsement purportedly from President Harry S. Truman. The annual work party boosted campus morale. The sight of President Haas dressed in jeans as she swept the sidewalk shattered stereotypes. A picnic, subsidized by the faculty, followed by evening skits in the auditorium, broke down barriers between students and faculty. Neil Wagner, class of 1952 and for many years dean of extension services, called it "A wonderful day . . . a catalyst for feeling of family."

Discussion over coffee at "The Hut." stimulated the most radical curriculum experiment. In 1958, four faculty members from different disciplines shared their unhappiness with the fragmentation of knowledge in academe, complaining that science, humanities, art, and music needed to be integrated. Led by charismatic Frederick Lowe of the English department, a recent recipient of a Ph.D. from Columbia University, this tiny band persuaded the faculty to let them introduce what was intended to be a four-year, interdisciplinary course sequence that would fulfill the general education requirement for elementary education students.

The first course, grandly entitled "Monuments of Culture," was offered to freshmen during the academic year 1958-59. Five days per week students and faculty either listened to lectures or participated in small group discussions examining from multiple perspectives four cultural artifacts: *The Education of Henry Adams*, Picasso's painting "Girl Before a Mirror," *The Communist Manifesto*, and Einstein's *Theory of Relativity*. In weekly preparation sessions, the core faculty—Lowe, historian Martha Counts, Jim Timmins of the art department, and scientists Lon Edwards and Chris Rafter—thrashed out ideas in the English department office in Berkshire Hall. Without secretarial support, they typed, duplicated, collated, and stapled bibliographies and syllabi. They recruited guest speakers from within and outside the faculty and even brought the students to New York City for a visit to the Hayden Planetarium and a performance of "West Side Story." The goal of all this dedicated effort was to bring students into direct (if forced) contact with great minds.

When asked forty years later how the students reacted to this onslaught, Martha Counts smiled and said candidly, "I think they were overwhelmed." A letter to the student newspaper written in January 1959 by "Some Down-Trod Frosh" confirmed this judgment. Clearly frustrated by the amount of work expected as much as by anything else, the students castigated the course as "A disorganized mass of general confusion." The criticism, though juvenile and intemperate, prompted a full-page rebuttal by Dean Burton Cook in the following issue of the *Echo*. The "Monuments of Culture" course had also generated reservations among the faculty, who voted to abandon it after a single year.

The premature termination of "Monuments of Culture" completed a retreat from experimentation. By the end of the decade, all of Danbury Teachers College's bold educational reforms had disappeared. Mimeographed copies of the "Elementary Teacher's Do's" gathered dust. The freshman and sophomore instructional teams expired in 1956. Interim ended a year later. Do-Day evolved into Spring Weekend—the party without the manual labor—at about the same time. Size alone altered the school's chemistry. What was feasible with four hundred students was unwieldy with twice that number. The Interim Committee, for example, found it impossible to find and administer suitable placements for three hundred freshmen and sophomores. A study of the program by a Columbia Teachers College graduate student in 1957 reinforced doubts about the value of makeshift internships. The enlargement of the faculty and the inevitable hardening of departmental boundaries contributed to a coolness toward interdisciplinary cooperation.

An even more fundamental reason for the demise of the educational experiments of the 1950s was the shift in the nature of the school from a teacher-training institution to a general-purpose college. The impetus for innovation at Danbury during the post-war years had come from the determination of President Haas and the faculty to produce better teachers. When the mission of the school expanded to embrace areas other than teacher preparation, this shared commitment, which had provided the cohesion and motivation responsible for reform, declined.

Throughout the 1950s, the state board resisted efforts to broaden the mandate of the teachers colleges. In 1956, the board rebuffed a request by the four presidents to eliminate the word "Teachers" from the name of each school, arguing that this would misrepresent the basic purpose of the institutions. Two years later, the new commissioner of education, William Sanders, agreed to alter the name of the schools, but he was adamant that all graduates must still meet teaching certification requirements. In 1959, the General Assembly by-passed the State Board. State Senator Norman Buzaid of Danbury, annoyed that many of his constituents had to leave home to finish their college education unless they wanted to be teachers, introduced a bill of far-reaching consequences. Not only would it make the cosmetic name change, but it would direct Danbury to grant four-year degrees in fields other than education. The bill, approved by the legislature, extended the name change and the new mission to all the teachers colleges. Despite the continued resistance of the state board, the legislature restructured higher education in Connecticut by making Danbury and its sister schools multiple-purpose state colleges. This rare intrusion of the Connecticut General Assembly into curriculum matters pushed Danbury State College into a new era. ■

Note On Sources

Documentation for this period of the university's history is plentiful. Fredericka Batchelor, Ruth Haas' niece, donated memorabilia connected with the career of her aunt to the Ruth Haas Library Archives. Among important items in this collection is a scrapbook of clippings and personal letters compiled by her mother, Fredericka Haas Batchelor. A 1975 Jack Friel interview with Haas, and one with Joseph Batchelor, her brother-in-law, conducted by the author in 1999, were essential. The personnel at the Syracuse University Archives helped locate items that illuminated Haas' years at the university. The well-organized files of the Student Dean Program were especially rich.

Do-day activities in 1948 (clockwise from left) A student work party concentrates on manicuring the lawn in front of Fairfield Hall. Navy veteran Thomas Curley attracted attention to his campaign for the post of dean of women by blocking the steps of Old Main with his jeep. After the work and play were over, the faculty provided refreshments. (WCSU Archives)

Faculty and students active at the Danbury Teachers College in the 1950s helped illuminate what was happening on campus during that dynamic decade. Gertrude Braun took time for three long interviews and never failed to respond promptly to letters and phone calls. Alfred and Claire Geddes cheerfully submitted to an interview and follow-up telephone questions. Edwin Rosenberg supplemented his oral history tape with a series of colorful written vignettes of his years on the Danbury faculty. In addition to traveling to Danbury for an informative interview, Martha Counts supplied a copy of the syllabus for the "Monuments of Culture" course. The following students shared their recollections of attending Danbury State Teachers College in this period: Harriet Blum, Ben DaSilva, Edyce Dashiff Hornig, Joseph Lehney, Harriet Rosenberg and Sheila Shearson. Twenty-five years ago, Jack Friel taped and placed in the archives indispensable interviews with the following faculty: F. Burton Cook, Alice Donnelly, William Espositio, John Tufts, William McKee, Neil Wagner, and Mervin Whitcomb.

I am grateful for the ardent record-keeping that accompanied the educational experiments of the 1950s, and for the sometimes-haphazard process that preserved these reports, minutes, and memos in the Haas Library Archives. The stories of the Teachers Do's, FITS and SITS, Interim, and the "Monuments of Culture" ventures were recovered from these mundane documents. The 1953 "Report to the American Association of Colleges For Teacher Education" affords a succinct summary of the roots of these reforms. Three bulging scrapbooks, compiled by an anonymous benefactor and carefully preserved in the Archives, constitute a valuable supplement to all the above. They contain newspaper clippings pertaining to campus events from 1950 to 1959.

Below: This late 1950s commencement parade, from Old Main along unpaved Roberts Avenue to the Osborne Street athletic field, underscores that Danbury State Teachers College was still a small school. (WCSU Archives)

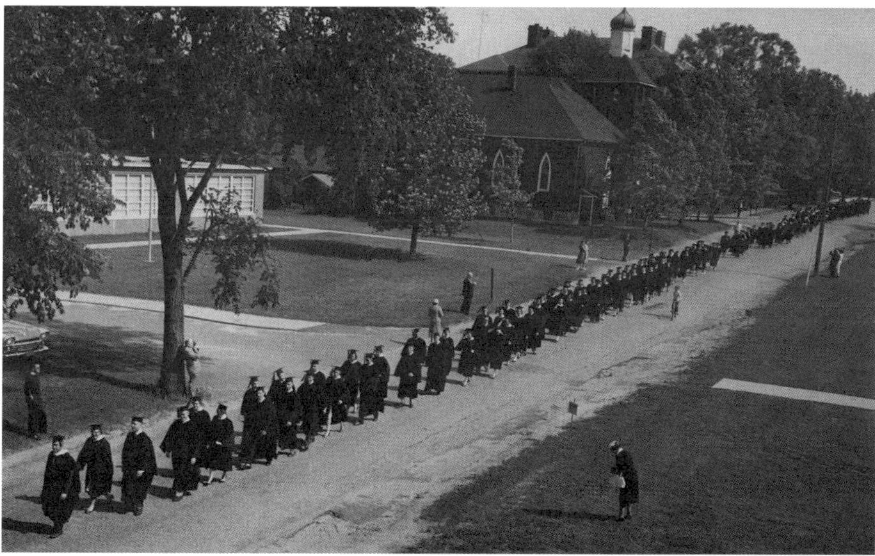

Above: The Vietnam War stirred opposition even among a basically conservative student body. (James Dyer Collection)

Opposite: Freshmen wearing "WCS" beanies register in 1967. (WCSU Archives)

CHAPTER SEVEN

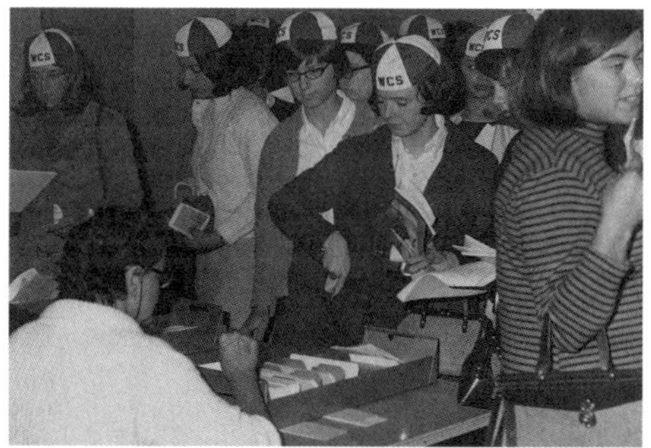

THE MORE THAT COME, THE FEWER I KNOW

Like all male students, Rick Asselta lived off campus while he attended Danbury State College in the mid-1960s. He depended upon a temperamental automobile, a bicycle, and public transportation to get from his home on Washington Avenue to school. On one bus ride, he struck up a conversation with another passenger who asked where he was going. When he responded that he was on his way to the college, the elderly woman replied, "Oh, you go to the Normal School!"

If the normal school image of a small, predominantly female, exclusively elementary-teacher-training institution lingered in the minds of some Danburians, by the 1960s it bore little relationship to reality. During this decade, the school became a large, multi-purpose college with the new name of Western Connecticut State College befitting its enlarged role.

The pace of growth was astonishing. In September 1965, the freshman class totaled 501 members, larger by one hundred than the entire student body ten years earlier. Faculty were added in unprecedented numbers. Between 1965 and 1968, seventy-five new teachers doubled the size of the staff. The menu of courses expanded; the 1960 catalog listed 114 courses, while the catalog for 1970 enumerated 372. Most students were no longer elementary education majors. After 1961, the school offered undergraduate degree programs in six liberal arts disciplines and began training secondary education teachers in the same subject fields. Other options were available, as well. When Danbury Hospital discontinued its nursing school in 1965, the college quickly inaugurated a four-year bachelor of science degree in nursing. A business administration major was added in 1968.

This massive change in the school's scale and complexity exacted high social costs. Rituals and procedures that had meaning to students when the college was small and homogeneous could not accommodate a larger and more varied student body. For the first time, many Danbury students remained detached from college life. On the other hand, the political turmoil of the 1960s, in particular the Civil Rights movement and the opposition to the Vietnam War, did not totally bypass this provincial campus. A committed minority of Danbury students, augmented by a few faculty members, marched and picketed in support of their social agenda, disrupting customary campus decorum. President Haas struggled, with considerable success but some frustration, to impose her traditional values on a school that was very different from the one she took over in 1947.

The children born in the post-World War II baby boom reached college age in the 1960s. To avoid swamping the state's higher education system, the Board of Education limited each of the four former teachers colleges to a maximum 10 percent annual increase in enrollment. Danbury State rejected seventy-five qualified applicants in 1960 to comply with this mandate, the first time it had experienced that painful luxury. At the start of each academic year, the *News-Times* used a variation of the headline "DSC GREETS BIGGEST CLASS" to keep its readers abreast of the rapid growth at the college. Full-time undergraduate enrollment passed one thousand in 1965 and two thousand in 1969. By 1970, the total vaulted close to twenty-five hundred. In addition, part-time students jammed the parking lot and classrooms from 4 to 10 p.m. on weekdays and on Saturday mornings. At the end of the decade, almost a thousand graduate students were working for master's degrees in either education, mathematics or English, and approximately five hundred undergraduates were enrolled in evening classes.

Faculty were hired en masse to accommodate this influx. The teaching staff more than quadrupled in the decade from forty-nine in 1960 to 221 in 1970. The bulk of this increase occurred after 1965, when the enrollment restrictions imposed by the State Board of Education no longer applied. At least twenty additional faculty arrived every fall from 1965 to 1970. In September 1969, a record thirty-seven newly employed instructors entered college classrooms. The hiring process was often hectic. English Professor Ray Baubles, who joined the faculty in 1967, remembered that although he had been interviewed in June, he did not receive a letter notifying him he had the job until late August, just before classes began. Baubles realized later that the last of a series of meetings during his early summer visit to Danbury—a session with Dr. Haas—was tantamount to being hired. Once on campus, he shared office space with nine other colleagues in a large room in the basement of Berkshire Hall.

In an unpublished paper with the apt title of "Observations on Growing Pains at WCSC," psychology professor Harold Burke summed up the impact of this constant expansion in one simple statistic. He pointed out that each year forty out of every one hundred students that appeared on the Danbury campus had never been there before. This meant that in 1969, when Burke made this observation, eight hundred students were strangers to Western Connecticut State College. They could not turn to a veteran faculty for guidance because, as Burke noted, each year about one sixth of the faculty were also on campus for the first time. "Little wonder," he concluded, "that traditional procedures began to waiver and shake each September."

Burke, in his capacity as dean of students, observed that many remained aloof from the extracurricular life of the college. They did not join clubs, participate in Spring Weekend, or attend sports events. Dormitories were empty from Friday to Monday. He concluded ruefully that many students "have 'outside' interests which are untouched by campus events." The *Echo*, the school newspaper, frequently complained about what it saw as student apathy. In November 1969, the newspaper called attention to its own staffing problems by printing an issue containing nothing but advertisements and blank pages with the admonition in bold print "THIS ISSUE CANCELED DUE TO LACK OF INTEREST." The paper followed this up in December 1970 by printing the names of the fifteen hundred students who had failed to vote in the last student government election. Even in agate type this "dis-honor roll" consumed three full pages.

No one was more concerned about this malaise than Ruth Haas. She was convinced that the key problem facing the school was how it could "grow to meet the needs of many students and still preserve the values of a small college." She attempted to maintain personal contact with students. In the face of daunting numbers, she still tried to learn their names and treat them as individuals. She frequently reminded students that her office was open to them and found other small ways to demonstrate her concern. Shortly after Rick Asselta missed the 1967 graduation ceremonies in order to fulfill his Peace Corps commitment in Micronesia, he was surprised and pleased to get a personal letter from Haas. Alumni like Ben DaSilva, class of 1952, appreciated the congratulatory note he received from the busy president each time he got a job promotion. But after the mid-1960s, Haas found it more difficult to maintain the prized sense of family. She worried that one of the harmful effects of expansion was the loss of what she termed "hominess." In 1966, as she spoke to a newspaper reporter about the future of the school, Haas confessed: "I personally don't know the students as well as I would like to." Then she lamented, "The more that come, the fewer I know."

The faculty, too, found it harder to become a part of the total life of the college. There were fewer opportunities for face-to-face interaction with colleagues. Classes were held in different buildings. Offices were scattered in odd corners all over the cramped campus. The customary monthly full-faculty meeting became cumbersome and inefficient; in 1967, it was replaced by a faculty senate made up of elected representatives.

President Haas combated faculty isolation by insisting that teachers be available to students at all times. Mandatory five-day class schedules insured instructors' visibility on campus. Faculty offices may have been decentralized, but all mail boxes were located in Old Main. Until the end of the decade, teachers had to pick up their mail outside Dr. Haas' office from which she could observe and summon them if necessary. Junior faculty soon learned that a blizzard was not an acceptable excuse for missing class. It was rumored that the president expected faculty who lived at a distance from Danbury to book a local hotel room if snow made travel difficult, because she would not close the school for that reason. An annual letter from the president's office, sent out each April, announced which teaching appointments were cancelled. Anticipation of its arrival reinforced faculty motivation.

In such a fluid environment, it was difficult to maintain the spirit of experimentation that had earlier characterized the Danbury State Teachers College curriculum. However, the fate of the "Monuments of Culture" course did not deter the influential curriculum committee, whose membership included many proponents of the 1950s innovations, from encouraging the faculty to devise a workable interdisciplinary sequence for all students. Between 1959 and 1961, the school labored to put in place liberal arts majors as ordered by the General Assembly. At the same time, a handful of dedicated faculty—Chester Anderson and Lee Jacobus of the English Department, scientist Lon Edwards, and H. Jonathan Greenwald of the psychology department—drew up and won approval for a mandatory eighteen-credit, four-year program designed to explore human nature from the scientific, aesthetic, social, and philosophic points of view. A separate interdisciplinary department headed by Greenwald* and made up of special faculty hired for this purpose, along with volunteers from other departments, administered "The Nature of Man," as the four-course sequence was called. Faculty enthusiasm for this ambitious effort to integrate knowledge, stimulated by the excitement of the best students, soared during the early years of the decade. At its peak, the interdisciplinary department had sixteen members. By 1969, however, the objections of career-oriented students, as well as faculty who desired more curriculum space for their own specialty, forced the cutback of "Nature of Man" to twelve hours. The courses would become optional in 1975.

The 1959 decision of the legislature mandating that the state schools offer liberal arts degrees put the four colleges on a collision course with the Connecticut State Board of Education, the overseer of all public education with the exception of the University of Connecticut. Over the years, the board had served the state colleges well, supporting expansion and providing for consider-

*Greenwald, an admirer of the Great Books approach pioneered by Robert Hutchins at the University of Chicago, insisted that the interdisciplinary label was inappropriate as a name for the department. He felt that faculty who participated in the program did so as specialists in a particular discipline who were willing to address a common problem. In the 1970s, the department changed its name to "Humanistic Studies."

able local autonomy. Ruth Haas was comfortable with the board's priorities, asserting as late as 1964 that she remained dedicated to the founding principles of the school. "As long as teachers are needed," she maintained, "our primary responsibility is the training of teachers." However, the issue of priorities came to a head in 1962, when the board rebuffed, on financial grounds, a request from the four presidents to reduce the individual faculty teaching load from fifteen to twelve semester hours. The board's action convinced the presidents, with Haas less enthusiastic than the others, the schools would be better off under a board devoted exclusively to their interests.

Prodded by the state college presidents, the legislature belatedly emulated thirty-seven other states and, in 1963, authorized a study commission to conduct a full examination of higher education in Connecticut. Handicapped by lack of budget and staff, the commission turned to the United States Office of Education for assistance. In the end, Connecticut rejected the federal recommendation to establish a single board of regents for all higher education, favoring instead a compromise more acceptable to existing institutions. Public Act 330, passed in 1965, established the Commission for Higher Education with overall coordinating, but not governing, responsibility. The University of Connecticut retained its board of trustees. A separate board was established for the four state colleges as a group, along with a third board that would govern the community and technical colleges previously under local control. The State College Board of Trustees began operation on June 30, 1965. It added an element of promise, but also of uncertainty, to this turbulent period.

One cosmetic alteration occurred quickly and without controversy. Prodded by State Senator T. Clark Hull, the legislature in 1967 eliminated reference to Danbury from the school's title. Changing the name to Western Connecticut State College, an action endorsed by President Haas, was intended to more accurately reflect the regional scope of the swiftly developing institution.

Other issues evaded simple solutions. On January 17, 1963, about forty people, including guidance personnel from area high schools, had journeyed to Danbury State College to attend a meeting seeking answers to the puzzle of why so few African-American students enrolled, or even applied for admission, at the college. Despite the prominence of several African-American graduates in the 1950s,* only three were in attendance in 1963. After a frank discussion of the issue, college officials agreed that they should no longer be content with waiting for minority students to come, but should actively recruit African-American candidates—no easy task, given the small pool of qualified candidates in the region. In 1966, for example, there were only nine African Americans in the Danbury High School graduating class of five hundred students.

During the next few years, the college worked hard to create what English Professor Chester Anderson, the head of the Human Relations Committee of the Danbury Area, described as a "warm image of welcome" for minority students. Only modest gains resulted. In October 1970, Western Connecticut State College reported to the Connecticut Commission on Civil Rights that thirty-four African Americans were currently registered.

The assassination of Martin Luther King in April 1968 galvanized the small band of African-American undergraduates on campus. Feeling the need to assert their identity, they formed the Afro-American Society and held their first meeting in early 1969. At the start of the 1970 academic year, the group—"not just another 'funzies' club," one member warned—was ready to be heard. On Monday morning, October 19th, they marched thirty strong into Dr. Haas' office to present her with ten "negotiable demands," which included establishing a Black Studies major and hiring more Black faculty as well as a full-time Black administrator. After ninety minutes of dialogue, an exasperated student suddenly adjourned the meeting by declaring, "We're not getting anything accomplished here. I'm sick of all this talk." What followed was the first instance of picketing to take place on the Danbury campus. For three days, African-American students paraded in front of Old Main waving hand-lettered placards with mock ferocious legends such as "STOP BEATING AROUND THE BUSH OR THE BUSH IS GOING TO BEAT AROUND YOU."

Ruth Haas handled this crisis the way she dealt with all militant students in

*Owen Pegler, class of 1954, and Richard Brown, class of 1958, were both officers of the Student Government Association. The 1958 yearbook was dedicated to Brown, who became a teacher in Stamford and the president of the Danbury NAACP.

this restless time. First, she was accessible and willing to listen calmly to what they had to say. She maintained that "Everyone has a right to say what they [sic] think." Haas then communicated her position in a direct, unambiguous manner. In this case, she rejected a Black Studies major because it "fails to prepare young people to make a living," but she was willing to implement a Black Studies minor. She promised to hire more minority faculty, although she would not agree to an exact timetable. Other requests for special treatment, such as a room for the exclusive use of the Afro-American Society, Haas dismissed with the admonition, "Take part in the college as a whole, living together, mixing with others." Like other protesting groups, the African-American students were unhappy but not offended.

Though mild in comparison with the demonstrations on many other campuses, outbursts provoked by the Vietnam War did occur at Western Connecticut State College. For most of the decade of the '60s, the college was a bastion of support for the government's handling of the war in Southeast Asia. The failure of the Tet Offensive in February 1968, however, altered the mood on campus. Led by its feisty president, Karen Burns, the Student Government Association conducted a referendum in support of the National Moratorium Against the War in Vietnam. Although only 856 students participated—about 40 percent of those eligible to vote—the moratorium won support by a three-to-one margin. On October 15, 1969, students took part in a mass rally in downtown Danbury, where they were addressed by Joseph Duffey, the president of Americans for Democratic Action. They marched in a candlelight procession up White Street to the campus and listened to a debate in Berkshire Auditorium between Professor Eric Roman of the history department, a passionate defender of government policy, and sociologist Arthur Levy, a critic. The overflow crowd spilled into the gymnasium where the proceedings were presented on closed circuit television. This controlled and civil response satisfied both a basically conservative campus and a wary President Haas.

The May 1970 tragedy at Kent State University provoked a more vehement anti-war protest in Danbury. Three hundred Western Connecticut State College students wearing black arm bands chanted "Peace Now!" as they paraded downtown to hold a rally in Rogers Park. An SGA referendum to boycott classes for two days as an act of mourning for the Kent State victims attracted twelve hundred voters, the largest figure in the school's history, and was approved by an overwhelming margin. Dr. Haas never revealed her position on the Vietnam War. She was content to support the students' "right to reflect their own honest opinions as long as they do so in an orderly way." But when the leaders of the student strike crowded into her office and demanded that grading rules for the spring semester be relaxed so as not to penalize those who missed class, Haas drew the line. "You made your choice. Don't ask us to accommodate ourselves to you. Don't ask for amnesty!" she snapped. The president refused to deviate from the position she had taken at the start of the controversy. "It is a matter of each student's conscience to decide what he does. College will be in session as usual; exams will be given as usual; and classes will be held as usual." After this unequivocal response, the chastened students quietly exited her office.

Male students who wanted a major change in the athletic program were more persistent with their demands. As a teachers college, the school had a meager tradition of intercollegiate athletic competition. When men had arrived in large numbers after World War II, the school had supported only two male sports —basketball and baseball—both in a low-key fashion. The basketball team was a nomadic tribe practicing in borrowed quarters at the high school gymnasium, or the VFW Hall on Osborne Street, or the West Street Armory, or, when desperate, in the narrow basement gym in Old Main. Home games were played at the armory or at Rogers Park War Memorial. The first full-time coach, hired in 1949, was the popular and capable Harvey Jessup who had one inviolable rule: "All team members must play in every game." This approach may have been democratic, but it was hardly a formula for a winning record. Baseball was more stable; the team played and practiced at Lee Field adjacent to the hat factory on Triangle Street, where the players themselves cut the grass and manicured the infield. Uniforms were sketchy. Neil Wagner, the outstanding player of the time in both sports, remembered that the baseball team wore khaki pants and Danbury State Teachers College sweatshirts in his first season.

During the 1950s and '60s, the basketball and baseball teams competed against area colleges with few winning seasons. Baseball showed improvement after Al Thomas took over as coach in 1961, and the team qualified for the National Association of Intercollegiate Athletics (NAIA) regional tournament in 1965 and 1967. Soccer was added as a third sport in 1957, when Professor Ed Rosenberg of the math department, a college player at Massachusetts Institute of Technology, volunteered to organize and coach the team.

This level of play satisfied the administration. Alice Donnelly, the resolute chairman of the health and physical education department, would not bend in her determination to give more financial and logistic support to physical education instruction and intramural sports than to intercollegiate athletics. She hired coaches who saw themselves primarily as physical education teachers. Dean Cook and President Haas endorsed this policy. "How Alice felt was exactly how I felt. We were in complete agreement," Cook told an interviewer years later. "It burned Alice to put a lot of money into intercollegiates because it had to come out of other funds."

A growing student demand for football first surfaced in the early 1960s, and challenged entrenched priorities. Despite the resistance of Donnelly, Dr. Haas seemed willing to accept football "if operated properly with all safety measures." In 1963, she told a *News-Times* reporter who was preparing a series of articles about the school's sixtieth anniversary that she looked forward to the time when the school had a marching band to perform at football games. Haas placed responsibility for dealing with this delicate issue in the hands of the Varsity Athletic Governing Board and its chairman, Neil Wagner, then head of the evening and extension program.

It took a student petition seeking to establish an informal "club football" team to spur the athletic board into action. In the spring of 1969, the board purchased equipment and staged a training period to determine the level of skill and commitment present in the student body. Fifty young men eager to show their enthusiasm for the game worked out during April under the eyes of a part-time coach. What discouraged Andy Robustelli, a former New York Giants star who was brought in as an unpaid consultant by the athletic board to evaluate the situation, was the "umbrella of non-enthusiasm" unfurled by an administration still convinced that the school lacked adequate facilities and sufficient money for a football program. Only after an SGA referendum approved a levy on students to pay for the construction of a metal building at the corner of the Osborne Street parking lot to serve as a locker room, would a reluctant administration permit football to proceed. The first varsity football game, a lopsided loss to Curry College, was played in September 1970.

The demise of Spring Weekend dramatized how much the college had changed in a single decade. Each May during the 1960s, the four classes at the school competed for creative honors by constructing floats, staging humorous skits, and producing musical extravaganzas. According to biology teacher William Esposito, the advisor of the class of 1968, the rivalry was "the cohesive element in keeping class spirit together. . . If you could win all three [Float Design, Skit Night, and 'Sing'] in one year," he explained, "it was like Yale beating Harvard, Princeton, and Brown all in the same afternoon." In May 1970, this unifying event became divisive. Two hundred black-clad, anti-war protesters, all students, carried cardboard coffins and silently trailed the parade of decorated floats. Cornelius Ivers and Jerry Maxim, co-chairmen of the evening skit competition, stunned the crowd gathered in Berkshire Auditorium by announcing their resignations. In the light of the Kent State tragedy, they declared, their consciences would not let them continue this frivolous activity. "You can't dance upon people's graves," insisted one of their supporters. At the entrance to the auditorium, anti-war students flanked two coffins draped in black cloth. They distributed invitations to a teach-in being held at the same time in Memorial Hall. Activist faculty solicited signatures on a petition calling for the end of the Vietnam conflict. Despite the eloquent plea of the elected "King" of the festivities, William Manfredonia ("If we can show that we can sing together in harmony then we can work together in harmony and peace"), the Spring Weekend tradition never fully recovered from this challenge. Within a few years it had disappeared.

The end of the 1960s was also a difficult time for Ruth Haas. She was approaching the mandatory retirement age of seventy. The school was no longer a close-knit family. Almost every administrative decision was contested. When a popular English professor's contract was not renewed in 1968, angry students responded by collecting five hundred signatures of protest. The Student Government Association conducted and published the results of its own evaluation of faculty teaching effectiveness in 1970. Haas had to have been hurt by an advertisement placed in a May 1969 issue of the *Echo* with the highly critical message: "Wanted: Skilled craftsman to remove dead wood from Old Main. Must be innovative, ingenious, and flexible. No Conservatives need apply." She certainly was shocked when arsonists ignited four small fires outside her office during the same week the ad appeared.

To many students and some faculty Haas appeared inflexible and old-fashioned during these years. She was adamant about what she defined as proper appearance and behavior. In 1969, when students wanted to go to Hartford and challenge legislative cuts in the higher education budget, Haas implored them to "Please be courteous." She did not hesitate to promulgate a strict dress code that

Above: Five busloads of Western students joined a rally in Hartford's Bushnell Park on November 10, 1971, to protest Governor Thomas Meskill's plan to raise tuition at state colleges. (James Dyer Collection)

ended with the injunction "All students should be advised that clean and proper grooming is important." She often chided male faculty members about long hair and scruffy beards because, in her opinion, they were not being good role models. Younger faculty, in particular, were uncomfortable with what they saw as the president's matriarchal tendencies.

It must have been with relief that Ruth Haas frequently had to turn away from internal campus woes to deal with the Danbury community and the state legislature, where her values were respected and her enormous political skills were remarkably effective. Although not an empire builder by inclination, her greatest accomplishment during the 1960s came in orchestrating the physical expansion of the downtown campus and the addition, under difficult circumstances, of a suburban campus. ■

NOTE ON SOURCES

Formal written documents in the college archives tell something of the life at Danbury State/Western Connecticut State College in the 1960s. The 1963 "Re-Evaluation Report to the New England Association of Colleges and Secondary Schools," and the "Re-Evaluation Report to the National Council for the Accreditation of Teacher Education" of the same year, summarize curriculum changes. A detailed thirteen-page memo about the "Nature of Man" program, prepared in 1967 by Professor H. Jonathan Greenwald, provides exhaustive detail about that innovative sequence. Dean of Students Harold Burke's "Observations on Growing Pains at WCSC" (1969) is insightful. An excellent undergraduate paper written in 1994 by Colleen Blair, "A Mild Shout: Anti-War Protest at Western Connecticut State College, 1967-1969," is based in part on interviews with participants.

Newspapers are a major source of information about happenings at the college during the period. The *News-Times* provided unusually detailed coverage. Reporter Don Fraser's five-part series in 1963 about the state of the college was particularly helpful. The three large folders of newspaper clippings in the Warner Collection eased the task of accessing the unindexed *News-Times*. The college newspaper, the *Echo*, published bi-weekly during this time, was for the most part thorough and even-handed in its coverage.

Recorded interviews with participants were vital. Jack Friel taped faculty members John Tufts, Neil Wagner, William Esposito, William McKee, Alice Donnelly, Mervin Whitcomb and F. Burton Cook in 1976. In 1999-2000, the author interviewed faculty members Ray Baubles, Martha Counts, Tom Doyle, Jean Kreizinger, Ed Rosenberg, and Neil Wagner; and students Rick Asselta, Jack Sikora, Harriet Rosenberg, Ben DaSilva, and Joseph Lehney.

Above: The Ruth Haas Library, an island surrounded by parked cars, opened in 1969. Its white color and modernistic design contrasted jarringly with other campus buildings. (WCSU Archives)

Opposite: The original library on the second floor of Old Main remained in use until replaced by the Haas Library in 1969.
(WCSU Archives)

CHAPTER EIGHT

WHAT DEAN HAAS WANTS, DEAN HAAS GETS!

Howard Durgy was a campus legend. By the time he retired from Danbury State College in 1955 as head custodian, he had spent a record fifty years in state service. Hired by John Perkins in 1905, the year Old Main opened, the crusty Durgy inspired countless stories from generations of alumni. Many remembered his willingness to remind architects, contractors, and school presidents that the soil on the White Street property was wet and unstable. He told all who would listen that as a boy he had fished in a stream that flowed where Berkshire Hall and the Higgins Hall additions were ultimately built.

Durgy's warnings about the spongy nature of the land in the center of Danbury underscored one of the obstacles that limited the ability of the downtown campus to accommodate the rapid growth in the student body in the 1960s. Given the need for technically complicated, expensive foundations, it did not make sense to build tall buildings. Few other options existed. The original campus was small, about twenty-eight acres. It was, in effect, an island, almost surrounded by downtown commercial buildings to the west, the railroad and the Still River to the south, and the Danbury Hospital complex to the north. Only the residential properties to the east offered the prospect of acquisition at reasonable cost. Until the late 1960s, the college had coped with growth by adding new buildings on the existing acreage, by purchasing the adjacent Danbury High

School from the city, and by buying land on White Street for construction of dormitories. The Board of Trustees, which assumed authority over the state colleges in 1965, forced Ruth Haas to consider a more radical alternative.

Since it began operation, the school had been hard-pressed to provide living arrangements for out-of-town students. In 1960, less than one-third of the 390 women undergraduates could be accommodated in the single college dormitory, Fairfield Hall, even after a 1957 addition had increased its capacity by 50 percent. All of the 308 men had to live off campus. To remedy this situation, the college in 1960 purchased land on White Street next to Old Main, demolished the homes on the property, and constructed two more women's dorms over the course of the decade. Financed by $2.7 million in bonds that would be paid off by user's fees, Litchfield Hall opened in 1964, followed by Newbury Hall in 1969. However, enrollment continued to soar ahead of available living space. Together the three campus residences housed 574 women, still only about one-third of the total female enrollment in 1970.

Stop-gap measures helped slightly. A privately owned and college-sanctioned dormitory on Beaver Brook Road, about a ten-minute walk from campus, lodged eighty women residents. In 1970, the financially shaky Danbury Motor Inn, built in the early 1960s on the Main Street site of the venerable Hotel Green, agreed to provide third-floor quarters for another one hundred women students. Probably as a result of the damage done to Fairfield Hall in the single year (1964-65) that it was used as a men's residence, the school made no effort to construct a male dormitory.

Classrooms were as scarce as dorm rooms on the cramped campus. But here an attractive solution beckoned. Danbury High School on White Street, separated from Fairfield Hall by a low fence, was woefully overcrowded. Built in 1927, the school had operated on double sessions since 1957 in order to handle skyrocketing enrollment. Danbury voters, goaded by angry parents, agreed to build a huge new high school on Clapboard Ridge in 1962 as the centerpiece of a school modernization program. Pressure mounted to erect the city's first junior high school. The Danbury Board of Education, Superintendent of Schools Walter Sweet (a close personal friend of Ruth Haas), and President Haas proposed an arrangement that would benefit the city and the college. The city would sell the obsolete high school to the state for renovation into desperately needed college classrooms. With the money from the sale of the high school, the city would finance construction of a junior high school on city-owned Broadview Farm, aided by a state subsidy that would defray one-third of the cost. Another appealing feature of this deal, from the city's point of view, was that no property would be removed from the tax roles as was the case whenever the college bought privately owned land for expansion.

The General Assembly and Danbury voters saw the wisdom of this scenario. In 1961, the legislature added $1 million to the original $1.5 million approved by the 1959 legislature for the purchase and conversion of the building. In 1963, the Connecticut State Bonding Commission bestowed its blessings. In June 1964, a special Danbury town meeting accepted $1.9 million as the sale price of the thirty-five-year-old high school.

The college wasted no time moving in. In September 1964, while energetic junior high school pupils fidgeted in classrooms in the front of the building, the music department, which had been squeezed in its former Berkshire Hall quarters, took possession of the rear section. It would take five more years and another $2 million before the renovation was complete; but the college had temporarily solved its classroom shortage. Alexander White Hall, named in honor of the donor of the original tract of land for the Normal School, contained twenty-five classrooms, more teaching space than in all of the other campus buildings combined. The former high school gymnasium was transformed into offices, instructional rooms, and practice space for the music department.* The 1920s-era auditorium began a new life as an up-to-date concert hall dedicated to Danbury composer Charles Ives.

Ruth Haas had long realized that the library, still in its original quarters (a dignified wood-paneled room with a balcony on the second floor of Old Main), was an embarrassment. Only the librarian, Marie Green, who had patiently coped

*Mervin Whitcomb, who succeeded Ruth deVillafranca as music department chair, joked that this was the first time music was not part of every class at the college. Previously in Old Main and Berkshire, the sound of music students practicing was carried by the ventilating systems into all other rooms.

with sub-standard conditions since 1936, had a private office; other employees shared work space with students at a few study tables. During the 1950s, the school spent just $40,000 on books, far short of the $110,000 recommended by the American Library Association. In 1959, the library took over the entire third floor of the administration building, where concern about the weight of the puny book collection of 50,000 volumes required storage of periodicals in the basement. Librarians scurried up and down three flights of stairs to retrieve and then re-shelve materials. Fortunately for the weary staff, the library could accommodate just one hundred and fifty students at a time.

The General Assembly responded to this glaring need in the 1963 session by appropriating $1.5 million to construct an adequate library on the northeast corner of the campus bordering Osborne Street on land that had previously been used as an athletic field. Complications slowed progress. Local architect William Webb Sunderland, whose buildings (and those designed by his father, Philip) are area landmarks, drew up plans for a severe four-story, marble-clad structure that many felt was not in keeping with the neighboring brick buildings on campus. When estimates indicated that construction costs would exceed the amount allotted by the legislature, Sunderland eliminated the marble in favor of white, pre-cast concrete panels. Dr. Haas transferred money set aside for purchasing books to help offset the shortfall. Bureaucratic red tape caused further delay. Federal funds, which were to pay for one-third the cost of the building, did not arrive until 1966. Ground breaking for this sorely needed facility did not take place until early 1967. When the completed building opened in May 1969, it was appropriately named the Ruth A. Haas Library, a fitting testament to the president's tenacity and patience.

The legislature treated Danbury State College generously in the 1960s. The total cost of construction on campus during the decade exceeded $10 million. In addition to the projects mentioned, the state authorized the remodeling of the student union building and a classroom and laboratory addition to Higgins Hall, finished in 1970. In part, a robust Cold War economy justified this spending; nevertheless, the energy and skill of Dr. Haas as a lobbyist for the college cannot be ignored.

Steve Collins, a shrewd and well connected observer of the Connecticut legislature, enjoyed telling a story that illustrates Haas' political clout in Hartford. The long-time editor of the *News-Times* took advantage of a chance encounter in the hallway of the state capitol with Representative Guido LaGrotta, the chairman of the House education committee, to lobby for a pending bill that Collins thought would benefit the college. LaGrotta had served terms in the legislature over a twenty-year period from the 1940s through the 1960s, and he knew Haas well—first as the dean and then as the college president. In fact, to emphasize their long-standing friendship, he continued to refer to her as 'Dean.' Collins had only begun to make his case when the Republican from New Preston interrupted him with the blunt question, "What does Dean Haas want?" LaGrotta paused, and then added with gusto, "What Dean Haas wants, Dean Haas gets!"

Much like her father, Ruth Haas had natural political instincts. She remembered names and catalogued details about people. Collins recalled that as soon as he got the Associated Press story reporting the committee assignments in the General Assembly at the start of each legislative session, he would call Haas with the information. As they went down the list, he was always astounded at the depth of her knowledge about key representatives and senators. Legislators were impressed that she was always meticulously prepared, never excessive in her requests, and pleasantly persistent. "Flint underneath the smile," commented T. Clark Hull of Danbury, a man who had been both a state senator and lieutenant governor during Haas' tenure at the school.

Haas had two other rare qualities that contributed to her political success. First, she was completely non-partisan. William Ratchford, a Democrat who represented Danbury in the General Assembly from 1963 to 1973, expressed an unchallenged judgment when he said, "Party didn't matter when it came to Ruth Haas." This neutrality served her well, particularly after 1965, when court-ordered legislative reapportionment broke the grip of the Republican Party on the lower House and led to fluctuating party control of state government. Second, she was self-effacing. Her reply to a 1946 request for personal information for a story in the Syracuse University alumni magazine was typical of the way she sought to avoid the limelight. Haas, who had just taken over as Danbury president at the time, answered, "I'm afraid you will not find anything worthy of recognition or anything very startling in my life history . . . I can't imagine anyone finding my activities very good reading." In the 1950s, Professor John Tufts of the English department, who also handled publicity for the college, wanted to send out a press release touting Haas as one of the few female presidents of a state college in the nation. Haas forbade it, with the reproach, "I am not unique!" In politics, as in all matters, she was content to work behind the scenes.

So many building projects were underway during the 1960s that the tiny campus resembled a single construction zone. Little space remained, either for more structures or for automobile parking. Proximity to the railroad—one of the reasons the school was originally located on White Street—was no longer an asset. Instead, parked cars, essential transportation for commuting students, choked the downtown property and the surrounding streets.

The City of Danbury, eager to make the college a participant in its downtown redevelopment plans, offered assistance. Established after the 1955 floods primarily to discipline the rambunctious Still River, the city's urban renewal program had expanded, with the help of generous federal grants, into a comprehensive blueprint to replace slums, improve roads, and revitalize business in the downtown. In 1964, the city initiated the Mid-Town East Redevelopment Project, which concentrated on upgrading two hundred acres near the college campus. One of the project's stated goals, inspired by the prospect of bonus money from the U.S. Department of Housing and Urban Development, was to "make land available to Western Connecticut State College for expansion purposes." Dr. Haas and city authorities explored at length the possibility of the college utilizing most of the eighty-acre strip of land between White Street and the Still River for off-street parking. The parcel stretched from the present location of the state courthouse eastward one-third of a mile to where Matz Lumber Company stands today. To show its support, the legislature appropriated $800,000 in 1965 to cover the purchase and development of this property. In the end, a combination of time-consuming federal procedures and pressure from the Board of Trustees to move in another direction ended this potential city-college partnership. In 1969, the state did buy four lots on the south side of White Street in the redevelopment tract where the present parking garage is situated.

Ruth Haas had her eyes on one other segment of land, the triangular parcel of one- and two-family houses bounded by Osborne Street, Locust Avenue, and Crane Street. The president intended to use this property, which extended northeast to Danbury Hospital, for additional dormitories, including a badly needed men's facility. Governor John Dempsey and the Democratic-controlled legislature in 1967 made available one million dollars to acquire the land for this purpose. Early in 1968, surprised residents received letters from the Connecticut Department of Public Works informing them that the state meant to purchase their homes. "It really floored me," complained one resident shortly afterwards, adding with resignation, "but I guess there is not much we can do about it."

This Osborne Street homeowner was too pessimistic. Real estate prices in the area sandwiched between the flourishing hospital and the thriving college had escalated. Professional appraisers hired by the DPW submitted figures indicating that the cost of buying this land, not including the demolition of the existing buildings, exceeded $125,000 per acre. Haas, already leery about displacing so many Danbury citizens, concluded that "the Osborne Street site was far too costly per acre," and dropped the plan in August 1968.

Almost from the time it assumed supervision of the state colleges in July 1965, the Board of Trustees had questioned the wisdom of expanding the downtown campus of Danbury State College. The board's own internal problems contributed to this opposition. At the urging of Ella Grasso, then secretary of state, who presided over the first organizational meeting, the board chose Walter Kennedy as its chairman. Although the Stamford attorney was competent and affable, he was also preoccupied with his job as commissioner of the National Basketball Association, which was struggling in its early years, and he allowed the board to drift. In an effort to provide direction, the board named John Langford, a former superintendent of schools in East Hartford, as executive secretary. Unfortunately, Langford died unexpectedly after one month on the job. In April 1966, the board selected his replacement, Central Connecticut State College faculty member Harold Bingham. Bingham provided energy, but his determination to centralize control over the four state colleges antagonized their presidents and a majority of the board. After a tumultuous year, he was forced to resign in May 1967, just two months after Kennedy had stepped down as chairman. The election of Bernice Niejadlik, a former teacher active in the Connecticut Education Association, as the new chairperson, and the subsequent appointment of retired Willimantic State College President J. Eugene Smith, as executive secretary, finally brought stability to the board.

It was during Bingham's troubled stewardship that resistance to Danbury State College's downtown expansion ambitions first surfaced among board members. In June 1966, the board's planning committee, headed by Redding resident (and Danbury attorney) Walter Werner, recommended that the present Danbury campus not be allowed to expand any further. The committee was appalled that the school would need to spend an estimated $43 million for more land and additional construction in order to accommodate the 1975 target of four thousand full-time students, an increase of twenty-eight hundred over the 1966 enrollment. If that expenditure were to be permitted, the cost of providing educational facilities for each student at Danbury threatened to jump to more than three times the cost at Central and Southern. The conclusion was inescapable: the Danbury campus was in the wrong place. The committee went further and recommended that a fifth state college be established somewhere "in southwestern Connecticut," on a piece of land three hundred to five hundred acres in size and located near express highways and heavy population centers. The Danbury property would be maintained as a state college with an enrollment capped at approximately two thousand to twenty-five hundred students. Even though Ruth Haas argued that a school this size could not be cost effective, the board approved the report and relayed it to the Connecticut Commission for Higher Education.

The Board of Trustees' next exercise in central coordination increased Haas' anxiety. In October 1966, the planning committee contracted with the Cambridge, Massachusetts, landscape architecture firm of Dober, Walquist, Harris, Inc. to develop a long-range growth plan for the entire state college system. The modest cost, $24,000, indicated that it could not be an exhaustive study. The firm's chief executive, Richard Dober, spent six months surveying the higher education needs of the state. His recommendations, contained in a document officially entitled "New Colleges for Connecticut," but usually referred to simply as the "Dober Report," were made public in April 1967. In the report, he urged that Danbury State College be relocated as soon as possible "to a site where it can more effectively serve the needs of both Danbury and the Southwestern Region." In even more ominous detail, the report specified that the new location should be convenient not only to Danbury but to "Greenwich, Stamford, Norwalk, and possibly parts of Greater Bridgeport." Basing his conclusion almost entirely on a 1966 study of Danbury conducted by Columbia University's Bureau of Applied Social Research (at the request of Danbury State College),* Dober suggested that the existing downtown campus could be re-used as a community or technical college. "The best course for Danbury to pursue in developing its public higher education facilities," Dober advised, "is to support a four-year comprehensive college of excellence within reasonable commuting distance of the City and launch a specialized college on the present campus of Danbury State College."

The Danbury community emphatically disagreed with Dober's analysis. The city's young, dynamic Democratic mayor, Gino Arconti, put the recommendations in historical perspective as yet another scheme of rival towns "to take the college out of Danbury." He encouraged local volunteer firemen to circulate petitions of protest. Steve Collins, another influential Democrat, criticized Dober's research as sloppy and inaccurate in angry *News-Times* editorials. Danbury was well represented at the state level by influential Democrats and Republicans who were sensitive to community fears. When the Democratic Party gained control of both branches of the General Assembly in 1968, veteran legislator William Ratchford, whose district included the college, became the Speaker of the House, a post he retained until 1973. Arconti, Collins, and Ratchford had ready access to Governor John Dempsey (1960-1970), a Democrat, as did the Commissioner of Public Works Charles Sweeney, who represented Danbury on the Democratic

*David Wilder, "An Assessment of the Community Needs of Danbury, Connecticut and the Potential Role of Danbury State College in Community Service," (Bureau of Applied Research, Columbia University, 1966). A federal grant supported this investigation.

State Central Committee. On the Republican side, T. Clark Hull of Danbury served in the Senate from 1963 until he was elected lieutenant governor in 1970. Francis Collins of Brookfield, a former Danbury State Teachers College student and an attorney who served four terms in the lower House, was minority leader in the 1971 session and Speaker in the following term. A. Searle Pinney of Brookfield was the chairman of the Republican State Central Committee from 1962 to 1967. The vagaries of politics provided Ruth Haas with many well-placed allies in her fight to keep a state college in Danbury.*

The fate of Western Connecticut State College lay in the balance during the summer of 1968. It was now painfully clear that the cost of acquiring land downtown was too high. The Dober recommendations made sense to many, including some of the Danbury faculty. When Walter Werner, the chairman of the planning committee of the Board of Trustees, came to Danbury to discuss the report with the school's teachers, he estimated that "a preponderance of those present seemed to favor moving."** There was lingering support in the Board of Trustees and the commission on higher education for establishing a fifth state college in southern Fairfield County.

At this point, Dr. Haas embraced the concept of a second campus in Danbury, suggested first by Steve Collins in a *News-Times* editorial two years earlier. Local political and business leaders (the Chamber of Commerce desperately wanted the school to remain in Danbury) rallied quietly in support of this solution. However, before approaching the governor and the General Assembly, Danbury boosters needed a piece of property suitable for a modern campus. Only three tracts in the city were large enough. The Charles D. Parks "Tarrywile" estate, like the current campus, was inconveniently located in the center city. The former Harold Farrington land on Mill Plain Road near the New York state border was tied up in litigation, as the owner had recently died.

*Hull and Ratchford jointly sponsored the bill that changed the school's name to Western Connecticut State College in 1967.

**At the end of the lengthy meeting, Werner asked the assembled faculty (many had already left) to vote on whether they favored moving the campus. There were enough objections to this procedure so that only a hasty and inconclusive voice vote was taken. A few days later, the *Echo* conducted an informal faculty poll. Of the fifteen faculty queried, eight expressed approval of relocation.

A 232-acre parcel of hilly pasture land, also on Mill Plain Road but near the intersection of the still-unfinished Interstate Route 84 and the north-south Route 7, slated to be upgraded soon to a high-speed, limited-access highway, offered the most promise. Known as Gregory Farm after the family (original Danbury settlers) who had owned it for more than 250 years, the land had been purchased in 1954 by prosperous businessman John Previdi as an investment for his two daughters. A Republican, Previdi had served as mayor of Danbury from 1951 to 1955. When approached by Haas, he agreed to sell the property to the state in order to save the college. He explained that he was motivated by gratitude to his sister Margaret, a graduate of the Danbury Normal School, who had "set the ideals for the family." "Besides," he added, "How can I say no to Ruth Haas? Nobody can say no to her!"

When classes began in September 1968, Dr. Haas announced the change in direction; the downtown campus would not be abandoned, and a second campus would be developed on Gregory Farm. The State Bond Commission, made up of Governor Dempsey's appointees,* immediately agreed that the $3.5 million in appropriations and self-liquidating bonds already approved for expansion of the White Street facility could be used for the new campus. Speaker of the House Ratchford opened the legislative session in January 1969 with a bill requesting $21 million for planning and construction of the suburban campus. In May 1969, the state agreed to the bargain price of $1.1 million for the land. Concern about the safety of a natural gas pipeline that crossed a corner of the property delayed final approval for several months. Ruth Haas interrupted a September 18, 1969, meeting to take a phone call from Hartford informing her that the bond commission had authorized the sale. When she returned to her desk she proclaimed to those in her office, "Now we've got some land on which to plan."

Arnold Hansen was in ecstasy. He had come to Danbury in 1950 to take over audio-visual services at the college when Burton Cook became dean. In 1965, as the pace of growth accelerated, Hansen was appointed director of institutional planning—primarily, as he readily admitted, because he had once worked in the

*Mayor Arconti recalled that Governor Dempsey had assured him in a private meeting, "You need not fear. Danbury is dear to my heart. So is Dr. Haas. We will purchase a site."

engineering department of the Boston and Maine railroad and could make sense of blueprints. Despite his skimpy background in planning, Hansen was an idealist who saw the acquisition of what he termed "the country campus" as a rare chance to achieve fundamental educational reform. For the first time in Connecticut's history, a state college could design a physical campus that would be a coherent expression of its educational philosophy. Hansen welcomed this opportunity.

Dr. Haas, though less utopian in her thinking, agreed the new campus should be planned as a total, efficient unit. She urged the faculty to suppress any cynicism and participate in the planning process. During the academic year 1969-70, departments labored over lengthy mission statements and facilities wish-lists that were relayed to Hansen. Questionnaires solicited more ideas about what the campus should look like from students, staff, and alumni. Classes were canceled on December 16, 1969, so students and faculty could participate in what Hansen termed "think tanks" devoted to such topics as "Should we emphasize a commuting or boarding school approach?" and "How innovative should the new campus be?" Hansen summarized, duplicated, and distributed the results of these discussions. While all this soul-searching was going on, the college retained the Statistical Utilization Division of the Dillingham Corporation to project how much space would be required to implement the present school curriculum in 1977, when an estimated fifty-five hundred students would be attending classes on the second campus.

Support for a comprehensive approach to designing the new facility came from an unexpected source not noted for creativity: the Connecticut Department of Public Works. Commissioner Charles Sweeney, a Danbury resident and an enlightened bureaucrat, insisted the college employ a prestigious architectural firm to draw up a master plan for the campus. Hansen paid tribute to Sweeney's role when he declared, "Nothing could have happened without him."

In a bold move, Sweeney chose John A. Johansen, an internationally acclaimed architect, to design a campus for the small regional college. One of a cluster of famous modern architects living in New Canaan, Connecticut, Johansen had studied under Bauhaus émigré Walter Gropius at the Harvard School of Design in the 1930s. Johansen maintained a midtown New York office as well as a teaching post at the Columbia University School of Architecture. His style was experimental, iconoclastic, and disturbing to conventional tastes. Critic Robert Hughes, writing in *Time* magazine, described the Mummer's Theater in Oklahoma City, which Johansen had finished shortly before accepting the Western Connecticut State College commission, in language that might have startled some Danburians. "Brash and incisive at first sight, it does not look like a theater at all. Johansen designed it in terms of distinct units—blocks of raw concrete with brightly painted steel cladding connected by tubes and catwalks."

Johansen plunged into the new campus project even before a contract with the state had been signed, pouring over the mountain of material that Hansen had gathered from all segments of the college community. In May 1970, he made his first visit to the wooded site with Hansen at his side. During the same month, the architect held two lengthy meetings with Haas and top school officials. Johansen's reputation had preceded him. According to the minutes of the first session, the president warned that "the architectural style should not be so experimental that it is obsolete before long; it should be durable." Johansen tried to reassure her that he would be "thinking primarily in terms of developing buildings so as to take greatest advantage of the natural features of the site, rather than in terms of developing an architectural style." In June, the firm made preliminary presentations to the faculty, the Department of Public Works, the Board of Trustees, and the Commission for Higher Education—complete with a model, slides, drawings, and a warning that more land should be purchased to avoid the need for multi-story parking garages. In November 1970, Johansen submitted the final Comprehensive Master Plan in two hefty volumes.

An examination of this document reveals that the celebrated architect had listened to his clients. Rather than impose a pre-conceived pattern on the site, he let the topography determine the design. The valley that ran through the property—the "chief amenity," as Johansen termed it—would be preserved in its pristine condition as the unifying element that balanced the man-made and the natural. The academic center, located on one side of the valley (the other side was reserved for future growth) would be the magnet that pulled together students, faculty, and administration. All classroom and office clusters would be arranged around, and connected by, "an interior pedestrian mall . . . a quasi-urban hub; a Main Street to which commuters, residents and faculty members could go whenever schedules permitted." Resembling a modern shopping center with echoes of a traditional New England town green, this "campus core" would contain all dining and social facilities. Johansen believed "the concentrated traffic and varied activities along the mall should foster more interaction than is normally made possible on the traditional campus." The plan called for the construction of twelve buildings in the first stage of a three-phase implementation. Each building would be designed by a different, preferably Connecticut-based, architect. Johansen's advice to these firms was to be content with a "simple and direct architectural statement capturing the purpose of academic life."

But economic and political reality suddenly intruded. On election day in November 1970, Connecticut voters chose Thomas Meskill, a two-term Republican congressman from New Britain, as governor. Even before he took office, Meskill, concerned about the size of the state deficit, asked retiring Governor Dempsey to freeze all state building projects. When Dempsey agreed to that request on December 4, 1970, the grand dream of a complete, rationally planned new campus for Western Connecticut State College, on Danbury's west side, died. ■

Note On Sources

The actions of the Board of Trustees during these formative years are recorded in "Minutes of the Board of Trustees, Connecticut State Colleges" (Connecticut State University System Office, Hartford). James Frost's "The Establishment of the Connecticut State University, 1965-1985: Notes and Reminiscences" (New Britain: Henry Barnard Foundation, 1991) is invaluable. Frost was the executive director of the Connecticut State Colleges from 1972 to 1982 and the first president of the Connecticut State University (1983-1985). Dober, Walquist, Harris, Inc., "New Colleges for Connecticut" (1967) was a study commissioned by the board. David Wilder's "An Assessment of the Community Needs of Danbury, Connecticut, and the Potential Role of Danbury State College in Community Service (Bureau of Applied Research, Columbia University, 1966) is a thoughtful study upon which the Dober Report strongly relied. I want to thank Pat Heslin of Technical Planning Associates of New Haven for providing me with a copy of that document.

The planning for the Westside campus is detailed in files kept by Arnold Hansen, former director of Institutional Planning and Development, which are now in the college archives. Hansen also authored a short pamphlet, "At the Gateway to New England" (1970), which proved helpful. He generously shared his memories of this exciting time in a long phone conversation with the author. John Johansen's autobiography, *John M. Johansen: A Life in the Continuum of Architecture* (Milan: Arca Edizioni, 1995), although it merely lists the Westside campus plan, is an excellent study of the architect's full career and contains a critical essay on his work. *The Master Plan: Western Connecticut State College, Volume I, "Research and Analysis"*; *Volume II, "Developed Plan"* (1970) is in the Haas Library Archives. Jean Kreizinger of the biology department made available to me a copy of a carefully researched paper done in 2000 by student Margaret Jackson, entitled "Land Use History of Westside Nature Preserve."

Jack Friel's 1976 interviews with Gino Arconti, Steve Collins, Francis Collins, John Deegan, T. Clark Hull, and William Ratchford were essential. Ron Douglas' 1976 interview with Marion Pfender provided an intimate picture of the operation of the library in its Old Main quarters. My oral history sessions with former state representatives Francis Collins and Clarice Osieki illuminated Connecticut politics in the 1960s and 1970s. Because of managing editor Steve Collins' friendship with Ruth Haas and his intimate knowledge of state and local politics, the *News-Times* editorials that he wrote during this period are informative and insightful.

Opposite: This interior mall was the heart of the master plan for a complete new Westside campus devised by renowned architect John Johansen in 1970. (WCSU Archives)

PART FOUR ❧ THE STATE UNIVERSITY

DANBURY: REGIONAL HUB

Opposite: Union Carbide moved from New York City to its sprawling corporate headquarters on Danbury's western edge in 1980. (Greater Danbury Chamber of Commerce)

DANBURY: REGIONAL HUB

In 1988, *Money* magazine named Danbury the best place in the country to live. In effusive prose, the publication ranked the Danbury metropolitan area ("situated in the lush Housatonic River Valley") above three hundred other American cities in nine categories: arts, crime, economy, education, housing, health, transit, weather, and leisure. The findings were subjective, of course; however, the fact that the city received such lofty praise from a reputable national magazine indicates how much Danbury had changed from its days as a single-industry mill town.

No longer a city set among isolated rural towns, Danbury was the core of a region where growth of the suburban periphery was more dynamic than that of the urban center. According to the 1990 census, the population of the Danbury "primary metropolitan statistical area"—the ten towns that the federal government considered an economic unit—totaled almost two hundred thousand. If the boundaries of the region were pushed slightly further in Connecticut and across the New York state border to include contiguous towns, another 130,000 people would be added to Danbury's orbit.

All these towns followed a similar demographic pattern. Their population was static or declining until after World War II, when rapid suburban migration began. Between 1950 and 1990, the towns in northern Fairfield and southern

Litchfield Counties grew spectacularly and lost their rural character. Farms, large estates, and village centers were transformed into the suburban fabric of single-family homes, retail stores, and campus-style offices so characteristic of present day Connecticut.

Brookfield, Danbury's northern neighbor, exemplified this trend. It took the tiny hamlet a full century to exceed its 1850 population peak of 1,359 residents. During the 1950s, the town's population doubled as subdivisions devoured former agricultural land and sprang up along the shores of Candlewood Lake. The pace of development increased in the next decade. From 1960 to 1970, Brookfield's population soared from 3,405 to 9,688, a rise of 184 percent, making it the fastest growing community in the state. To provide the schools, roads, and sewers needed to accommodate this influx, the town's annual budget escalated from $770,000 in 1960 to $3.7 million in 1970. The economic base of the community grew. According to the census of 1990, almost six thousand people worked in the businesses and industries that had located in Brookfield. By the time *Money* magazine discovered "the lush Housatonic Valley," the population of the town approached fourteen thousand and only sixty-one acres of farm land remained within its borders.

While the image of the autonomous, self-sufficient town still had a strong emotional appeal, residents of the suburban ring around Danbury recognized that they faced many common problems. In 1968, Danbury and its neighbors voluntarily formed the Housatonic Valley Council of Elected Officials to coordinate regional planning efforts. Headquartered in Brookfield, the HVCEO has played a leading role in dealing with such vital issues as transportation, solid waste disposal, and water resource management.

The network of modern highways constructed after World War II, even though incomplete in Connecticut, facilitated the suburbanization of the western part of the state. The opening of Interstate Route 84 in the 1960s tied together communities to the east and west, and in the process disregarded the Connecticut-New York political border. After I-684 was completed in 1970, employees of the large corporations that had migrated from New York City into southern Fairfield and northern Westchester Counties could live in the Danbury region. Construction in the 1970s of a 4.5-mile, multiple-lane segment of Route 7 (from Danbury to Brookfield) pushed suburban sprawl to the north.

Danbury remained the economic hub of this rapidly growing region. In 1986, the largest indoor shopping mall in New England opened on the seven-hundred-acre site of the historic Danbury Fair. An exit from the Route 7 expressway near the intersection of I-84 funneled the automobiles of suburban consumers into a gargantuan, seven-thousand-car parking lot and three-story garage to facilitate shopping at four major department stores and hundreds of specialty shops. It is significant that the largest commercial development in Danbury's history, like the Westside campus of Western Connecticut State University, was built on the edge of the city where both could serve a burgeoning suburban population.

There were many other indications that Danbury needed to be viewed in regional terms. In 1963, the venerable *Danbury News-Times* abbreviated its name to *The News-Times* to emphasize that it now saw itself as primarily a regional newspaper. Twenty years later, in 1983, it changed its publishing time from afternoon to morning to accommodate the schedules of suburban readers. At the same time, the newspaper resisted pressure to move its headquarters out of the central business district, remodeling instead the former supermarket on Danbury's Main Street, where the newspaper had been published since 1967.

Danbury Hospital resembled the college and the newspaper as a major institution with a regional focus. During the 1970s, the hospital added three large buildings to its hilltop complex, located in downtown Danbury close to the Midtown campus. This included construction of the multi-million-dollar Tower Building. With two thousand employees and a staff of more than 250 physicians, the hospital would provide medical care for the western part of the state. A new courthouse, built on White Street a short distance from the college in the early 1980s, preserved the city's traditional position as judicial center for the region.

The large companies that moved their headquarters into the city in the 1970s and 1980s also selected suburban locations convenient to major highways. In these two decades, German pharmaceutical giant Boehringer-Ingelheim, as well as Grolier, Pitney Bowes, Ethan Allen, and Duracell, built impressive facilities in Danbury. International Business Machines (IBM) purchased land on the Ridgefield-Danbury border for a conference center in the 1970s. Occupying temporary quarters in Danbury in the early 1980s, IBM had, by 1989, filled its sprawling new complex overlooking I-84 in Southbury with 2,500 employees. However, Union Carbide, then America's twenty-fifth largest corporation, was the most prestigious newcomer. In the late 1970s, the company abandoned its midtown Manhattan skyscraper and began construction of a massive headquarters on a 674-acre parcel of land on the west side of Danbury, in the Mill Plain district abutting New York state. Two thousand employees per day used the special exit off I-84 to reach the $23-million architectural gem that opened in 1980. Few of them realized that the building was located on land that only twenty-five years before had been an active dairy farm. None could have predicted Union Carbide would no longer exist within another twenty-five years and the glamorous facility—the largest free-standing building in the state—would be orphaned.

Danbury lost its character as a factory town in the 1970s. Even though hatting had faded as the backbone of the local economy after World War II, the city had remained an industrial center. An influx of small-to-medium-sized companies in the 1950s and 1960s employed skilled workers to manufacture specialized technical products. The industrial park replaced the hat factory. But by 1980, a majority of the employees of the ten largest companies in the city held white collar jobs in corporate offices and research facilities. Most were new arrivals to the area and did not live in Danbury. According to the 1990 census, 56 percent of those employed in Danbury resided outside the city.

In one important respect, the central city of the region did not change. It was still a mecca for less affluent newcomers. The support of the Association of Religious Communities and the prevalence of entry-level jobs attracted many Cambodians and other Southeast Asians in the mid 1970s and the 1980s. African Americans continued to come to Danbury, though in fewer numbers. By 1990, they constituted about 7 percent of the city's population. Although not segregated into distinct neighborhoods, they did face difficulty finding adequate housing and racial tension surfaced in the schools. During the 1970s, Danbury High School closed on four occasions, once for a full week, because of race-related violence.

Hispanics, many of them undocumented, flocked into the city. From 1970 to 1990, the size of this group increased five times to almost five thousand persons. Figures from the 2000 census put the Hispanic population in that year at twelve thousand. Experts estimate that if unrecorded illegal aliens were to be included, the total might reach twenty thousand. In addition, a large and fluid stream of Brazilian nationals mingle with the established Portuguese community. Close to half of the immigrant children registered in the Danbury public schools at the beginning of the twenty-first century were born in Brazil. Formerly vacant downtown stores now house businesses such as restaurants, markets, and travel agencies that cater to a Hispanic and Brazilian clientele. The Danbury Public Library, in recognition of this trend, has developed a special section adapted to Brazilian interests, and a Brazilian weekly newspaper is published in the city.

Danbury's government has endeavored to maintain the downtown as the heart of a progressive and prosperous community by combining the new and the old. A modern city hall and library remain at its center. The remnant of land cleared in the urban renewal enthusiasm of the 1960s now contains a municipal parking garage and, after much controversy and delay, a state-of-the-art ice skating rink. At the same time, historic buildings have been restored and given productive uses, many as upscale restaurants.

Intense regional development has altered both the college and its host city. Danbury is no longer a frayed, primarily blue-collar, hat-making town located in a sparsely populated corner of rural Connecticut. Instead, it is a diverse, energetic and growing suburban place with a population of seventy-five thousand and a prosperous mixed economy. Nor is the school simply a local college: it has become Western Connecticut State University in recognition of its enlarged scope. ■

Above: A weary President Haas speaking on September 20, 1974, at the ground breaking for an access road on the Westside campus. Directly behind and to her right is Governor Thomas Meskill applauding. (WCSU Archives)

Opposite: No buildings appeared on the Westside campus until seven years after the access road had been constructed in 1975. (WCSU Archives)

CHAPTER NINE

THE ROAD TO NOWHERE

For three days in March 1973, a team of veteran educators representing the New England Association of Schools and Colleges visited Western Connecticut State College to evaluate the school. It was the final step of the re-accreditation process that took place every ten years. The team's report was generally positive. In particular, it applauded the institution's continuity of leadership, noting that only two presidents had served over the past almost-four decades. Dr. Haas was praised for inspiring the trust and affection of the faculty. The visitors identified the president, then celebrating her twenty-fifth year in office, as "the principal integrating force on campus." In their conclusion, however, the committee expressed concern for the welfare of the institution when Dr. Haas stepped down, asserting that "the involvement of the faculty in the life of the college is not at an organizational level which can insure a stable environment when the President's retirement becomes a reality."

The Board of Trustees also worried about what would happen when Ruth Haas left office, but for a different reason. The unsettled status of the new campus convinced the board to exempt Haas for two years from the state policy that called for mandatory retirement at age seventy. In granting her another one-year extension until July 1, 1975, Governor Meskill emphasized that continued progress on the second campus required Haas' tested leadership.

Unfortunately, Haas' final years as president coincided with a prolonged downturn in the national economy—magnified in Connecticut—that frustrated her efforts to begin construction on the Mill Plain property. For most of the 1970s, "stagflation," the term given to a contradictory combination of recession and inflation, plagued the country. Unemployment, oil prices, the inflation rate and the federal deficit all soared while the gross national product sagged. Connecticut, heavily dependent on military contracts, was particularly vulnerable to national economic and political trends. The de-escalation of the Vietnam War hurt the aerospace and defense industries so important to the state's economic vitality. Obsolete manufacturing facilities and high energy costs put Connecticut at a competitive disadvantage with other parts of the country. Between 1968 and 1975, twenty-one aged factories closed in the state with a loss of more than nineteen thousand jobs.

The effect of the economic decline on state government, whose primary source of income was the sales tax, was predictable. Both conservative Republican Governor Thomas Meskill (1971-1975) and liberal Democratic Governor Ella Grasso (1975-1980) expressed shock at the size of the state deficit when they assumed office. Both responded to the fiscal crisis by attempting to increase revenue and reduce spending. The state sales tax went up as high as 7 percent within the decade. Dividend and capital gains taxes were levied. In the summer of 1971, a divided General Assembly in a special session enacted and, after five weeks, repealed an income tax. Meskill and Grasso imposed an austerity regime on the state and cut support for human services including education. They kept tight control over bonded indebtedness. Clearly this was an inauspicious time to advocate building a multi-million-dollar campus at public expense.

Western Connecticut State College had to travel a long, tortuous route to obtain funding for capital projects. First, the Board of Trustees had to give its blessing. In the case of the Westside campus, the board loyally championed the necessary appropriations, for a time even holding back the building requests of the other three state colleges to avoid competition for scarce dollars. The second step, gaining the support of the Connecticut State Commission for Higher Education, where the private colleges in the state had great influence, was trickier.

Ultimately, the commission would be a serious obstacle to the school's growth; but during the early 1970s it, too, endorsed the second campus project.

Only after the board and the commission had signed on could the college seek a line in the governor's budget, a daunting prospect in a time of recession, even with the support of Lieutenant Governor T. Clark Hull of Danbury. The General Assembly then had an opportunity to alter the governor's recommendations. Danbury-area representatives remained in influential positions in the General Assembly until 1974. During the 1971 and 1972 legislative sessions, Bill Ratchford of Danbury was the Speaker of the House and Fran Collins of Brookfield was the minority leader. When the Republicans wrested control of the legislature in 1972, the two local men switched positions for the next two years.

The final hurdle for the Westside campus proved to be especially formidable. Most of the money authorized by the legislature for capital projects was in the form of bonded indebtedness. Therefore, the State Bond Commission, chaired by the governor, who controlled the agency's agenda and appointed a majority of its members, had the final say on the timing of the release of funds. Neither Meskill nor Grasso was eager to bond the sizable amounts needed for the Westside campus.

Despite ample evidence that economizing was the order of the day, President Haas never abandoned her original vision of a complete new campus. She pressured Governor Meskill to follow the recommendation, made by architect Johansen in the master plan, to purchase an additional sixty acres that would provide access to Mill Plain Road. "Dismaying" was the term she used to describe the state's 1972 decision to buy only thirty-four acres. Prodded by area representatives, the legislature, against the wishes of the governor, appropriated more bond money for the campus in 1971 and 1972. This was added to the sums appropriated in the 1965 and 1967 sessions—an amount that remained largely unspent.

Dr. Haas began her last full year in office in 1974. It was the year the new campus was supposed to open, according to the original schedule, and yet no construction had yet taken place on the hilltop acreage overlooking the Danbury airport. The exasperated president decided to launch an offensive. That March, she led a contingent of area legislators, businessmen, students, and faculty to Hartford to ask the finance committee of the General Assembly to provide enough money to get the full campus built. Joseph Taylor, the head of the Danbury Chamber of Commerce, captured the mood of the delegation when he announced that the group was eager to go to the capitol because "we're disgusted with getting nothing but promises" from the state. Haas was a bit less combative. "I'm sure you have a shocked feeling about forty million dollars," she told the lawmakers in her disarmingly candid manner. "So do I, but I had nothing to do with it. We need this facility very, very badly and we have been patient a very long time." According to Haas, the $40 million she requested, added to the $21 million already authorized, was the minimum necessary to provide core facilities on the second campus. Before adjourning, the General Assembly appropriated in excess of $25 million for this purpose—again in the elusive bonding category.

During the summer of 1974, the Board of Trustees gave a boost to Haas' efforts. Worried about the slowdown in enrollment, the board contemplated abandoning the suburban campus in Danbury. Instead, after a full review of enrollment projections, it concluded that "in the long run, Connecticut would be served better by building a new campus and phasing out the old." It reaffirmed that construction of the first phase of the campus plan—site development and eight buildings—was fully justified, despite the high cost. Actually, the board was already backing away from a commitment to implement the total master plan. Influenced by a cautious report of its planning committee and the skepticism of Executive Director James Frost, the board, in September 1974, agreed that "further expenditures on the new campus would be dealt with on a year-by-year basis in the light of experience." In his 1991 history of the Connecticut State University System, Frost would write, "It was very hard to oppose this beloved and able lady, but I could not justify in my own mind construction as costly and spacious as she desired."

Encouraged by the board's partial vote of confidence, President Haas now utilized a tactic that was alien to her style. At her own expense, she ordered the printing of a small pamphlet entitled *Why Build It Now*, which summarized in crisp terms the arguments for proceeding with the construction of the second campus as planned. The conclusion, emblazoned on the first page in bold print, was that the only four-year college in the fastest growing part of the state should not be ignored. "The answer is obvious," the text proclaimed. "THE JOB MUST BE DONE NOW!"

Her efforts bore some fruit. The state took a small step toward making the new campus a reality. On September 20, 1974, Governor Meskill came to Danbury to participate in the ground breaking for a one-and-a-half-mile access road on the Westside property. In remarks delivered at the ceremony, he acknowledged Haas' persistence. "She's been on my back throughout my entire term," he joked. Then, in a more serious vein, he admitted the road was overdue. "Perhaps it's been too long in coming," he explained, "but everything in government these days is too long in coming." Meskill's words were a dose of reality. No building would appear at the end of that four-lane entrance road for eight more years. It would not be long before skeptical WestConn students and faculty would begin to refer to the abandoned stretch of pavement as "The road to nowhere."

Ruth Haas, tired and discouraged, would retire less than nine months after work began on the access road. "I'm just too old," she confessed to a Bridgeport *Post* reporter. "The college needs younger and more vital leadership." Danbury expressed its gratitude for her service in large and small ways. The first week in June 1975—officially Ruth Haas Week—culminated on June 6th, in a four-hour testimonial dinner at the Amber Room, the city's largest banquet facility. Dignitaries present included Congressman Ronald Sarasin, who read a citation printed in the *Congressional Record*. Recently elected Governor Ella Grasso gave the principal speech. Written tributes arrived from President Gerald Ford and Connecticut Senators Abraham Ribicoff and Lowell Weicker. Over fifty thousand dollars for college needs were raised in her honor. But the gift that probably touched her most was the quilt embroidered with 256 signatures of faculty and staff, presented by the group of friends who had sewn it. The women had spent two years completing the quilt, and it was the spirit behind its creation that inspired Haas' after-dinner comments as she summed up her tenure with the simple statement, "I wanted us to feel like one big family."

The elaborate quest for Dr. Haas' successor, begun a full year before her retirement, differed from any job search the school had experienced. First, it was nationwide in scope, attracting approximately 350 applicants. Second, the campus community for the first time played a key role in choosing the president. An advisory committee made up of faculty, students, administration and alumni, and headed by Gloria Brunell of the mathematics department, spent months narrowing the list of candidates to a final dozen. Only then did they meet with the state Board of Trustees. The two groups jointly agreed on the five finalists, who were invited to visit Danbury. The board suggested that several acceptable candidates be identified from this select number, but the campus representatives unanimously and enthusiastically made Dr. Robert Bersi, the associate vice president of California State University at Dominguez Hills, their single choice.

One unprecedented step followed. Two members of the board, along with two members of the advisory committee, Brunell and Registrar Bill McKee, flew to Los Angeles for what Brunell remembered as "one super-full day," during which the group visited the Dominguez Hills campus. When they returned to Danbury in the early hours of the morning after a forty-eight-hour marathon jaunt, Brunell and McKee went directly to the Washington Avenue home of Chemistry Professor Paul Hines, where the rest of the advisory committee was gathered, eager to get a report on the trip. Jim Dyer, the alumni representative, at whose urging the Student Government Association had appropriated funds to cover the travel expenses of the WestConn representatives, recalled that even at 5 a.m. the group was jubilant to hear "that Bersi was all we thought he was."

The advisory committee had done a good job: Bersi's strengths matched Western Connecticut State College's needs. The rangy, handsome, forty-three-year-old westerner grew up in Lodi, California, on a ranch that was part of a cooperative winery. His parents spoke the same Italian dialect as Ella Grasso, a minor but not insignificant asset in Connecticut. Bersi had attended the University of the Pacific on a debating team scholarship and, in his senior year, had served as head of the Student Government Association. Urged by the university's president to consider a career in educational administration, Bersi moved on to Stanford University, where his graduate program was broad. In addition to education courses, he had participated in a rigorous tutorial program directed by W.H.

Cowley, former president of Hamilton College. He also earned thirty-six credits at the law school. In 1965, Bersi had received a Ph.D. in higher education. His dissertation had focused on the economic and political workings of a modern university.

But it was the ten years Bersi spent in the California State University system that best prepared him for the Connecticut assignment. In 1966, he became the special assistant to Dr. Leo Cain, the first president of California State College at Dominguez Hills. When Bersi arrived, the school was operating out of temporary quarters in a bank in Palos Verdes while officials searched for a permanent home in the suburbs southwest of Los Angeles. In the aftermath of the Watts riots, the school moved to a flat, 346-acre tract (occupied mostly by defunct oil wells) because it was accessible to inner-city minorities. President Cain delegated many tasks to the personable Bersi, who, as the public relations officer, wrote a weekly column for a local newspaper, the *South Bay Daily Breeze*. He negotiated with the oil companies to remove the wells from the school property, met with representatives of the Asian and Black communities, and journeyed to Sacramento to defend the school's budget. He set up courses in public libraries, day care centers and corporate headquarters. In 1975, when Bersi left California State Dominguez Hills (by then a university of more than eight thousand students), he took with him experience in every phase of campus-building.

The young Californian understood why he had been hired: the Westside campus had to become more than an enticing promise. But Bersi defined his challenge in broader terms: he needed to change the state government's perception of the school. While the economy of Connecticut was in the doldrums, the economy of Fairfield County, a magnet for corporations fleeing New York City, flourished. The governor, the legislature, and higher education bureaucrats had to be shown that corporations were coming to western Connecticut in part because of the college. He had to convince them that "we were an outpost that had to be reinforced," Bersi said, years later. Dr. Frost, the executive director of the Board of Trustees, agreed with Bersi's analysis. The corporations moving into the state didn't "see Western as 'Danbury Normal School,'" Frost observed, "they see it as a multi-purpose small university."

To alter the public image of Western, Bersi had to devote most of his time and attention to off-campus matters. He delegated responsibility for the internal affairs of the school to others. Bersi appointed Dean Gertrude Braun as academic vice president with total control over educational matters, while Carl Robinson, vice president for administrative affairs, dealt with all non-academic issues. Braun recalled that Bersi's detachment from the mundane details of the school's operation was so complete that it was often hard to get his attention to resolve occasional disputes. Neil Wagner, the director of extension services, who enjoyed working with Bersi because he "let me do the job," gave an example of the president's style. When confronted with a threat from the University of Bridgeport to offer MBA courses in Danbury, Bersi told Wagner bluntly and without details, "I don't want it. Keep it out." The faculty and students liked the affable president, but saw little of him. Unlike Haas, he attended Faculty Senate meetings only when invited. Gloria Brunell, the head of the advisory committee that had recommended Bersi for the president's post, made a telling comparison between the Californian and his predecessor. "It was easier to get in to see Dr. Haas, and I miss it," she lamented in 1976. "The open door is gone!" But she immediately put that regret in perspective by pointing out that Bersi, in his first year on the job, had convinced the Board of Trustees to promote twenty-six faculty members; none had been promoted the previous year. "You don't mind if the door is closed if you get promoted," Brunell concluded. "It's probably the price you have to pay for growth."

This president had to lower his sights in order to hasten growth of the Westside campus. When the Board of Trustees voted in 1975 to concentrate on building just two buildings—a classroom structure and a dormitory—rather than a total campus, Bersi accepted the decision as "a realistic game plan." He spent the rest of his administration trying to dispel the myth that Western wanted a grand and outlandishly expensive Westside complex. In 1979, he tried to dispose of what he termed "the 200-million-dollar straw man" by gaining board approval for a ten-year, limited-growth plan for both campuses that would cost less than $40 million.

The Commission for Higher Education proved to be the locus of the most consistent opposition to Western's expansion. Shortly after Bersi's arrival in the summer of 1975, Vice Chancellor Louis Rabineau advised Governor Grasso not to include funds for the new campus on her list of bonding priorities because the 1960s master plan was based on outdated and inaccurate enrollment estimates. His suggestion that the Westside property be sold shocked and angered the Board of Trustees. The commission was attuned to the needs of private colleges, particularly those newer institutions eager to recruit more students. Members listened to people like Philip Kaplan, the outspoken president of the University of New Haven, who dismissed Western's ambitions as "grandiose and absurd." Kaplan had a vested interest in checking the school's growth. He convinced the commission to delay approval of Western's MA in Administrative Science on the grounds that it would rival the Master of Business Administration program taught by University of New Haven faculty in rented space in Danbury.

The future of the commission itself was far from secure. At the start of the Grasso administration, for the fourth time since the 1930s, Connecticut considered placing control of higher education in the hands of a single board of regents, similar to the system used in New York state. Both John Filer, the chairman of the board of Aetna Life and Casualty, who had been commissioned by Governor Grasso to make suggestions for streamlining state government, and Samuel Gould, the former chancellor of education in New York, now retained as a consultant by the Board of Trustees, recommended such a unified approach. The General Assembly rejected this advice and instead, in the 1977 session, substituted a stronger, twenty-member Connecticut Board of Higher Education for the unpopular commission.

Bersi took advantage of this unsettled situation to restructure the college into three schools, each headed by a dean. He combined the eleven liberal arts departments into the School of Arts and Sciences under the direction of Gloria Brunell. Psychology Professor Fred O'Neill became the first dean of the School of Professional Studies, which encompassed the departments of education, music and nursing. Stephen Feldman, the dean of the business school at Hofstra University, was hired to direct the School of Business Administration. This reorganization was primarily a defensive maneuver designed to foil assimilation into a single higher education system. "We are now a lot more difficult to swallow than we were a year ago," Bersi quipped in 1977. However, creating an organizational chart suitable for a large university also was part of his relentless campaign to accentuate Danbury's growth potential.

The other pocket of resistance to what Bersi referred to as Western's need to "break out" was located in the Connecticut General Assembly. Two New Haven legislators, Representative Irving Stolberg, a Democrat, and Senator Laurence DeNardis, a Republican (not coincidentally college professors at Southern Connecticut State and Albertus Magnus respectively), did everything they could to cut off funds for the new campus. Whatever their private motivation, they publicly based their opposition on a controversial 1974 report written by David Basch, the former planning director of the Board of Trustees. The report showed that full-time enrollment at Western sagged far below the early predictions of 1968, when the Westside campus was conceived. Stolberg and DeNardis were particularly "dangerous" because they were members of the Connecticut State Bond Commission.

Governor Grasso was an enigma. She was publicly sympathetic to Western's needs. On many occasions—in each of her election campaigns, and in her remarks at Ruth Haas' retirement dinner, for example—she pledged support for the second campus. However, she failed to back up her words with action. On October 24, 1976, just two weeks before election day, Grasso's rhetoric became more specific. After three Western student leaders, briefed by Bersi, presented the governor with data on the high cost of living in Danbury, she promised to build a dormitory on the new campus. This assurance notwithstanding, Grasso, a realistic politician, was determined not to let the state slip back into large deficits. In October 1978, nevertheless, the governor finally directed the State Bond Commission, over the objections of Stolberg and DeNardis, to release $5.2 million for construction of a classroom building. The road on the Westside was closer to having a destination.

One more battle, a microcosm of the long struggle, had to be fought. When the low bid for construction came in at nearly $8 million, the Connecticut Department of Public Works had to ask the State Bond Commission for extra funds.

In February 1979, the governor inexplicably sent the request for more money back to the Board of Higher Education for review. Critics there resumed agitating for limited expansion of the Midtown campus only. Deputy Commissioner of Education Nan Robertson even brought a state engineer to Danbury to evaluate the long-rejected option of high-rise buildings on the White Street property.

At this point, the Student Government Association stepped in. On March 9th, a procession of 250 cars and buses filled with students—most of whom had never seen the normally padlocked Mill Plain Road campus site—tied up traffic in the city for over an hour as it wound its way from the Student Union on the Midtown campus to the Westside. Heading the cortege was a hearse carrying a coffin labeled "The Death of Higher Education in Danbury." As television cameras rolled, student pall bearers under a protective canopy lowered the coffin into a freshly dug grave. Before Ray Lubus, the energetic SGA president who had masterminded the event, played taps on his trumpet, Bersi gave a eulogy in which he predicted, "We will all be out here in the near future to resurrect WestConn."

The president proved to be a prophet. A few weeks after the mock funeral, an irate Governor Grasso dismissed Board of Higher Education objections and ordered the State Bond Commission to act. By a six-to-four vote, with the legislative members including Stolberg and DeNardis in the minority, the Bond Commission released an additional $4.5 million for the first building on the Westside campus. Construction began in April 1979, almost a decade after the state had purchased the property.

The fame of Danbury native Charles Ives provided an unexpected opportunity for Bersi to simultaneously push the Westside campus forward and gain public notice for the college. On July 4, 1974, a crowd of seven thousand people had endured sitting in the sweltering grandstand at the Danbury Fairgrounds to listen to the American Symphony Orchestra, under the direction of Leonard Bernstein, perform the works of the avant-garde composer born in Danbury one hundred years earlier. National media had covered and praised the event. Western Music Professor Howard Tuvelle, one of the organizers of this Centennial tribute, had an even more ambitious agenda. He saw the concert as the first step toward establishing, on the Westside campus, a permanent cultural center dedicated to

Charles Ives, and to modern music and art. Armed with a small grant from the National Endowment for the Arts and backed by an organization of local arts figures, including the internationally famous soprano Marion Anderson, Tuvelle took his idea to the new president.

Bersi was enthusiastic, sensing political as well as artistic gains. Asking Tuvelle to detail his concept in text and sketches, the president then commissioned John Johansen's architectural firm, responsible for the now-defunct Westside master plan, to draw up a preliminary design proposal for a cultural center. The study, funded by Union Carbide Corporation, which was soon to settle in Danbury, impressed Governor Grasso. It was hard to resist a cultural complex that included a three-thousand-seat outdoor pavilion (which Leonard Bernstein agreed could be named after him), two indoor concert halls, a multimedia theater, a music library, and offices for the departments of music and art—especially if the state did not have to pay the estimated $5 million cost for its construction. In 1977, the governor granted the Charles Ives Center, Inc. permission to build and operate, but not own, a performing arts center on a thirty-nine-acre plot located on the edge of the Westside campus. Regardless of the ultimate fate of the Ives Center, the immediate impact advanced Bersi's agenda by enhancing the public image of Western Connecticut State College.

Bersi believed the Ives Center formula—private financial support of public educational institutions, common in western states but rare in staid Connecticut—could make Western Connecticut State College "an institution to be reckoned with." From the time he arrived in the state, Bersi had cultivated the large corporations headquartered within the orbit of the college; in 1978, he formed the Corporate College Council. Members were top executives of area companies who would meet quarterly to offer advice about ways the school could assist the business community. Corporations appreciated this access. One CEO remarked approvingly, "When we sit for breakfast and discuss various projects for the college, we're an integral part of the direction the college takes. It's great to have the ear of the school. It's sort of [like] being the Board of Directors."

Bersi's investment paid its first major dividend in 1980, when Nathan Ancell, the seventy-one-year-old chairman of the board of Ethan Allen Company, contributed $600,000 in company stock to the college. The furniture manufacturing giant had recently moved its corporate offices from New York City to acreage adjacent to the Westside campus on Mill Plain Road. In return for the contribution, Bersi agreed to make the Westside building under construction, originally designated for the behavioral sciences, the home of a business school to be named after Ancell. The grant was announced at a press conference in the company board room while area corporate executives dined on shrimp and champagne. It inaugurated a $5-million-fund-raising drive. Within the next year, the family of Robert Young, the late president of Fairfield Processing Corporation, gave an unspecified but substantial amount for a business library, and the Perkin-Elmer Corporation followed suit with a gift of a computer system worth more than $300,000.

But there were abundant signs that Robert Bersi did not intend to stay long in Connecticut. His sights were trained on greener pastures. From 1978 on, he was among top candidates for consideration to head universities in Arizona, California, North Carolina, New Hampshire, Tennessee, and Virginia. In each case, Bersi ultimately withdrew his name from consideration, clarifying for the benefit of concerned Connecticut citizens that he had not applied for the position but had been nominated by an outside party. However, in February 1980, Bersi announced he was returning to the West. In part to be near his terminally ill father, he accepted the post of chancellor of the University of Nevada's seven-college system.

Bersi had been at Western for less than six years. Yet in that brief span, he had accomplished his political and public-relations goals. The first building was taking shape on the new campus. A few months after his resignation, construction began on the second structure: a 230-bed dormitory to be named, at the urging of Western undergraduates, for Ella Grasso, who had died of cancer in early 1981. By enticing major corporate financial contributions, Bersi had altered the image of the school. When asked in a November 2000 interview about the significance of these private donations to Western Connecticut State College, the former president contended that they represented Western's announcement to the state that "We have arrived; don't ignore us anymore. Listen to us!" ■

Note On Sources

The many tributes to Ruth Haas on her retirement as president are in the Haas Papers in the University Archives. In addition, the Archives has a copy of the 1973 Re-accreditation Self Study and the Re-evaluation Report of the New England Association of Schools and Colleges. A copy of the 1974 pamphlet, *Why Build it Now*, is in the Warner Papers in the Archives. The Archives also contains the Warner clipping file and copies of the *Echo*, which is of particularly high quality for these years.

President Bersi generously granted me a long telephone interview, in which he reviewed in detail the events of his administration. Karen Jean Hunt, the head of the Archives and Special Collections Department at California State University at Dominguez Hills Library, provided me with a copy of Judson Grenier's *The Rainbow Years 1960-1985: The First Quarter Century of California State University, Dominguez Hills* (1985). She also supplied me with segments of Professor Grenier's oral history interviews with Dominguez Hills' first president, Leo Cain. Grenier himself made helpful additional comments by e-mail. The process of Bersi's selection as the school's third president is detailed in oral history interviews with Gloria Brunell and James Dyer in 1976, shortly after Bersi took over.

Connecticut politics in the 1970s is covered in Joseph Lieberman's *The Legacy; Connecticut Politics, 1930-1980* (1981). Francis Collins and Clarice Osiecki, both Republican members of the Connecticut House of Representatives during this decade, provided behind-the-scenes details of legislative maneuvering as part of their lengthy oral history interviews. The Connecticut economy during this period is not nearly as well documented. The best survey is *The Connecticut Economy, 1950-1975: An Overview*, produced by the Economic Development Planning Division of the Connecticut Department of Commerce in 1978.

Above: President Robert Bersi brought a youthful zest and a touch of the American West to his Danbury office. The longhorns and roll-top desk were family treasures. (WCSU Archives)

Above: In 1980 Nathan Ancell, the chairman of the board of Ethan Allen Company, donated $600,000 to Western. Ancell, President Bersi, Governor Ella Grasso, and Business School Dean Stephen Feldman (l to r) celebrate this unprecedented partnership.

Howard Tuvelle gave me access to the extensive correspondence, reports, and clippings he has collected in relation to the founding and development of the Charles Ives Center. Of particular interest is the November 2, 1977, letter from Leonard Bernstein expressing eagerness to have the outdoor pavilion at the proposed Ives Center named after him. Tuvelle elaborated on these materials in a candid taped interview. His papers and the interview tape have been deposited in the Haas Library Archives.

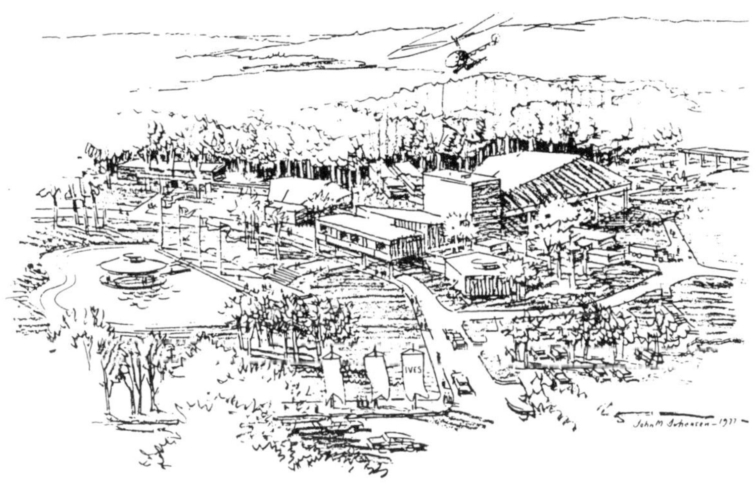

Above: This sketch by architect John Johansen helped convince state authorities in 1977 to permit a private organization to build and operate the Charles Ives Center on the Westside campus. (WCSU Archives)

Above: On March 9, 1979, the Student Government Association, with the backing of President Bersi, staged a mock funeral for higher education on the normally padlocked Westside campus. Attendant publicity helped spur action on the second campus. (James Dyer Collection)

Above: The physical facility completed for the Charles Ives Center was much more modest than the original concept. (Photo by Peggy Stewart)

Above: President Bersi, Governor Grasso and members of the Board of Trustees inspect the bedraggled Midtown campus in 1979. (James Dyer Collection)

Opposite: President Bersi gives visiting Governor Grasso a look at the sad state of the science labs in Higgins Hall. (WCSU Archives)

CHAPTER TEN

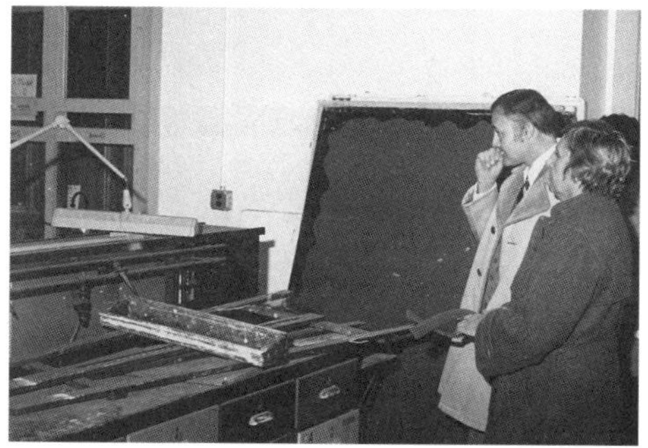

THE MIRACLE OF WESCONN*

At the end of March 1977, the *News-Times* published a five-part series that the newspaper headlined "Wesconn Report Card." The author, Kristin Nord, who would later teach journalism at the school, pulled no punches in describing the bedraggled Midtown campus. An opening sentence of the first article set the tone: "During these late winter months, the campus is at its worst: muddy hallways, leaky roofs, dingy corridors and icy parking lots." Much of the story is a depressing litany of deferred maintenance, slashed budgets, low salaries, and worn equipment. No one reading Nord's account would give the physical aspects of life at Western Connecticut State College a passing grade.

However, the young reporter was perceptive enough to notice another side of the college. In talking to students and faculty, she found eager learners and talented teachers. Pat Rogan, a middle-aged mother of seven who had returned to school in 1975, told Nord, "This is a tired old campus that's badly run down. The only thing that's keeping it going is the teaching and the motivation." Chemistry Professor Paul Hines confessed that because of "the incredible amount of enthusiasm, dedication and intellectual giving that exists under really strained

*In 1978, President Bersi, acting on the advice of advertising consultants, decreed that the school's nickname would become "WestConn," rather than the commonly used "Wesconn," to emphasize the institution's commitment to the region.

conditions," teaching at Western was an "exhilarating experience for me." Hines added, "I call it the miracle of Wesconn." The flourishing of education despite inadequate facilities may not have been miraculous, but it did characterize Western Connecticut State College in the 1970s.

The economic recession that plagued Connecticut during the decade did more than postpone construction on the Westside campus, it intensified the problems of an aged and overcrowded downtown facility. In an effort to pare the state deficit, Governor Meskill imposed a hiring freeze on all state agencies and, in a maneuver of questionable legality, eliminated for one year the guaranteed salary increment for state college faculty. He and his successor, Ella Grasso, regularly cut funding for the four state colleges. Western's share of the total state college budget during this period amounted to about 15 percent. Central and Southern together received 75 percent of the available money. Inflation magnified the impact of reduced spending. Between 1974 and 1980, for example, the cost of heating campus buildings rose 515 percent while the number of full-time students increased by just 1 percent.

Connecticut officials could not resist the temptation to make students carry more of the financial burden of operating the state colleges, reversing the time-honored tenet that public education was a taxpayer responsibility. When Governor Meskill (glorying in his sobriquet of "Tough Tommy") took office in 1971, Connecticut residents paid an annual one-hundred-dollar fee, imposed by the Board of Trustees, to attend a state college. This levy was not classified as tuition. Out-of-state students paid a four-hundred-dollar fee plus three hundred dollars in tuition. When he asked the General Assembly to impose a tuition charge of six hundred dollars per year on Connecticut students, Meskill met resistance. Western Connecticut student and future Danbury mayor, Jim Dyer, who was named the first undergraduate member of the Board of Trustees in 1970, organized the Keep Tuition Down Committee that bombarded the legislature with a ten-thousand-signature petition of protest from angry parents and students from all parts of the state. Five hundred Western students participated in a 1971 anti-tuition rally in Hartford's Bushnell Park. Dyer, castigating the Republican governor for "looking to the campus to remedy the state's financial woes," helped force a compromise. Beginning in 1972, for the first time, in-state students paid tuition amounting to $300 a year in addition to an annual $150 fee. The total yearly cost for non-Connecticut students nearly doubled to $1,350. This cost structure remained in place until 1979, when the state boosted the annual charge for those living outside of Connecticut to a substantial $1,720. Connecticut students entering WestConn in that year had to come up with $730, seven times more than their brothers and sisters who had started at Danbury ten years earlier.

Though moderate compared with the price of private colleges, the higher tuition and fee schedule of the Connecticut system had an adverse effect on Western's enrollment. Throughout the 1960s, the school had set attendance records each year. Starting in 1971, numbers began to level off. In part, this was a tuition-induced decline in clientele from adjacent New York state. Westchester and Putnam Counties, because of convenient highway access to Danbury and a lack of affordable local public higher education facilities, had traditionally provided a large number of students.

The increase in tuition also forced more in- and out-of-state students into part-time status, thereby changing the composition of the Danbury student body. As full-time enrollment fell, part-time attendance rose until, by 1975, there was a difference of less than five hundred in the total student population of fifty-two hundred. Thanks to this surge in part-time study, the overall enrollment at Western continued to climb slowly during the 1970s.

Other factors were even more important in cooling the school's rate of growth. A sharp decline in the number of school-age children in Connecticut led to a surplus of teachers in the state. In response to this trend, wary students turned away from a career in education. By 1975, only 831 undergraduates at Western majored in education, a drop of 40 percent from the 1971 figure. However, the main reason more students didn't come to Danbury in the 1970s was a familiar one: they didn't have any place to live. Off-campus apartments were scarce and expensive. Director of Admissions Les LaFond summed up the bleak campus situation in a 1976 interview, pointing out that the college had dormitory space for just 588 students, including room for 124 men in Newbury Hall. There were so few vacancies that his staff could accommodate only 116 of the 1,239 housing applications received in the fall semester. The harried LaFond observed that, based on national standards, the entire school had reached its saturation point in the mid-1960s and currently had 10 to 15 percent more students than the tiny White Street property could handle.

Lean budgets took a toll on academic programs. Physics and French were dropped as majors in the early '70s. The demise of French, a staple of traditional liberal arts curricula, prompted sharp criticism from the New England Association of Schools and Colleges, the regional accrediting body, as well as loud complaints from the recently formed campus chapter of the American Federation of Teachers. In the spring of 1973, ten faculty members, including four with tenure, were let go—a shocking development, since only three years earlier almost forty new faculty had been hired. When one of the dismissed teachers (a Caucasian professor of history) charged reverse-racial discrimination, citing the simultaneous hiring of an African-American teacher by the department, students, stirred up by some faculty, staged protest rallies. Their general frustration with cutbacks was expressed on signs they carried at these gatherings with legends such as "You can get more courses at a Chinese restaurant than at Wesconn!"

Most of the harm done to education at the college during the 1970s was more irritating than lethal. The supplies and equipment budget was cut to the bone. Ruth Kohl, the chair of the nursing department, told reporter Nord that her fifteen-hundred-dollar annual allotment "gets used up in a month." Students were amused, and often distracted, when mimeographed class materials appeared on the reverse side of already used paper. Faculty were definitely not amused when introductory classes suddenly ballooned to one hundred students. Fortunately, the dimensions of most existing classrooms prevented flagrant recourse to this economy measure. Classes were often delayed because the school could not afford to have the parking lots plowed in the early morning after winter snow storms.

The library provided an inviting target for retrenchment. During this period, the book budget was severely curtailed. Subscriptions to scholarly journals lapsed. Professional positions went unfilled. There was no money for student help. At the start of the 1978 academic year, beleaguered library Director Robert

Blaisdell, his staff short three professionals, touched off a student rebellion by closing the library on Sundays and restricting Saturday opening to a mere four hours. After enduring complaints for one month, President Bersi found a way to restore normal service.

No subject was more incendiary at this predominately commuter school than automobile parking. Grass became an endangered species on campus because almost every area not occupied by a building was paved for vehicle use. Nevertheless, the seven hundred available parking spaces fell far short of demand. Frustrated students rushing to class left their vehicles in prohibited areas along city streets, irritating homeowners. During the first three weeks of the fall 1976 semester, campus and city police issued 550 parking tickets to Western students. The previous year, the school scholarship fund had benefited from a windfall of fourteen hundred dollars in parking fines. No help came from the state. The Department of Public Works consistently found reasons not to pave the college-owned land on the south side of White Street, derisively referred to by students as "The Pit." Those who were bold or frantic enough to leave their cars there had to cope with ruts, hub-cap-deep mud, and vandalism. The supreme irony came in 1979, when Mayor Donald Boughton drove to the school to discuss parking problems and was ticketed by campus police for leaving his city vehicle in a restricted fire zone. A picture of the mayor's car resting in an illegal parking spot emblazoned on the front page of the *Echo* provoked laughter but little sympathy.

Left: Automobiles mired in the mud in the unpaved parking lot on the south side of White Street (present location of the parking garage). The lot was sarcastically referred to as "The Pit." (WCSU Archives)

Probably the most depressing feature of the campus environment was the dilapidated condition of the buildings. Again, the state routinely ignored requests for money for emergency repairs. Governor Grasso's 1976 budget cut of over one million dollars from the state college system translated into the loss of four maintenance employees at Western. The remaining custodial staff could barely keep up with routine cleaning. Individual buildings, even those that were comparatively new, needed attention. Joyce Luongo Flanagan, a music major from Yorktown Heights, New York, remembered that her parents would inevitably ask, "Are we paying for *this*?" when she took them into White Hall, where most of her classes were taught. Less than ten years after the former high school building had been renovated, it suffered from disintegrating stairways, peeling paint, holes in blackboards, broken venetian blinds, and clocks that did not work. Other buildings suffered similarly. An anonymous wag penciled "San Wesconn Fault" beneath a gaping crack in the cinderblock wall on the third floor of Higgins Hall. Professor Donald Groff, who taught geology, explained that the most recent addition to the science building was slowly sinking into what once had been a glacial swamp. Professor John Tufts spoke about Berkshire Hall, which housed the English department, in biting terms. He charged that "any home owner who allowed his home to go to pieces as Berkshire [is] would be known as a slum lord." Dormitories were in better condition, although Vice President for Administrative Affairs Carl Robinson estimated in 1977 that it would take approximately $250,000 to bring fifty-year-old Fairfield Hall up to modern standards. The Student Union could accommodate the needs of a maximum of twelve hundred students, a figure the school had exceeded as far back as 1964. When state inspectors in 1978 discovered numerous fire code violations in campus buildings, the problem escalated from inconvenience to safety. Suddenly even the most economy-minded officials found the money to remedy these deficiencies.

No activities suffered more from financial stringency during these years than physical education and athletics. All students were required to take four physical education courses. In addition, the college offered an intercollegiate athletic program of five men's and five women's sports. Facilities for classes and athletics were deplorable. Joyce Luongo Flanagan, class of 1978, has vivid memories of the

Left: Athletics faced many obstacles in the 1970s. The baseball team attracted few spectators to its home games played at the shabby Lee hat factory field on Triangle Street. (WCSU Archives)

chaos involved when the women's field hockey team, the men's soccer team, and the men's football squad attempted to practice simultaneously on the school's single athletic field. Dr. Haas (hardly a booster of varsity sports), shortly before her retirement, complained to the Board of Trustees that the baseball team was forced to play on a sandlot field behind a hat factory, and the football team depended on the good will of the city to use the substandard Osborne Street property. Members of the basketball team, she said, risked injury by banging into the walls of the school's tiny court. Her resentment at this situation leaps from the page of the September 1974 board minutes: "Miss Haas wished the record to show that the request for physical education facilities was not based on a desire for better facilities—but stems from the position of having nothing."

WestConn's shortcomings were obvious; its strengths were real but less apparent. Despite economic stringency, the college offered the most diverse set of courses of any of the four state institutions. The music and nursing programs were the best in Connecticut. New programs in areas such as business administration and criminal justice, added in response to regional demands, flourished. Community pressure also prompted the establishment of a joint Master of Business Administration program with the University of Connecticut in 1974. Despite the objections of suspicious UConn officials who charged it was a "disguised MBA," President Bersi won approval for a Masters of Science in Administration curriculum in 1977, to serve the needs of local corporations.

Music was, and still is, WestConn's jewel. Designated as the music school

Above: Western music professor and accomplished composer James Furman rehearses the school's chorus. (WCSU Archives)

for the state system in 1945, the school offered degrees in music education and professional performance. Limited in size by available practice and rehearsal space, both programs were highly competitive, requiring an audition besides the normal admissions procedure. Many were turned away. In 1973, for example, only 75 of the 140 applicants were accepted. A young and energetic faculty of sixteen full-time members at its peak, aided by a corps of accomplished adjuncts, molded these talented students into a variety of performance groups ranging from a symphony orchestra to a jazz ensemble. The concert choir performed such original works as Professor James Furman's oratorio, "I Have a Dream," inspired by the life of his friend Martin Luther King. The choir sang at the April 1977 premiere of Furman's tone poem, "Declaration of Independence," which was narrated by Governor Grasso. Furman, a specialist in African-American gospel music, was a mainstay of the department from 1965 until his death in 1989.

The 20th Century Arts Festival typified the creative energy present at Western Connecticut State College during this period. Begun by the music department in 1966 to honor Charles Ives, the annual four-day March event aimed to foster "understanding and appreciation of the living arts in our own time." The focus was originally on the music of Ives, but it rapidly expanded to include other forms of modern music, such as jazz, along with art, dance, drama, poetry, and architecture. At its peak from 1974 to 1979, the Festival brought a famous composer to the campus each year, including some who lived in the area.

Aaron Copland, Virgil Thomson, John Cage, Lucas Foss, and Karel Husa in succession delighted audiences and inspired students.

These famous musicians came to Danbury as teachers as well as performers. Officially "artists in residence," they participated in seminars and informal discussions with students and faculty, and rehearsed student musical groups in preparation for public concerts of the visiting composers' own work. The educational contribution of these renowned artists justified Student Government Association financing of the Festival.

The general public flocked to the new Ives Concert Hall—dedicated in 1970—for these free performances. Some were put off by the early avant-garde emphasis. The music critic of the *News-Times* described the audience reaction to "an electronic theater collage of sound and movement" in 1967 as "one of mass nervousness, an uneasiness that was accompanied by fidgeting and writhing." She added, "Sensitive music lovers had to remove their fingers from their ears to applaud." In 1974, when the festival was revived after a three-year hiatus, it offered less extreme, and therefore more popular, fare. Several hours before Aaron Copland was scheduled to lead the student orchestra, wind ensemble, concert choir, and chorus in a performance of "Lincoln Portrait" in 1975, the lobby of Ives Auditorium was jammed with people trying to get tickets.

Like the music major, the nursing program at the school had originated in the immediate post-World War II era. In 1945, the college began to offer liberal arts courses to assist registered nurses who had been trained in three-year hospital programs but desired bachelor of science degrees. Twenty years later, professional medical opinion had shifted toward requiring all nurses have a college degree. Danbury Hospital, eager to close its School of Nursing, urged WestConn to develop a four-year nursing baccalaureate syllabus that would use the hospital's facilities. Dr. Haas seized the opportunity to make the school the third college in the state to offer an undergraduate nursing degree (the University of Connecticut and the University of Bridgeport also offered four-year nursing degrees at this time). It immediately became the most selective major on campus.

Beginning with the first class admitted in 1966, all students, with the exception of a few carefully chosen minority candidates who showed potential despite a flawed academic background, were ranked in the upper half of their high school graduating class. By 1975, the program could accept only sixty-two (including a handful of men) of the 425 who applied that year. Faculty had grown to eighteen members. Under the leadership of Dr. Ruth Kohl, the former director of nursing at Danbury Hospital, Western Connecticut State College received, in 1980, an eight-year period of accreditation, the longest duration granted by the National League of Nursing.

The specialized facilities that were available limited the number of students that the music and nursing departments could accept. No such restrictions curbed the business administration major. Begun in 1969 with fifteen students and retired business executive John Raglan as chair and sole faculty member, that department grew to four hundred students and a staff of four in less than five years. In 1977, President Bersi made the School of Business and Public Administration one of the three base units of his reorganization scheme. Dean Stephen Feldman, in an end-of-the-decade progress report, enumerated the accomplishments of what would soon become the Ancell School: it had twenty-four faculty members, all with Ph.D.s or CPAs; it had raised admission standards; it had an honors program open to the top 15 percent of high school graduates. "In two years," Feldman predicted, "we'll probably be turning away undergraduate students."

The University of Connecticut's claim that it had a statutory monopoly on state-supported advanced study in this professional discipline stymied the equally intense demand for graduate training in business administration at WestConn. The Commission for Higher Education approved a temporary arrangement that permitted UConn to offer two graduate courses leading to the MBA degree each semester on the WCSC campus. One course would be staffed by a professor from Storrs, the other by a WestConn faculty member. By the time the first courses were offered in September 1971, forty persons had registered in the program, an indication of the urgent need for such a service in this region. The Board of Trustees agreed this was a stop-gap measure, useful only until the state college was permitted to fashion its own graduate business curriculum.

That was not a simple objective. Private institutions like the University of New Haven and the University of Hartford, along with the University of Connecticut, had strong objections to giving WestConn permission to launch professional programs in any discipline, but particularly in business.* To get around this resistance, the college designed a Master of Science in Administration degree that President Bersi insisted was complementary, not competitive, with established programs because it catered to the job needs of corporate middle management, a group not served by MBA courses. The backing of large area corporations helped persuade the commission to grant approval of this unique degree in 1977.

In the 1970s, the morale of the dedicated faculty was tested. Salaries had slipped far behind the inflation rate. Department chairs organized to deal more equitably with the administration. Kathleen McGrory, the forceful and highly competent chair of the English department, was a spokesperson for the group that was bound together by the "shared frustrations" of meager authority, skimpy department budgets—two hundred dollars per year was the norm and deficient support services. Discouragement over these obstacles led her to leave Danbury in 1979 to become the dean at Eastern Connecticut State College, and afterwards the president of Hartford College For Women. The overwhelming Faculty Senate vote to adjourn indefinitely in 1978 occurred because, as Senate President Ray Baubles put it, "We are getting absolutely nowhere." It was simply another barometer of faculty frustration.

Hesitantly, the faculty turned to unionization in hopes of solving its problems of pay and power. For many years, the campus professional organizations (the Connecticut State Employees Association [CSEA], the Connecticut Education Association [CEA], and the American Association of University Professors [AAUP]) had brought grievances to the attention of the Board of Trustees through a Faculty Advisory Council. In 1970, the American Federation of Teachers [AFT] challenged this genteel approach—ridiculed by Math Professor Wallace Lee as "collective begging"—by establishing a union chapter at the college. Led by Lee and John Eichrodt of the English department, Local 2136

*The objections of University of New Haven President Philip Kaplan also delayed Commission endorsement of Western's application to offer a criminal justice undergraduate degree in 1974.

publicly criticized the administration's responses to budget reductions, often in intemperate language, and engaged in informational picketing on campus. Their aggressiveness attracted considerable faculty support. The AFT claimed in January 1972 that seventy-seven faculty members endorsed the group's tactics. Others dismissed this agitation as irrelevant because Connecticut teachers were not allowed to unionize.

In 1975, the General Assembly, pressured by President John Driscoll of the Connecticut State Labor Council AFL-CIO and a power in the Democratic Party, changed the rules of the game by passing a law permitting public employees to form unions. The Board of Trustees did not contest this action but insisted that a single union had to represent the faculty at all four colleges. The first vote to choose a bargaining agent in February 1975 was won by the AFT; but the margin was so close that a second ballot, a month later, was required by law. This time the AAUP eked out a narrow 567-500 victory. While the tabulation from each campus was never revealed, it is certain that Western was a hotbed of AFT support.* The choice of the AAUP indicated a preference among the majority of state college faculty for moderate professionalism over militant confrontation.

Negotiations for the first contract consumed most of 1976. The Western team of science professors Alan Adler and Jean Kreizinger and their counterparts from the other campuses met weekly with the representatives of the board. Sessions were intense but civilized. Kreizinger tells of being invited to spend the night at the home of the young woman lawyer representing the board when deliberations ran so late that Kreizinger could not get back to Danbury. The finished product, approved by the legislature in May 1977, was a model three-year contract both in its salary provisions and in its clearly defined faculty rights and obligations. The contract called for a 6.6 percent pay raise retroactive to December 1976; a 7 percent increase in 1977-78; and a 5.8 percent boost in 1978-79.

Most of this maneuvering was probably unnoticed by students, many of

*Informal accounts agree that Western and Southern backed the AFT. Anthony Ficarra of the Western foreign language department exemplified the zeal of the AFT boosters. He insisted on being transported to the campus despite a broken hip so he could cast his ballot.

whom had come to Western by unorthodox paths. Beginning in 1973, approximately 150 young people with weak high school records and sub-standard SAT scores were admitted each year to a remedial two-year regime known as Basic Studies. The primary goal of this track—described by its initial director, Psychology Professor Sister Mary Friel, as "a community college inside the baccalaureate program"—was to move students into regular courses. The proportion of older students also swelled during these years. Director of Admissions LaFond estimated in 1976 that two thousand of the school's fifty-two hundred students fell into this category, referred to as "Non-Trad," in Western parlance. The median age of this group was thirty-four years. LaFond's successor, Del Kinney, reported that in 1982, 16 percent of the full-time students were Non-Trads. A significant segment of the student body had begun college elsewhere. Almost three hundred students transferred to Danbury from other colleges annually. Any Connecticut community college graduate with a 2.0 average could automatically move into a four-year Connecticut state college.

Basic Studies was a product of necessity and altruism. In the early 1970s, as declining enrollment threatened faculty positions, the administration searched for a way to attract more students without lowering admissions standards. An appropriate model already existed. Each summer from 1970 to 1973, a special qualifying program directed by Constance Terry Wilds prepared twenty disadvantaged students from Connecticut urban ghettos to enter Western. As a result of this intensive training, minority registration more than doubled. Even though motivated in part by job security, the faculty took Basic Studies seriously. Only those committed to the program taught in it. They concentrated on remedial work in small classes, on building study skills, and on individual advisement. Stephen Flanagan, who had pursued a vocational course at Danbury High School, entered Basic Studies in 1974 with apprehension, but recalled that he encountered four of Western's best teachers in his first semester. After a single year, he moved into the regular program, graduating three years later with honors. His achievement was not unusual. Professor of Education John Devine reviewed the first ten years of the program's history and found Basic Studies students graduated at the same rate as those admitted under traditional rules.

Mary Friel did not need a scientific study to tell her what was happening. In 1983, she attached a proud note to a newspaper article about Steve Flanagan's candidacy for the Danbury Common Council (he would serve three terms on this body) and sent it to Dean of Arts and Sciences James Pegolotti. The note read, "I thought you would enjoy knowing one of many success stories because of Basic Studies availability."

Those who came to Western Connecticut State College during this period, either to teach or to study, noticed and commented on the strong bond that existed between students and faculty. Teachers kept generous office hours and students took advantage of this opportunity to discuss common interests. The establishment of White Hall's Elbert Gross Library, named in honor of the recently deceased chair of the social sciences department, was a joint student-faculty initiative, as was *Clio*, the history department magazine, which was first published in 1973. Many courses had elements of active learning that featured collaboration between faculty and students. Author and foreign correspondent Arnold Brackman taught journalism from the late 1970s until his death in 1983, and used the school newspaper as the training ground for his protégés. History students enrolled in Professor David Detzer's "Crime and Punishment" course produced a carefully researched film on Danbury's "crime of the century," the 1970 bombing and bank robbery that involved brothers James and John Pardue. The film was clearly effective; in 1977, Connecticut's attorney general, responding to complaints of the lawyers for the Pardues that the film could prejudice their clients' trial, banned a public showing of the documentary.

Left: Members of the WestConn chapter of the American Federation of Teachers, organized in 1970, engage in informational picketing along White Street. (James Dyer Collection)

William Devlin, a history and environmental science major, transferred to the school in 1976 and welcomed the contrast with the more orthodox curriculum of his previous college. In each of his two years at WestConn, he pursued a project tailored to his interests. Geology Professor Donald Groff supervised a study of the operation of wetlands commissions in area towns that led to Devlin's appointment to the Brookfield commission. The history department mentored an exhibit on early Danbury craftsmen that he curated at the Scott-Fanton Museum. Looking back at his college career, Devlin, now a teacher himself, commented that at Western he had been "able to explore and not feel tied down." His assessment captured the strength of Western Connecticut State College in the 1970s. ■

Note On Sources

The Danbury *News-Times* was an indispensable source of information about this transition period of Western's history. Use of the unindexed local newspaper is eased by the existence of folders of clippings pertaining to the college and arranged in chronological order in the Warner Papers. Special files containing newspaper stories about members of the administration, the faculty, and individual students, as well as select topics such as the Arts Festival and Basic Studies, are also in the Warner Papers. It should be noted that the *News-Times,* during these years, published several in-depth reports about the college, such as Kristin Nord's five-part piece (March 27-31, 1977) and Wayne Shepperd's four-part investigation of WestConn's athletic woes (November 21-24, 1976). Under Arnold Brackman's guidance, the college newspaper adhered to high journalistic standards. The *Echo* file in the Haas Library Archives, therefore, is a particularly full and reliable historical source for this period.

Former Arts and Sciences Dean James Pegolotti gave me access to his file on Basic Studies that included the results of the valuable investigation of the program he asked John Devine to undertake: "The Basic Studies Program: The First Ten Years" (1982). Howard Tuvelle's clipping file on the Arts Festival was also useful. In addition, four emeriti professors in the nursing department—Helen Mizer, Lilla Dean, Harriette Tax, and Elizabeth Olsen—compiled a short but helpful history of nursing at Western.

The recollections of the following faculty and students, who were interviewed either by Jack Friel or myself, contributed to this chapter: Ray Baubles, Gertrude Braun, Gloria Brunell, William Devlin, Joyce Luongo Flanagan, Stephen Flanagan, Sister Mary Friel, Donald Groff, Ruth Kohl, Jean Kreizinger, Les LaFond, Wallace Lee, Raymond Lubus, Kathleen McGrory, and Howard Tuvelle.

Above: After fifteen years of anticipation, the first building on the Westside campus, the home of the Ancell School of Business, opened in January 1982. (WCSU Archives)

Opposite: (l to r) President Stephen Feldman, Governor William O'Neill, and former presidents Ruth Haas and Robert Bersi attend the 1982 dedication of the Westside classroom building. (WCSU Archives)

CHAPTER ELEVEN

GROWING PAINS

By the start of the 1989 spring semester, the relationship between Western President Stephen Feldman and the university faculty had soured. Rather than calling for a vote of "no confidence" in the chief executive, a move that was seriously contemplated, the school's chapter of the AAUP decided to ask its members to evaluate Feldman's performance as a leader. Ninety-seven full-time faculty completed an elaborate five-page survey that gave them the opportunity to rate the president in sixty-seven categories. The results were devastating. Feldman graded high in a few important areas, such as obtaining outside funding and increasing minority enrollment; however, the faculty judged his overall performance to be unsatisfactory. An April 1989 AAUP press release charged that "Feldman scores particularly low in promoting good morale among faculty, chosing [sic] and monitoring administrative subordinates, understanding faculty points of view, and providing open and honest explanations for his actions." The *News-Times* alerted its readers to the situation on campus with an alliterative and inflammatory headline: "FELDMAN IS FLUNKED BY FACULTY."

This acrimony contrasted with the upbeat mood in the summer of 1981 when Feldman, the capable and respected dean of the Ancell School, had assumed the presidency. Outgoing President Bersi favored him for the job. The Board of Trustees, who had great confidence in Bersi's judgment, endorsed his choice.

James Frost, the executive director of the board, felt so strongly about Feldman's ability that he had nominated him for the vacant post of president of Southern Connecticut State College shortly before the WestConn position became available. After a brief three-month search, an advisory committee representing WestConn's faculty, administration, students, alumni, and the local community agreed—though not unanimously—that he was by far the strongest of the 130 candidates for the job. James Dyer, then mayor of Danbury, who had also been a member of the search committee that had chosen Bersi, judged that "Overall, Dr. Feldman clearly had the best credentials and the greatest diversity of experience" of the six finalists. The Danbury newspaper editorially praised the selection, saying that the thirty-six year old dean appeared to be "exceptionally perceptive of where the college itself and western Connecticut in general could and should be heading."

The story of Feldman's rise to the college's presidency resembled a Horatio Alger saga. Born in 1945, he grew up in the blue-collar Crown Heights section of Brooklyn, where he shared a cramped, one-bedroom apartment with his parents and his sister. The family was close and supportive, but poor. His father, a Jewish immigrant from Odessa, Russia, worked long hours without vacations as a waiter in New York City restaurants. Young Stephen attended local public schools and, along with other boys in the neighborhood, spent most of his leisure time playing sports in the schoolyard playground. During the summer, he worked as a messenger in midtown Manhattan. His strong academic record at Wingate High School earned him admission to City College of New York, where tuition amounted to a mere eight dollars a year.

CCNY provided a springboard to upward mobility for Feldman as it did for thousands of children of immigrants in New York City. He lived at home, commuted by subway to the college, and majored in accounting not because the field enthralled him, but because he felt it offered the best prospect for a respectable job. His strategy seemed justified when, as an undergraduate, he obtained a part-time, entry-level accounting position with Columbia Pictures, which required him to wear a suit and tie. Feldman, an honor student, took full advantage of the placement services at City College. The school arranged sessions with prospective employers, and tutored the eager young man on the techniques of preparing a resume and handling an interview. Thanks to this guidance, Feldman, in his senior year, received an attractive job offer from the prestigious accounting firm of Price Waterhouse. He intended to accept this position and then earn his CPA by attending night classes. When asked later about his career goals at the time of his graduation, he answered with passion, "Never in one hundred years did I think of graduate school; I thought it was great to finish college!"

At this point an unexpected opportunity presented itself. International financier Bernard Baruch, a CCNY alumnus, had recently left a large bequest to his alma mater to fund a graduate program in economics. Encouraged by his teachers, Feldman applied for one of the full-tuition scholarships and a generous living stipend underwritten by this gift. Only after he had been accepted for graduate study did he consider the possibility of life as a college professor for the first time.

Feldman would later refer to the years that followed as the "euphoric period" of his life. Working as hard as ever, he completed his master's degree and his doctorate, teaching for one year at Hunter College while writing his dissertation. In 1969, recently married, he joined the Hofstra University faculty where he remained for the next eight years teaching banking and investments. He authored a book and several articles in his specialty and, during the last four years at Hofstra, served as the chairman of the seven-person banking, finance and investments department. Despite some uneasiness with a more privileged but less motivated student body than he had met at CCNY, Feldman said he "felt like royalty" at Hofstra. He and his wife owned their own home in Queens and were able to purchase a new car. The couple took full advantage of the cultural events on the Long Island campus of the private school.

Though proud of his accomplishments, Feldman aimed higher. As he saw it, a deanship constituted the next logical step up the academic ladder for an enterprising department chairman. Blocked at Hofstra by the presence of a young and capable dean, Feldman realized that to move up he would have to move out. Ordinarily the prospect of leaving New York City, where he had spent his entire life, would have intimidated him. However, his experience as a management consultant for International Business Machines (whose employees at this time joked that IBM, the company initials, stood for "I've Been Moved") convinced him that physical mobility, at least along the eastern seaboard, need not be hazardous. When he spotted an advertisement for a position at Western Connecticut State College, a school located a comfortable distance from Gotham, he applied. In the summer of 1977, Feldman, only thirty-two years old, became the first dean of the recently established School of Business and Professional Administration.

The transplanted New Yorker moved into the dean's office on the third floor of Old Main at an opportune time. During the 1970s and 1980s, business schools all over the country flourished. The migration of large corporations into western Fairfield and northern Westchester Counties created an especially strong market in the region for college graduates trained in business. *Business Week* magazine reported that Union Carbide Corporation had relocated to Danbury in part because of the presence of Western's business school. Enrollment in the business school increased, as did the number of faculty. By the early 1980s, the business school enrolled about one-third of the full-time students and close to half of the part-timers at Western. The faculty of the School of Business and Public Administration totaled almost thirty full-time members with double that number of adjunct instructors. Undergraduates majoring in business could choose from among six specialized concentrations: accounting, business economics, finance, management science, marketing, and personnel. Feldman was particularly proud of the honors program he established so the brightest high school graduates could earn a bachelor's and a master's degree in four years. Remembering his own impoverished background, he persuaded local corporations (Timex was the first) to subsidize participants by hiring them to well-paid summer jobs. With the encouragement of President Bersi, and using the contacts of veteran Director of Public Affairs Raymond Trimpert, Dean Feldman spent much of his time off-campus cultivating corporate executives.

The friendships he forged with local business leaders would serve him well when he succeeded Bersi in 1981. As the college president, Feldman looked, thought, and acted like the chief executive officer of a large corporation. He was always impeccably dressed, usually in a dark business suit, white shirt, and red tie. His gold Mercedes automobile stood out as the most flamboyant element of his persona. Intense, ambitious, hard driving, he was characterized as "100 percent business" by his key assistant, Frank Muska. Feldman had a utilitarian frame of reference that exalted the accomplishment of tangible material objectives. A manager, not an educator, he had no aptitude for, or interest in, nourishing the intellectual life of the university. One administrator described him as a "things" president—as in "he gets things done"—who saw people primarily as instruments employed to reach his goals. Feldman had little patience for the tedious and messy collegial decision-making process so revered by academics. Uncomfortable in unstructured social situations, he preferred to make decisions at the top with the advice of a small cadre of trusted lieutenants who understood that their boss viewed disagreement as perilously akin to disloyalty.

This leadership style, though not popular, seemed to be effective. One success after another marked the first half of Feldman's tenure. After fifteen years of anticipation, the Westside campus welcomed its first students in January 1982. The following year, the second building on the new campus opened, the apartment-style, 273-bed dormitory named after deceased Governor Ella Grasso. In May 1983, as part of the legislative package that realigned higher education in Connecticut, the four state colleges gained university status. Feldman was instrumental in bringing this about. He and State Senator Wayne Baker of Danbury drafted the amendment to the reorganization bill that elevated the four state colleges to university rank. Anticipated opposition from the University of Connecticut did not materialize, possibly because resisting the establishment of a centralized board of regents for all public higher education in the state preoccupied Storrs officials.

The corporate community, impressed with this progress, continued to make generous financial contributions to the new university—the only unit of the state system to benefit from this private largesse on a large scale. IBM, Boehringer-Ingelheim, and the Perkin Elmer Corporation donated sophisticated laboratory and computing equipment. IBM also loaned company executives to work on special projects at the college and established an experimental technology classroom. Northeast Utilities subsidized the university weather center. IBM financed a series of public policy debates for the Ancell School, bringing prominent figures such as General Alexander Haig, Robert Reich, Donald Rumsfeld, Arthur Laffer, and Lester Thurow to the Westside campus. The administration organized the WestConn One Hundred Society (the name calls attention to the modest $100 annual membership fee) to solicit gifts from smaller businesses.

At a time when the number of high school students in the state declined and consequently the enrollment at many Connecticut colleges sagged, WestConn grew. During the 1980s, despite significant tuition increases and dormitory space so limited that a lottery system had to be used to allocate available rooms, WestConn became more and more selective in its admissions policy. In 1981, the school accepted 69 percent of those who applied. Ten years later, only 42 percent gained admission. It required an average SAT score of 933 to win a place in the freshman class at Danbury in 1991, compared with a score of 860 a decade earlier. President Feldman was elated when the 1984 edition of Barrons *Profile of American Colleges* elevated the university to a "Competitive Plus" category, a distinction shared with the University of Connecticut. This lofty ranking was short-lived, however; by 1986, the school was rated "Competitive" along with the other three Connecticut State universities.

The president welcomed comparisons with the Storrs institution. Nothing pleased him more than finally eliminating the MBA classes that UConn had conducted in Danbury since 1974. Having persuaded the Connecticut State Board of Governors for Higher Education to permit WestConn to offer this advanced degree beginning in September 1987, he sought money from area corporations to augment the salaries of star professors he hoped to recruit for this prestigious program. Unlike many of the business faculty, Feldman did not fear that the state-imposed requirement to seek accreditation from the American Assembly of Collegiate Schools of Business would re-orient the Ancell School toward research and away from teaching.

Improvements in athletics also occupied a top spot on the president's agenda. Feldman considered the mediocre win-loss record of WestConn's intercollegiate athletic teams a blemish that needed to be erased from the school's image. As a sign of his determination to upgrade sports, he placed athletic affairs under the direction of his executive assistant, Frank Muska. In 1985, he separated the athletic department from the physical education department so that coaches no longer had to teach courses and could direct their full attention to coaching. Two highly competent young coaches, Jody Rajcula, hired in 1981, and Bob Campbell, hired in 1984, rejuvenated the women's and men's basketball programs. Twenty-win seasons and tournament bids became routine. The peak of accomplishment came in 1990, when both teams competed in the NCAA Division III tournaments. The men's squad, ranked sixth in the nation with a gaudy 28-2 record, reached the playoff quarterfinals.

The administration's commitment to athletics transformed the beleaguered football program almost overnight. In 1980, the sport had barely survived a vote of the varsity policy committee to end its troubled existence at the school. The hapless team had won only two games in the four seasons that preceded the coming of charismatic Paul Pasqualoni as head coach in 1982. The dedicated, personable, and meticulously organized former Penn State linebacker, who had been defensive coordinator at Southern Connecticut State University, brought in a large staff of assistants and courted talented high school players, while demanding improved facilities from the university. A Booster Club, established with seed money from the WestConn One Hundred Society in 1985, financed the installation of lights and the expansion of seating at the Osborne Street field, so home games could be played there instead of on the Danbury High School field. Four winning seasons followed a shaky transition year. The campus and community, accustomed to futility on the local gridiron, were amazed when the 1985 team capped a 10-1 season with an invitation to the NCAA tournament, the first time a New England team had received this honor. But success did not last long. When Pasqualoni moved to Syracuse University in 1987 after a five-season 34-17 record, the WestConn football program returned to its doldrums.

Construction of a badly needed field house on the Westside campus required all the president's tenacity as well as the lobbying skills of Frank Muska of the justice and law administration department, appointed as Feldman's executive assistant because of his family's political connections within the Democratic Party. Muska's lobbying with members of Governor O'Neill's administration helped to win support for the field house. Although architectural plans for a ten-million-dollar athletic facility were ready in 1981, the building did not open until 1994. Many factors caused the long delay. The plans had to be redesigned several times. In the mid-1980s, the continued growth of the school made necessary an increase in the size and cost of the proposed structure. The state belatedly realized that it had to abandon the original building site because it threatened protected wetlands. The State Bond Commission, worried by the familiar prospect of budget deficits, waited until 1989 to release $14.8 million for the construction of the 80,000-square-foot William A. O'Neill Athletic and Convocation Center. Finally, in what would become a depressing pattern, the general contractor, R. W. Granger and Sons, allowed the project to fall further behind schedule.

Even though the school had just begun to adjust to university rank, the eight-person committee representing the New England Association of Schools and Colleges, in its ten-year accreditation inspection in October 1983, gave WestConn high marks. While pointing out areas that needed improvement (such as student services), the team of scholars lavished praise on the school. The group's exit interview and final report sparkled with accolades, such as "The atmosphere is upbeat," "The university has developed a renewed optimism about the future and the people have a new spring in their steps," and "A genuine sense of trust [exists] among all levels of administration and faculty." Much of the credit for this healthy state went to President Feldman. "Confidence in institutional leadership is high," the visiting experts declared.

Feldman trumpeted these accomplishments at every opportunity. His rhetoric was enthusiastic and often overblown, especially when applied to the business school. He told the Bridgeport *Post* in 1983 that "our admissions standards have gone through the roof" due to the luster of university status and the pull of a strong business program. "People want to go with a winner," he asserted. A thirty-page advertising brochure about the college, published by the *News-Times* in 1983, typified the hyperbole employed by the administration. Headlines proclaimed: "ENROLLMENT BURGEONS," "REGISTRATION SOARS," "PROGRAMS EXPAND," "DONATIONS POUR INTO UNIVERSITY," and "STANDARDS ARE TIGHTENED."

Though camouflaged by euphoria, signs of trouble had existed even in

Feldman's early years. Almost as soon as he became president, the school's most experienced and powerful administrator, Academic Vice President Gertrude Braun, retiring after thirty-seven years of service, expressed apprehension about what she considered an overemphasis on the Ancell School. In a later interview, Braun confirmed that she left partly because she questioned Feldman's priorities; specifically, she worried about the president's apparent lack of appreciation for the value of the humanities in the preparation of students for careers in business. Almost simultaneously, in early 1983, Fred O'Neill, dean of the School of Professional Studies, and James Pegolotti, dean of the School of Arts and Sciences, announced their resignations. Pegolotti's threatened exit after less than two years on the job so shocked faculty members that they successfully petitioned him to reconsider. This overwhelming show of support for a dean with an open, self-effacing, academically oriented style must have baffled the aggressive, pragmatic, guarded Feldman.

One other resignation had even more ominous overtones. Ruth Kohl, the veteran director of the nursing department and the only member of the presidential search committee who had not favored the selection of Feldman, chose to retire in August 1984 in order to spare her department what she considered retribution from a vindictive president.

Unnoticed by the accrediting committee and largely ignored by President Feldman, the WestConn faculty based on the frayed Midtown campus had grown restive. The members of the School of Arts and Sciences, who constituted almost 60 percent of the teaching staff, were particularly uneasy. The rapid change from a small teachers college to a multipurpose, six-thousand-student university had produced tensions both symbolized and exacerbated by the existence of two separate campuses. The liberal arts faculty resented the takeover by the upstart Ancell School of what had long been originally earmarked as a behavioral sciences classroom building on the Westside. The sudden allocation of the modern new structure to the business school by President Bersi, a condition of the Ancell gift, had rankled. Suspicious faculty, forced to "teach in crumbling classrooms maintained at random temperatures" (as a 1984 issue of the *AAUP Newsletter* put it), saw the deal, and the simultaneous neglect of the downtown campus, as proof of the decline of the humanities at WestConn. Feldman's background and obvious comfort level with the corporate community fed the perception that he had abandoned the school's historic liberal arts focus in favor of business training.

Physical separation intensified mistrust. It soon became apparent that faculty would have offices and would teach on one campus or another. Formal or even casual interchange was minimal. Practicality also convinced students to concentrate their courses on a particular campus each semester. There was little anticipation of the problems of a split campus. In one small example, students rebelled at the administration's original plan of charging them fifty cents a trip to travel on a despised yellow school bus between campuses. Officials ultimately decided to provide free transportation on a bus without the grade school connotation, thereby removing the irritant. Western had become a university divided into two separate but unequal parts.

Beginning in 1987, this hostility burst into open, almost continuous, conflict between the president and the mainly Midtown faculty. In a major miscalculation, Feldman fired popular Dean Pegolotti, believing him to be a disloyal member of the "management team" because, in the president's view, he coddled the Arts and Sciences faculty. In reality, Feldman's action removed the safety-valve that moderated the growing unhappiness of this substantial group of faculty. Pegolotti's decision to keep private the details of his ouster and subsequent reassignment averted a public uproar. He contented himself with a strong letter to the *News-Times,* in which he praised the liberal arts teachers as "the firm 'rock' upon which all education is built at Western."

When students entered the fray, matters became very public. In April 1987, they objected to the program format devised by a wary administration intent on preventing the audience from asking questions of controversial guest speaker Henry Kissinger. Students asserted that restricting participation to professional television reporters demonstrated a lack of confidence in them. The editor of the *Echo* castigated the president personally, charging, "He doesn't care about education. What he wants is to get on the eleven o'clock news." A last-minute compromise arranged by Executive Dean Fred Leuthauser, another Feldman confidant, permitting one student to be a member of the panel that questioned Kissinger, did not stop about one hundred students from picketing the event carrying signs that asked, "WHAT EVER HAPPENED TO LEARNING BY DOING?" More quietly, student Tony Barrett contacted the state's Freedom of Information Commission during the summer of 1987, in an effort to force the school to make public the records of the University Foundation, the vehicle that enabled a state school to accept private donations. By refusing for several years to open the Foundation books despite the urging of the FOI, the administration had raised unnecessary suspicions.

The atmosphere became more tense during the fall 1987 semester when six issues of *The WasteCann*, an anonymous anti-administration broadside, appeared in faculty mail boxes and at school newspaper pick-up points. The scurrilous tone of the paper, and in particular the crude masthead that depicted President Feldman with a Hitler-type mustache, disgusted many on campus. Nevertheless, there was wide agreement that issues raised by the paper needed to be addressed. When, without explanation, material printed on campus copy machines appeared with cryptic symbols in the corner of each page, suspicious faculty interpreted this as a clumsy administration device to detect the source of the underground newspaper so unwanted criticism could be muzzled. *The Chronicle of Higher Education*, in a November 1987 story about the turmoil, quoted English Professor Steven Neuwirth's conclusion that "a wall of mistrust" existed between the faculty and the administration.

Both Feldman and the faculty sought to pull down this wall. The president began to visit individual academic departments. He conferred with the leadership of the Faculty Senate and the AAUP, and he readily accepted their suggestion that a faculty ombudsman should be selected who would attend the president's cabinet meetings and have free access to the chief executive. Howard Russock of the biology department received released time to serve in this capacity. Feldman promised to pay more attention to the condition of the Midtown campus. He even retreated slightly from his rigid stance on the sanctity of University Foundation records by releasing information about how donations to the WestConn One Hundred Society had been disbursed. This data indicated that 62 percent of the money went to projects sponsored by Arts and Sciences faculty.

After a brief lull, controversy escalated when Feldman, ignoring the recommendations of the social sciences department and the Tenure and Promotions Committee, refused to grant tenure to activist Professor Saul Mekies who taught economics. Feldman had legality on his side in this dispute because Mekies had failed to finish his dissertation as his contract stipulated. There was strong feeling on campus, however, that this case warranted flexibility because of Mekies' record as a dedicated student advocate responsible for bringing about pro-student innovations, such as a book exchange, a credit union, and a legal referral service. Nevertheless, the young teacher had one overriding liability; he was an outspoken critic of the president and had especially infuriated the administration by assisting students in their struggle to remove the secrecy surrounding the University Foundation's finances. Students and faculty signed petitions supporting Mekies. Many wrote letters such as the one in the Danbury paper that described the young academic as "a hero who is fighting for all of us." Mekies' status rose to that of a martyr for civil liberties when campus police surreptitiously video-taped a rally in support of his tenure, held on the lawn in front of Old Main. The Faculty Senate and the Student Government Association condemned the surveillance as "an instrument of intimidation," calling it "morally reprehensible." Even though Feldman immediately disavowed these tactics and ordered the tapes destroyed, major damage had been done. Looking back on the episode, the former president conceded that he had "paid a tremendous price" for his unwillingness to bend the tenure regulations.

Frank Muska, one of Feldman's inner circle and the man the president had appointed dean of personnel in 1986, became another lightning rod for faculty frustration. A simmering dispute with a campus union over Muska's handling of grievance issues culminated in an October 1988 AAUP vote of "no confidence" in the dean and a request that the president remove him from his position. Muska made matters worse by defending himself in intemperate language, identifying his critics as "a small core of union officials who act like pan-handlers selling snake oil." This time the president took a hard line. He told the faculty in a curt memo that the dean was doing "a superb job," that he would not be removed, and that the faculty should go back to teaching. When a mail ballot overwhelmingly supported the position of the union leadership on Muska, Feldman responded angrily. "The union can pass any resolution it wishes," he snapped. "I have absolutely no intention of removing him." The Faculty Senate and the AAUP countered by sending a delegation to the office of Connecticut State University System President Dallas Beal; they received a respectful hearing.

The Board of Trustees never wavered in its support of Feldman. Chairman Lawrence Davidson was a particularly staunch backer of the president. Davidson informed the members of the board that he had visited Danbury on November 22, 1988, and had encouraged Feldman "to continue to act in a professional manner in dealing with current campus tensions." A few weeks later, Beal warned AAUP President John Fitzsimmons to avoid a "test of wills" with the board.

In a lengthy interview with *News-Times* reporter Lynne Royce, who covered these controversies in painful detail, the president summarized his attitude toward the faculty in blunt words: "Last year I tried to understand their concerns and concluded they were not substantial. I will make no concessions. They work for me. I don't work for them."

The 1988-89 Christmas season did not bring peace to WestConn. When President Feldman entered the Hartford Lounge in the Student Union to deliver his traditional semester-opening, state-of-the-college remarks on January 25, 1989, the room was packed with angry faculty members. He began with a prepared statement stressing such positive items as progress on construction of the field house and Danbury Hospital's decision to provide financial subsidies for nursing students. He then invited audience comments. Professor Paul Hines of the chemistry department, one of the school's most admired teachers, asked the question on everyone's mind: what was the president going to do to end the state of war between faculty and the administration? "I wanted to give him the opportunity to show that he was not just president of bricks and mortar but president of people," Hines recalled. Feldman's curt rejoinder and sudden adjournment of the meeting worsened the impasse. "We don't trust them, and they don't trust us," concluded Professor John Fitzsimmons of the Ancell School, the head of the AAUP and a former confidant of the university president. It was in this poisoned atmosphere that the AAUP conducted its evaluation of President Feldman.

An uneasy truce, prompted more by exhaustion than understanding, followed. After a year of discussion, a joint administration and faculty committee in May 1990 could agree only on benign generalities such as "the faculty and administration of a university are engaged in a partnership of equals," but not on the specific steps that would move WestConn toward this goal. Many faculty simply retreated into their classrooms. Ombudsman Howard Russock complained that interest in the Faculty Senate had declined. No candidates sought membership on eight committees in the 1990 elections, while twenty-two other committees had only a single aspirant each.

For his part, President Feldman now began to show a bit more sensitivity to faculty opinion. Ever since the Connecticut Department of Higher Education had, in 1985, set percentage goals for registration of minorities in the state's public colleges, he had worked diligently to increase the number of Black and Hispanic students at WestConn. Beginning in 1988, the school spent fifty thousand dollars each summer to fund a five-week residential preparation program for primarily inner-city students. Nevertheless, Western had only 491 minority students in 1991, an increase of 50 percent in ten years but still far below the goal set by the state.

Given his attention to this issue, the president must have been upset when Edwina Chance, a Black admissions officer, resigned in 1988, accusing the school of turning the Basic Studies program into a haven for unqualified minority football players who had little hope of graduating. Feldman strongly disagreed with the *News-Times*' characterization of the university's conduct in this matter as "exploitation pure and simple." Yet, instead of a defensive response, he asked the Faculty Senate to investigate the charges and withheld all comment until that body released its findings in May 1990. Even though the report condemned the use of athletics as a minority recruiting tool at Western, Feldman accepted this verdict and tried to implement reforms. In 1990, after its seventeen years of existence, he eliminated Basic Studies as a set of special courses in favor of augmented support services for all marginal students.

Feldman also did his best to address the physical needs of the Midtown campus. In January 1987, he convinced the Board of Trustees to approve a ten-year, $48-million master plan that called for modernization of existing buildings, construction of a desperately needed and long-deferred parking garage, and expansion of the Ruth Haas Library. Unfortunately, the state's fiscal crisis in the final years of the administration of Governor O'Neill forced postponement of most of this construction. The drastic budget cuts imposed by his successor, former Republican Lowell Weicker, elected in 1990 on a third party ticket, worsened the situation. However, Feldman still spent $7.5 million on renovation of the Midtown campus while he was in office.

In February 1992, Stephen Feldman announced that he would leave Connecticut at the end of the academic year to become president of Nova University in Fort Lauderdale, Florida. Faculty greeted the news of his resignation with relief. "We just wanted him to go," declared one long-time science professor in a September 2000 interview. Her tone carried a bitter edge, despite the passage of almost ten years. The Board of Trustees felt differently. During a farewell luncheon held at the Ethan Allan Inn on June 5, 1992, and attended by about 250 businessmen and civic leaders but few faculty, Board Chairman A. Searle Pinney of Danbury announced that the basketball facility in the new field house would be named the "Stephen Feldman Arena" in honor of the president's dogged, decade-long effort to bring that building into existence. This combination of faculty disenchantment and material progress characterized the Feldman years at Western Connecticut State University. ■

Left: Former Secretary of State Henry Kissinger's April 1987 lecture at Western sparked student protest. In this photo, Kissinger chats with President Feldman and an unidentified guest. (WCSU Archives)

Note On Sources

Many WestConn faculty and administrators who lived through these tumultuous years shared their memories with me. I am especially grateful to former President Feldman, who made time in his busy schedule for a lengthy phone interview and also supplied written answers to my questions. This chapter relies heavily on oral history interviews with faculty members Jerry Bannister, Ray Baubles, Tom Doyle, Paul Hines, Ted Hines, Norine Jalbert, Jean Kreizinger, John Leopold, Vijay Nair, and Harry Schramm; and administrators Gertrude Braun, James Pegolotti, Jean Main, Philip Steinkrauss, Neil Wagner, and Constance Wilds.

The volume of printed material collected and saved by some of these individuals—much of it ephemeral—testifies to the importance they attached to the turmoil of the 1980s at WestConn. The following colleagues shared this carefully hoarded primary historical evidence with me: John Leopold, Jean Kreizinger, Barbara Obeda, and former Academic Vice President Philip Steinkrauss contributed bulging folders rich with such items as personal letters to President Feldman, materials connected with the faculty evaluation of the president, copies of the underground newspaper, and notes on the off-campus meetings of a group of concerned senior faculty; former Arts and Sciences Dean James Pegolotti contributed several unpublished student retention studies conducted by his office; and Vijay Nair, the current president of the WestConn chapter of the AAUP, opened union files to me without restriction.

Over the years, the Danbury newspaper has thoroughly covered events at WestConn. However, during this period, the *News-Times* for the first time assigned one reporter, education specialist Lynne Royce, to monitor the university, thus giving her an opportunity to develop contacts and gain essential background on controversial issues. Even though members of the administration considered many of her stories unduly negative, I appreciate Royce's aggressive and objective journalism.

Above: State and local dignitaries watch former Governor William O'Neill dedicate the Stephen Feldman Arena in the O'Neill Athletic Center. Feldman is at O'Neill's left. (WCSU Archives)

Left: WestConn's intercollegiate athletic teams improved dramatically in the 1980s. Coaches Bob Campbell (top row extreme left) and Jody Rajcula (top row extreme right) led the men's and women's basketball teams to the NCAA Division III tournaments in the 1989-90 season.(Athletics Department Photo)

Above: In September 2000, students and faculty, pleased and surprised by the rapid construction process, began using the modernized and enlarged Ruth Haas Library. (Photo by Peggy Stewart)

Opposite: Students utilizing state-of-the-art computer technology in the expanded Haas Library. (Photo by Peggy Stewart)

CHAPTER TWELVE

HEALING

The tension between faculty and administration that had gripped Western Connecticut State University during the late 1980s subsided in the early 1990s when Governor Lowell Weicker's severe budget cuts brought previous antagonists together to oppose a common threat. However, the resignation of President Feldman (announced in February 1992 to be effective July 1 of that year) re-ignited controversy as factions on campus and in the community mobilized to influence the choice of his successor. The most contentious presidential selection process in the school's history followed.

In outline, the procedure seemed routine. Two committees, one made up of six members of the Board of Trustees and an eight-person campus advisory panel headed by John Jakabauski, the director of personnel, winnowed the 120 applicants down to six finalists. All came to Danbury for interviews. The campus advisory group on July 1 recommended two candidates to the Board of Trustees. A month later, the trustees selected, as Western's fifth president, Dr. James Roach, who at the time was serving as the president of the University of Maine at Presque Isle.

In reality, the process was highly politicized. Some minority faculty and the Danbury branch of the NAACP favored the African-American female candidate who was one of the six finalists. They backed up their sentiments with public comments and letters to the Board of Trustees. Another top contender, former dean Frank Muska—elevated to vice president for student affairs, personnel, and external affairs by a grateful Feldman just before he left for Florida—waged an even more aggressive fight to succeed his mentor. Approaching the process as if it were a political campaign, he solicited support from students, alumni, members of the university clerical union, and even local corporate executives who had met each of the candidates privately at early morning breakfast sessions. Only four years earlier, the faculty had demanded Muska be removed as dean after a nasty grievance dispute; they could not be won over now. At a tense open meeting called to review the qualifications of the six finalists, many teachers told the advisory committee they had not changed their opinion of Muska. English Professor Steven Neuwirth expressed the unbending opposition of most of the faculty when he wrote to the Board of Trustees: "I do not believe Dr. Muska is qualified to be this university's academic head. He has not made a contribution to the academic life of this campus."

When the advisory committee sent the names of both Muska and Roach to the board as acceptable candidates, Muska stepped up his high-pressure campaign. A dozen top state Democratic Party politicians, including Attorney General Richard Blumenthal and Connecticut Senate President John Larson, bombarded the board with phone and written endorsements. Muska defended his strategy. He told the press that "Politics does play an important part [in academic life] and should. A university must be able to develop strong liaisons with the legislature." The board resisted, and may have resented, the WestConn administrator's tactics. In the end, only Trustee Robert Cartoceti, a Southbury lawyer whose unsuccessful 1990 campaign for the state senate was managed by Muska, refused to support the board's choice of Roach.

The trustees hoped that Roach, an experienced educator with a conciliatory style, would bring healing to troubled Western Connecticut State University. The new president was largely unaware of the political maneuvering that had preceded his appointment. He had professional and personal reasons for wanting to come to Danbury. After six years as president at Presque Isle, he craved fresh academic challenges. In addition, Roach and his wife Dr. Denise Hogan (who taught philosophy at Presque Isle), had tired of the frigid winters and physical isolation of northern Maine. The couple welcomed a move to a more urban and cosmopolitan environment.

Dr. Roach came to Danbury at sixty, after a lengthy career as a state college professor and administrator. His résumé bulged with credentials that dovetailed with Western's needs. His working-class background was similar to that of many past and present Western students. Brought up in a large, Irish-Catholic family in the gritty Boston neighborhood of Roxbury, he had attended parochial elementary school and Boston College High School. After graduation, without funds for college, he worked for two years as a stock boy and salesman in a home-furnishings store in downtown Boston before entering the Navy in 1952. Two years of active duty as a weather forecaster gave him free time to explore the riches of the library at the Norfolk Naval Base and fed his appetite for a college education.

Discharged in 1954, and now eligible for assistance through the GI Bill, Roach enrolled in the recently established Boston College School of Education. He lived at home and took public transportation to the Chestnut Hill school, then primarily a commuter institution. He worked the night shift at a factory, dipping lighting fixtures into a cleansing chemical bath. During the summers he earned generous overtime pay as a union helper on his father's brewery truck. After a practice-teaching stint at Boston Latin School, the young graduate headed for a career as a high school English teacher.

Instead, his path veered in a different direction. With a classmate, he volunteered to spend a year teaching at a high school in a rural section of the Caribbean island of Jamaica where the Jesuit order prepared promising native youth to take entrance examinations for universities in England. This missionary experience convinced him to enter St. John's Seminary in Boston to study for the Roman Catholic priesthood, a vocation he had long contemplated. Six years later, after his ordination as a priest, the Archdiocese of Boston assigned him to be the first full-time Newman Club Chaplain at Salem State College in Massachusetts. From 1963 to 1972, Roach, caught up in the spirit of post-Vatican II Catholicism, centered his activities around an ecumenical center located in a house near the campus purchased by the college for this purpose.

Over these years, much of Roach's admitted Boston provincialism (though not his Boston accent) wore away. Eager to teach at the college level, he enrolled in the mid 1960s in a doctoral program in World Religions—Hinduism, Buddhism, Islam—at Boston University. Dividing his time between ministry at Salem State and study at Boston University, he received his Ph.D. in 1972. His work so impressed his teachers that they arranged for him to spend a semester at the University of Geneva Ecumenical Institute in Switzerland, where he associated with scholars from all parts of the world. A keen interest in international education resulted from this exposure.

At this point, Roach made a second career shift. He resigned from the priesthood and took a position teaching philosophy and serving as an academic counselor at North Adams State College in western Massachusetts, where a long-time Salem State colleague recently had been appointed president. Three years later, Roach became academic dean at the college, which was struggling for survival in the sparsely populated Berkshire region. In order to boost enrollment, the school built dormitories, and Roach, as the chief academic officer, traveled all over the state recruiting students by dangling before them the twin lures of low tuition and a safe, beautiful campus that was within a three-hour drive of Boston. He enjoyed his job. His wife, whom he had met at Boston University, was content with her full-time, tenure-track teaching position in the philosophy department at the school. After a dozen years, Roach fully expected to end his career at the now-flourishing North Adams State College.

A surprise telephone call altered his plans. In 1986, a Washington D.C. placement firm, retained by the State of Maine to help find a president for the university branch at Presque Isle, called Roach and urged him to apply for the post. Later, reflecting on his feelings at this critical juncture in his life, Roach quipped that whatever career aspirations he'd had at the time involved moving "eastward [toward Boston], not upward!" However, with the encouragement of his wife, he headed north to a farming community of about thirty thousand people in distant Aroostook County, not far from the Canadian border.

What he found there was a rural college with major problems. Located a five-hour drive beyond Portland, Presque Isle was so remote that Roach had to rely on a chartered airplane to transport him to periodic meetings with the heads of the other Maine state colleges. The school was small—only about sixteen hundred students when Roach left—with a forlorn, poorly planned campus. When asked years later about his first impression of WestConn, he replied that he had been struck by how much the random accumulation of buildings on the Midtown campus had resembled, on a larger scale, the Presque Isle physical layout that he had inherited, the principal difference being that an ugly parking lot, rather than ancient tennis courts, served as the inappropriate focal point. Roach redesigned the Maine campus, much as he would do in Connecticut. He relocated the entrance, constructed a central mall, built new roads, and refurbished buildings. His most ambitious undertaking at Presque Isle was a $2.5 million student center that opened just before he resigned in 1992.

During his six years as president at Presque Isle, Roach demonstrated qualities that impressed the Western search committee and the board of trustees. He had brought disparate constituencies together. In order to build the student center at the Maine school, he had convinced state government, city officials, and the student body to contribute a portion of the cost. Each student agreed to pay an additional eighty-dollar fee for this purpose. Every segment of the Presque Isle community praised his accessibility. He regularly entertained faculty, students, and civic leaders in his campus home. When WestConn faculty heard he had a policy of always leaving his office door open, they thought back nostalgically to the days of Ruth Haas. It reassured many in Danbury when a Presque Isle professor told a *News-Times* reporter that President Roach "never played favorites and always listened to our concerns."

The new president justified Connecticut's expectations by quickly altering the mood on the Western campus. Administrative holdovers from the Feldman regime pledged cooperation. Roach was highly visible, friendly, and eager to talk about academics. Students welcomed and took advantage of his Thursday walk-in office hours. Faculty noted with approval his attendance at all Faculty Senate meetings. Outside experts noticed the difference. Barely a year after Roach took office, a committee representing the New England Association of Schools and Colleges came to Danbury to conduct the regular ten-year evaluation of the university. In their report, the educators asserted that Roach had brought to the school a fresh "leadership style which emphasizes communication, collegiality, consensus-building and a willingness to put the University's problems on the table and address them directly." After four days of intensive investigation in October 1993, the team concluded that "The concept of 'college community' appears to be real, not just a buzzword," at WestConn.

Roach had not had a chance to place one particular topic on the table: the Danbury branch of the NAACP dropped the issue of racial diversity on his desk the morning he took over at Western. At eight o'clock on Monday morning, September 28, 1992, as the president entered his office in Old Main for the first time, he was greeted by an angry delegation of about twenty local NAACP members, none of whom he had ever met. The group had a long list of what they saw as flaws at Western. There were too few minority students, they charged, and the attrition rate among the even smaller percentage of minority faculty and staff was shockingly high. The absence of an affirmative action officer in the administration especially infuriated them. The startled president, fresh from an ethnically homogeneous Maine campus, had to spend considerable time and energy addressing racial matters in his first years in Connecticut.

Racial diversity had always been an elusive goal at Western. The school drew most of its students from within a thirty-mile radius of Danbury, an area with comparatively few minority residents. Inadequate campus boarding facilities hampered efforts to attract students, including minorities, from other places. Despite the earnest efforts of President Feldman, which doubled minority representation during the 1980s, WestConn still could not reach the target established by the Connecticut Department of Higher Education in 1985. When Feldman left Danbury in 1992, 10.3 percent of the full-time undergraduates were African American or Hispanic. Under President Roach, slow progress continued toward the objective of a student population at Western more accurately reflective of the state's racial composition. As the twentieth century ended, the percentage of full-time minority students had inched up to 13.1 percent.

However, it was the racial makeup of the WestConn faculty, not the composition of the student body, that most offended critics. The local branch of the

NAACP was unhappy that only twelve of the 179 full-time teachers were African Americans or Hispanics, and was even more upset at what it saw as a pattern of hiring minority faculty but failing to grant them tenure. A harsh report, entitled "NAACP Investigation of Racial Tolerance and Retention of Minority Faculty and Administrators at WCSU," claimed that five African Americans had been denied tenure at the school during the past five years. Stanford Smith, the author of the document, concluded "Essentially what they're doing is bringing them in the front door and sending them out through the back." A national magazine, *Black Issues in Higher Education*, put the number of Black faculty who had been "forced out" at seven in the past two years. Associate Dean of Student Affairs Richard Dozier, one of six African-American administrators at the school, saw himself as the most prominent victim of discrimination. When his contract was not renewed in 1993, Dozier made his entire personnel file available for public inspection at the Haas Library in an effort to prove that "institutional racism is so ingrained at Western." He also filed a complaint with the state Commission on Human Rights and Opportunities. An underground newspaper, *The Jim Crow Times*, anonymously repeated charges of racial prejudice at "White Street U."

President Roach responded to his first crisis in what came to be a characteristic pattern of small steps and more study. He asked Dean of Professional Studies Walter Bernstein to institute a faculty mentoring program, and attached a two-page letter to a faculty paycheck that pledged his commitment to affirmative action. He found additional money to pay expenses of minority faculty candidates to travel to Danbury for interviews. He brought consultant Kevin Slater to the campus for two days in May 1993 to appraise the racial climate at Western. Slater's fourteen-page report, distributed to faculty, students, and interested community members, contained the expected generic recommendations to expand affirmative action and provide diversity training.

The president's most substantial action, an effort to solve several race-related problems, boomeranged. Caleb Nichols, an African-American professor, failed to win tenure in 1993 after six years of teaching in the justice and law administration department. Hesitant to cut loose yet another minority faculty member, and persuaded that Nichols' law degree was an appropriate credential, Roach named the Virginian to a new post as the temporary director of affirmative action. Loud protests erupted. The NAACP charged that Nichols was both unqualified and overburdened with responsibility for providing assistance to disabled students and coordinating multicultural affairs in addition to affirmative action matters. Nichols irritated the Affirmative Action Employee Advisory Committee by ignoring their suggestions. The state's Commission on Human Rights and Opportunities (CHRO), which held several hearings in Danbury during this period, further weakened Nichols' position in August 1994 by rejecting his massive, four-hundred-page Affirmative Action Plan for the university. In the face of this opposition, the president decided to hold a nation-wide search for a permanent director of affirmative action. When the search committee, after considering the qualifications of sixty candidates, decided in January 1995 by a one-vote margin to recommend the harried Nichols for the job, Roach balked and ordered a second search. In a March 2001 interview, the president explained that he made this decision primarily because not a single faculty member on the committee supported Nichols. Six months later, the school hired Barbara Barnwell to fill this sensitive position.

As a veteran state employee with fifteen years experience as the director of affirmative action for the State Department of Mental Health, Barnwell understood politics. Within weeks, the CHRO approved a revamped Affirmative Action Plan. Barnwell placated the Affirmative Action Employee Advisory Committee and skillfully defused charges of discrimination that continued to be raised periodically by minority employees in such places as the Financial Aid Office and the Ruth Haas Library. Only the bias suit of Lionel Bascom, an African-American journalism teacher who claimed he was not considered for the position of director of communications because of his race, attracted much publicity. More significantly, the school increased its effort to find and guide qualified minority faculty. By the year 2000, twenty-six of the 186 full-time faculty were members of a racial minority.

Race was only the most visible problem that President Roach inherited. Winning the allegiance of his top administrators, all holdovers from the Feldman years, including several who had been rival candidates themselves for the presidency, proved to be an equally difficult, though less dramatic, challenge. Feldman's twelfth-hour elevation of Deans Fred Leuthauser and Frank Muska to vice-presidential status complicated matters almost as much as did Roach's unwillingness to bring in his own staff. When asked by the author why he came into office from the outside without being accompanied by at least one trusted assistant who could serve as his eyes and ears, Roach replied that he had never considered that option. "It's not my university," he said. "I serve the university." It was not until 1997 and 1998 that the president replaced Leuthauser, Muska, and Philip Steinkrauss (who had been academic vice president for fifteen years) with people who shared his administrative style.

The university needed internal cohesion in order to deal effectively with the educational challenges of the 1990s. Since the end of World War II, Western had grown at a steady, and often substantial, rate. Only in the harsh economic climate of the 1970s did the pace slow, but then a spurt in the number of part-time students more than offset the dip in full-time attendance. When the economy of the state revived in the 1980s, enrollment shot up, topping six thousand for the first time in 1985. The number of full-time undergraduates rose to more than three thousand, also a record high. But in 1991, the school began a decline in enrollment that lasted throughout the decade. The number of full-time students plummeted and, unlike the 1970s, the number of part-timers fell even faster. One comparison illustrates the scale of the change. In September 1988, 721 freshmen started their college careers at WestConn; three years later, only 349 first-year students began at the school. In order to change this pattern, the CSU System Office and President Roach, in 1999, hired a Virginia consulting firm to develop a marketing plan for the shrinking university.

With help from a cresting baby boom, the downward curve started to reverse in 1999. The largest entering class in twenty years—822 freshmen—registered at the start of the fall 2000 semester. More transfer students, particularly from community colleges in Westchester and Dutchess counties in New York, accounted for part of this increase, although numbers were far lower than the 1980s' average of four hundred transfers per year. Maintaining a growth rate above 5 percent per year, as the university has done from 1999 to this writing, involved risk. The school admitted some applicants with combined Scholastic Aptitude Test scores below 900 and weak high school records. More than half of the entering students needed remedial work in mathematics. Retention rates were low. One-third of the freshman class dropped out of school after one year. Those who remained often failed to receive a degree. Currently less than 40 percent of students graduate after six years of study. While these figures are close to the national average for public colleges, they are deeply troubling.

The faculty also experienced a high degree of turnover. Enticed by the incentives offered by an economy-minded state government, a large number of faculty hired in the 1960s retired in the 1990s. The total number of full-time faculty positions, however, changed little. In 1993, there were 179 full-time faculty. Only nine more positions were added during the rest of the decade. Though the standard teaching load remained at twelve hours per week, an increase in the quantity of released time for research demanded by university status reduced the number of teachers available for classroom duty. Western, like most universities, relies heavily on part-time instructors. Fortunately, the AAUP contract stipulates that no more than 20 percent of the courses can be taught by adjunct faculty.

President Roach's oft-repeated warning about the folly of trying to change more than 5 percent of any institution guaranteed the traditional nature of the school curriculum. The core courses required of all students had not changed since 1986. The subjects offered in the School of Arts and Sciences, where more than 60 percent of the students were registered, did not look much different than they had in the 1960s when the liberal arts majors were inaugurated. Most of the changes in the curriculum were at the graduate level. The Master of Fine Arts and the Doctor of Education programs, both authorized in 2001, marked the school's first effort to offer the highest academic degree in those fields.

President Roach did not have to be an educational innovator. The economic recession that afflicted Connecticut in the late 1980s and early 1990s altered the job description of a state university president. Additional private money had to be raised, despite steep tuition increases that placed that figure, by the end of the decade, at nearly $4,000 per year for in-state students and $9,500 for out-of-state residents. Western's need was especially acute. In 1995, the Board of Trustees decided to allocate funds for the state universities based solely on the number of full-time students registered. This formula penalized WestConn, a school with two campuses and 40 percent part-time enrollment. At the same time, the trustees directed Roach to spend 40 percent of his time cultivating private donors. In the perceptive phrasing of the New England Association of Schools and Colleges' 1993 Accreditation Report, Western had changed "from a 'state supported' into a 'state assisted' institution."

Given these economic circumstances, it is amazing that the most intensive building boom in the school's history took place in the 1990s. The 1987 master plan had laid the foundation for this expansion by officially abandoning the 1970 goal of relocating the entire college to the Westside, and calling for $70 million to be used primarily in upgrading the long-neglected Midtown campus. Both political parties contributed to Western's good fortune. Danbury Democratic State Senator James Maloney helped convince the General Assembly to approve substantial bonding money for this purpose. In 1997, Governor John Rowland, a Republican, stinging from criticism that his administration favored the University of Connecticut, pushed through the legislature a $640-million package to be used for upgrading the state universities and the technical and community colleges. Western's share of this money amounted to more than $40 million.

President Roach used this bonanza to improve the physical aspects of the two campuses as a way of boosting faculty and student morale—a formula he had used so effectively in Maine. A six-story, apartment-style dormitory on the edge of the Westside campus, offering panoramic views of the Connecticut and New York state countryside, opened in 1999. Named after A. Searle Pinney, the Danbury attorney and politician who had been a member of the Board of Trustees for eighteen years, the huge facility accommodated more than four hundred students. Now more than one-third of the full-time undergraduates could live in university housing, altering Western's identity as primarily a commuter school.

The strategy of curbing discontent by improving the environment worked most effectively on the forlorn Midtown campus. Six buildings on the tiny White Street property were either built, enlarged, or purchased from private owners and renovated during the 1990s. Although the construction process was complicated by unexpected delays, and in one case by legal action, the eventual appearance of the buildings did ease frustration and communicate to the entire community that Connecticut cared about public higher education. Roach's most inspired move was to attend to the spaces around the buildings. Starting in 1996, while Midtown was still cluttered with construction debris, he began to knit the campus together with grass, brick walkways, trees, shrubs, benches, sculpture, lighting fixtures, and colorful banners. He converted the crumbling central parking lot and the area formerly occupied by Seventh Avenue below Roberts Avenue (closed by the city at the request of the college in 1993) into attractive quadrangles. Cynics scoffed at the "Campus Pride" slogan that accompanied this beautification effort, but by century's end most students and faculty agreed that a stroll across the now-unified and attractive campus uplifted the spirit.

Construction of a parking garage made a coherent campus design possible. Since the early 1980s, the Connecticut Department of Public Works had consistently deferred action on the plan to build a multi-level parking facility on the site of the maligned White Street parking lot sarcastically referred to by generations of students as "The Pit." When work finally began on the urgently needed structure in 1993, foundation problems forced a redesign and more delay. The three-story structure, with spaces for nine hundred automobiles and linked to the main campus by a covered walkway over busy White Street, did not begin operation until 1996. When the doors finally opened, the most persistent student complaint, repeated by thousands of frustrated commuters over a half century, had at last been addressed.

Memorial Hall, the cramped 1950s vintage student center, ranked a close second on the students' list of campus deficiencies. In November 1994, construction began on a 22,000-square-foot expansion of the outmoded facility, with the expectation that students would be able to use the new building at the start of the 1996 spring semester. Yet, when that time arrived, only 25 percent of the structure had been completed. The Department of Public Works, irritated at the delay and then alarmed when tests of the concrete foundation slab revealed weakness, removed the contractor in April. Another company, Konover Construction, resumed work a few months later and completed the job in record time. However, when the building opened in 1998, it was three years behind schedule. Students and faculty had been deprived of full access to the facility for almost five years.

It was difficult to function on WestConn's downtown campus during the mid-1990s. Key buildings were inaccessible. Piles of dirt and construction material blocked normal traffic routes. Fortunately, the school at this time acquired two long-coveted buildings located on the edge of the campus. In 1996, when the construction of the student union stalled, the state purchased a commercial office building that had been erected in the 1980s by private investors. Located on the south side of White Street near the parking garage, and renamed University Hall, the up-to-date, three-story structure now houses the office of the president and other members of the administration. Its first use was as a safety valve. At the annual Leadership Banquet in May 1996, President Roach, conscious of student frustration with campus conditions, announced the building would be used as a temporary student center until Memorial Hall was ready for occupancy. The purchase of St. Nicholas Church at the corner of Roberts and Seventh Avenues in 1993, and its conversion into a meeting and reception area designated in 1997 as Alumni Hall, also helped ease public space pressures. It became the home of the Child Care Center, a desperately needed facility that had been under discussion for almost two decades.

Few would argue that the library was the most inadequate building on campus. When the Ruth Haas Library opened in 1969, it served the needs of two thousand full-time undergraduates and about one thousand part-time graduate students working for advanced degrees in education. Twenty-three years later, in 1992, when James Roach got his first look at the building, it strained to meet the needs of about one-third more full-time undergraduates and graduate students (some full-time) in master's degree programs in administration, business, English, health administration, history, mathematics, nursing, and oceanography, as well as education. Dr. Roach summed up his initial reaction to the condition of the building in one word: desperate. Plans for an enlarged library were ready by 1990, but the combination of a weak Connecticut economy and then former President Feldman's lack of enthusiasm for the project had blocked action. In contrast, President Roach wished to make a large, technologically sophisticated library the centerpiece of his campus revitalization. The discovery of reliable Konover Construction (the firm that had rescued Memorial Hall) seemed to guarantee the speedy completion of a 40,000-square-foot addition that would double the size of this key university building.

One obstacle remained. Engineers insisted that the library had to be vacated during construction. A base for an interim library—one that could serve for an estimated two years—had to be found. Options were limited. The university considered and rejected the dingy former Armory on West Street, recently acquired as surplus state property. At the urging of concerned faculty, President Roach decided to tolerate delay and first build a companion building, located between White Hall and the Haas Library, to serve as temporary quarters for the library and later fulfill other unspecified university needs. The decision not to use the Armory proved fortuitous: the small quantity of books and other library materials that were stored in the Armory's basement during library construction were destroyed when heavy rains flooded that part of the old building.

Above: President James Roach made an effort to be available to all elements of the campus community. Here he visits informally with students. (WCSU Archives)

A complex but refreshingly efficient construction process began in the summer of 1998, when work started on both the library expansion and the neighboring structure. During the 1999 spring break (a single week), moving-company personnel, augmented by dozens of students, transported the contents of the library fifty yards into the completed building next door. The library would function smoothly here until its new home was finished. Little more than a year later, months ahead of schedule, the now 90,000-square-foot Ruth Haas Library was ready, and the parade of books reversed its direction. Even though a few unhappy students decided to use the October 2000 dedication of the building as an opportunity to jeer Governor Rowland for what they perceived as his lack of support for higher education, most of the university community welcomed the replacement of the old, inadequate, and poorly planned library with this roomy modern facility.

From the time the O'Neill Center at last began operation in 1994, to the end of the decade, Western Connecticut State University completed nine major building projects costing more than $70 million. As hoped, faculty and student attitudes changed markedly with the transformation of the campus environment.

One small part of the construction story underscores the extent of this mood shift. The attractive, three-story structure that had been the interim home of the library carried the accurate, if uninspiring, designation of "Swing-Space Building" on campus maps. At the urging of President Roach, the Board of Trustees in 2000 agreed to name the building "Truman A. Warner Hall" in honor of the unique alumnus, administrator, and senior faculty member who had died in 1997. Celebrating in this visible way a teacher respected for his dedication to students and service to his colleagues and community would have been inconceivable ten years earlier. Now, at the start of the new century, enthusiastic approval greeted the choice of this name as a unifying symbol for the school. ■

Note On Sources

Many people supplied information for this chapter. President James Roach graciously submitted to a lengthy interview, as did the following faculty members: Ray Baubles, Ed Hagan, Paul Hines, Vijay Nair, James Pegolotti, Howard Russock, Harry Schramm, and Jim Wohlever. Vice President for Academic Affairs Philip Steinkrauss supplemented his interview with a collection of important documents. Among them are: "The Report of the Evaluation Team Representing the Commission on Institutions of Higher Education of the New England Association of Schools and Colleges" (1993); "The Western Connecticut State University Strategic Plan" (1993); and Dr. James Roach's 1997 report, "The State of the University, 1992-1996."

As usual, newspapers were an essential guide. Complete files of the weekly student newspaper, the *Echo*, are in the Ruth Haas Library Archives. Use of the *News-Times* is more difficult, because the paper lacks any type of index. Fortunately, Truman Warner continued to collect and file articles about the university from the local newspaper almost to the time of his death in 1997. They are available, well catalogued, in the Warner Collection in the Haas Library Archives. The newspaper clipping file of Western's Public Relations Department contains copies of all newspaper stories about Western Connecticut State University printed in Connecticut newspapers from 1980 to the present, organized by year. I want to thank Junis Nicholson for maintaining this file (now located in the Haas Library Archives) until 1997, and for Koryoe Anim-Wright, director of public relations, for continuing the process and granting me access to this valuable resource. Jerry Wilcox, director of institutional research and assessment, supplied me with a statistical profile of the university for the period 1980-2000, and provided guidance as to the meaning of the data.

Above: Extensive new construction on the Midtown campus in the 1990s, and especially beautification of the landscape, led to improved morale. (Photo by Peggy Stewart)

Above: The new pedestrian entrance to the Midtown campus is located on White Street between the school's oldest buildings: Old Main (background) and Fairfield Hall (out of view, to the left). (Photo by Peggy Stewart)

Opposite: Originally built to provide temporary library quarters during renovation of the Ruth Haas Library, Truman Warner Hall was named for a revered faculty member. (Photo by Peggy Stewart)

EPILOGUE

A PEOPLE'S UNIVERSITY

Warner Hall is more than a symbol of unity; it is a link with the past. Named after an alumnus whose life touched the school at every stage of its evolution, the building is firmly rooted in history. However, the meaning of Warner Hall goes beyond chronology. The name highlights two dominant themes that resonate through the first century of WestConn's existence. First, the school has served people in the region, young and old, who otherwise would not have been able to benefit from a college education. Truman Warner came to WestConn because he had no other option. The grandson of a hatter and son of a house painter, the young man could not afford to attend a private college. When Danbury High School urged its stellar student to set his sights on Yale University, Warner responded that the low tuition and convenience of Danbury State Teachers College, now offering a bachelor's degree and eager to have more male students, better fit his financial situation. Years later, long after he had become a professor of anthropology at his alma mater, he admitted to an interviewer that he had enrolled at the teachers college "in some ways by default."

Similar WestConn success stories would fill a book much larger than this one. A few examples will suffice to make the point that the school has always been accessible to those in the area who had ability but limited alternatives.

Katherine Augusta Sutton taught in a one-room school house in New

Canaan to support her two young sons after the sudden death of her husband. She entered the Normal School in 1920 to earn state certification and never left. Dr. Sutton, who received her doctorate from New York University, became the most revered teacher at the Danbury institution until her retirement in 1946.

In the 1950s, Danbury State Teachers College gave Liz Timmons Nkonoki-Ward the opportunity to become the first African-American graduate with a music education degree. She went on to a distinguished teaching career in Hamden, Branford, New Britain, Newington, and Hartford. In a 1999 letter to the WCSU alumni office, she confessed that she would have withdrawn from school as a freshman if the head of the music department, Ruth deVillafranca, had not "made me realize the responsibility I had to her, the college, my people, my family, and me."

Following his graduation from Stratford High School, Al Montecalvo, aspiring to be a professional drummer, enrolled in the Berkeley School of Music in Boston. One year of study at the prestigious private school depleted his bank account and forced him to transfer to the affordable music education program at Danbury State. During his student-teaching assignment, he discovered that he was a "natural teacher." "It was the turning point of my life," he conceded. After graduation from this school in 1964, Montecalvo went on to a thirty-five-year career as music teacher and director of music in the Carmel, New York, school system.

His fascination with automobiles led Stephen Flanagan to select vocational courses at Danbury High School. After graduation, he worked for several years at blue-collar jobs "before I realized that I wanted more from life than I was prepared for." Fortunately, the newly established Basic Studies program at WestConn welcomed late bloomers like this. Flanagan spent one year in remedial courses before moving into the regular academic program and graduating with honors in 1978. Since then, he has earned two master's degrees and is completing his doctorate in history at the University of Connecticut. New Milford High School named him its teacher of the year in 1997.

Sister Mary Francis, after years of badgering her superiors at the Community of the Holy Spirit in Brewster, New York, for permission to attend the nearby college, finally prevailed. In 1993, she graduated from Western Connecticut State University as an honor student in English.

Forty-one-year-old Maud MacArthur, honored as the Alumnus of the Year by the School of Arts and Sciences in 2001, came to Danbury from her native Haiti at the age of sixteen with a minimal grasp of English. She worked to pay her tuition at Western where Psychology Professor Philip Lom encouraged her to follow a career in that field. Today, she counsels women inmates at the Federal Correctional Institution in Danbury.

Educating students is the primary mission of any school, but Warner Hall also signifies that Western's influence has reached beyond its campus classrooms. Truman Warner did not keep his scholarship locked in an ivory tower; he devoted a lifetime to educating adult audiences in the Danbury area through lectures, seminars, and museum exhibits. His public service, though quiet and unostentatious, illustrates the second dominant theme in Western's history: the college has not just been located in Danbury, it has been an integral part of the cultural and intellectual life of the community. In art galleries, concert halls, auditoriums, and meeting rooms, Western faculty have enriched the lives of all the people of the western part of the state.

In 1939, the *Danbury News-Times*, filled with pride that its city now had a full four-year college, acknowledged the vitality of the town-gown relationship in a glowing editorial. The newspaper claimed that the college faculty "contribute to the social life in our city in an even greater degree than our lawyers, doctors, or bankers do." While this tribute was exaggerated, Danbury-area citizens have consistently acknowledged the importance of the college by their actions. Whenever rival cities, penurious legislators, or hostile bureaucrats have threatened the welfare of the school, the region has united to repulse the menace. Each chapter of this book contains examples of crucial community support for the college. Only the citizens' role in blocking the most serious threat to the school's existence will be recalled here by way of illustration. In the late 1960s, the newly established Board of Trustees considered moving the entire college out of downtown Danbury to a more spacious site in populous southern Fairfield County. As at so many other points in WestConn's history, a coalition of civic and political leaders banded together to find a solution—in this case a second campus—that would permit the college to remain and flourish in Danbury.

Winston Churchill, a gifted crafter of symbols, understood that buildings provide more than shelter. He emphasized that they are also carriers of cultural meaning when he said, "We shape our buildings and afterwards our buildings shape us." The architects designed the newest building on campus to be attractive and fulfill many of the practical needs of today's students and faculty. The decision to name the structure Warner Hall, coming near the end of the school's first century, completes the shaping process by reminding the entire community of the school's legacy as "A people's university." ■

INDEX

D